NARC
Convictions of a DEA Agent

by

Sal M. Martinez

*There are always three sides to every story –
the two versions of the opposing parties and the truth.*

Revised 2.26.2019

FOREWORD

It was mid-summer of 1991 when I transferred to El Paso, Texas, after serving seven years in Mexico with the DEA. I was working side by side with Mexican Government officials in some of the most notorious international drug investigations at the time. One included the follow-up investigation of Kiki Camarena, a fellow agent who had been kidnapped, brutally tortured, and killed in Guadalajara, Mexico, in 1985. Throughout those years, and in an effort to accomplish the necessary results of any investigation, I had to quickly adapt to a cruel, manipulative, and culturally corrupt country.

Mexico took a toll on me. I felt I needed a break to spend time in my hometown and spend some quality time with my family as my parents were aging. I needed some cool down time and to place myself in a comfort zone before I moved on. Wrong! The intrigue and desire that compelled me to work all those years in Mexico was once again in my near horizon, right across the border in Ciudad Juarez. Mexico was my niche, and once again, I found myself sticking my nose where it didn't belong.

At the time, no U.S. agency was working in Cd. Juarez and the territory was wide open. Only mere intelligence reports were coming out of Juarez. I was ordered to physically go across the border and make contacts with the Federal Police to ascertain who the big players were. I needed a backup, a partner with experience working in Mexico, but none existed in the El Paso DEA region.

Sal Martinez was a few weeks from graduating at the DEA academy. I heard he had a working knowledge of the Spanish language, was a former State Trooper, and originally from El Paso. I thought to myself, "Maybe this guy would accompany me into Mexico. Kind of just hang on my coattail and follow my lead as most FNG's (Fucking New Guys) were taught to do."

Upon first meeting Sal, I quickly learned this guy was not your ordinary run of the mill FNG. He had an air of confidence coupled with a regimented demeanor complemented by his contagious smile and laughter. He would laugh at things that I never thought were remotely funny or amusing. But then again, I was considered the "serious, overly agitated, never smile" type of agent. I thought, "Shit, what a partnership!"

Sal was eager to take on his new responsibilities with a keen sense of enthusiasm at a time when other veteran agents were still investigating "kiddie dope cases". My first advice for Sal, as I explained to him, was to stand in a shower stall, turn the water on full throttle and rinse away all the State Trooper, regimented cop shit off the surface. Now is time to absorb all the crazy shit you are about to encounter on the streets of Juarez. "The cruelty of the game". I further explained "After all, you can't catch the devil with an angel. You need the devil to catch the devil."

It didn't take long for Sal to acquire an intimate working knowledge of Mexico and the manipulative infrastructure that accompanied it. He created contacts and sources with a simple smile and genuine laughter that put people at ease and created a sense of confidence with our foreign counterparts. In his book, you will read about some of the "unappreciated" ops we did in cross border cases that were actually the catalyst for the current existence of many projects and cross border offices that exist today. Sal's compassion and dedication for the job never left him after so many years, nor did his friends who maintain the upmost respect for him.

All of us go through life altering dilemmas, I certainly did. Some of us know how to maintain a level of composure through it all. Sal certainly has and still does to this day. Everyone has a breaking point, but some never reach that pinnacle. Somehow, through all the shit Sal went through, combined with on-the-job training skills he acquired at the level we worked, he managed to maintain his professionalism, character and innate sense of self-preservation.

I recently travelled to visit Sal and his loving family in his beautiful modest home. His home office is adorned with DEA memorabilia and several awards of accomplishment to give him a sense of empowerment of who he really once was. Something to be proud of!

Vindication comes in many forms whether it be legally, morally, or any other exonerating life event. Sal never had to earn vindication. In the eyes of his family and true friends he had always been vindicated. Love you my brother!!!

A.K.A.   Paul Rodriguez

CONTENTS

INTRODUCTION

Police officers and investigators have extraordinary stories to tell. I was responsible for confiscating large quantities of illicit drugs and arresting countless criminals that can be matched by only a few in law enforcement. However, my story ends with me enduring something that nobody wants to live through.

It took me several years to piece the events together in developing this book. I handled it like a hobby because I needed to focus my efforts on being a stay-at-home father and trying to make a living. In the process of describing what I experienced, I had to keep my emotions in check because the animosities attempted to sway the storytelling with a poisoned perspective. You will understand as you progress through the book.

Some people wanted me to glamorize factual experiences and classify my book as fiction. I consider myself a realist and simply wanted to tell it like it was. Everything written in this story is based on actual events. There is documentation and witness testimony to prove my story. I merged actual characters in a couple of situations so as not leave out unique personal experiences. The characters are based on real people. The true names of most of the characters were replaced with names of special people in my life like childhood friends, relatives, and those who stepped up to help me before and during my forced "sabbatical".

My first draft was formatted in third person because I was used to writing that way as a law enforcement officer. I changed it to first person because I am no longer a cop. There may be indications of the transition in this text. Forgive me for any errors and my novice style of writing as I completed this without any professional editing.

Music can be the soundtrack to memories of our lives. I infused some of the greatest classic rock music in my manuscript. The music and lyrics of this genre inspired me throughout my life especially as an undercover agent.

One last thing, the first several chapters describe the adventures of a young State Trooper and Special Agent. It provides the foundation for the journey that my life took. My thoughts and vocabulary transform with the times that I revered and eventually endured.

SPECIAL THANKS

For those who helped me and my family during the darkest hours:

My Mom and Dad, Anna and Dan Telles, Rudy and Dora Garza, Vincent and Susie Garza, Claudia Garza, Mary Jane Garza, Robert Lopez, Melissa Davis, Yvette Brusuelas, Aunt Tencha Enriquez, Jennifer Ramirez, Steve and Felicia Holgate, Kemi Monahan, Joe Dubois, Jack Geller, Bill Beyers, Donnie Garcia, and Charles Bowden.

For those who helped me with the transition after my sabbatical:

Rhett Stein, Rick Russell, Samuel Bayless, Richard and Martha McGee, Jacob Gaona, Sheriff Joe D. Tackitt, Jr., Wilson County Sheriff's Department (especially Booking), Chief Lorenzo Herrera, Judge's Marvin Quinney, Richard Jackson, Johnny Villarreal, Sara Canady, Clara Rutland, Orlando Carrasco, Dolores Cordova; Pam Woodmansee, Andres Cedillos, Stephen C. Barrera, Margaret Garcia, De'Ann Belicek, Clarice Trinidad, Linda Schulz, David Cordova, Dale Gilliam, Elaine Kolodziej, Jim and Donna Miller.

Most importantly, I want to express my sincerest admiration for Suzie. She was my greatest advocate, my foundation, and provided me with the greatest gift of all, Vincent.

PART ONE
DOMESTIC OPERATIONS

Chapter 1 – Just Another Day At The Office

I kissed my wife on the lips and said I should be home for dinner. I attempted to distract her when she noticed the large dent on the driver's side of the maroon GMC pickup. I would never tell her about last night's high-speed chase after the two assassins through the streets of Ciudad Juarez, Mexico.

She glanced at me wondering how it got there. Like most wives of law enforcement officers, she knows it is better not to ask what their husbands do at work. She forced a fake smile then looked in the rearview mirror before backing out of the driveway.

Behind every good man is a good woman. Lily was the only genuine aspect in my life. She was my moral compass. Living a life of deception, I wondered how I deserved someone so patient and trusting. I would leave her with innocence and not poison her with my exploits.

She majored in Political Science at Southwest Texas State University with ambitions of becoming a lawyer. I talked her out of becoming an ambulance chaser. Cops despise those who help criminals beat the American judicial system like defense attorneys and bail bondsmen.

Lily respected my opinion and pursued a career as an educator. Public educators are one of the most unappreciated and underpaid professions in the U.S. More importantly, her not entering the legal profession would be an ill-advised dissuasion later regretted by both of us.

Placing the Glock 9mm pistol under my shirt, I looked down to make sure a bulge was not evident. I carried the government-issued weapon everywhere I went. I believed it was an earned privilege and the responsibility as a peace officer to carry a weapon to protect others. I was always ready for the unexpected especially with all the lunatics in the world.

Lily gave me a hard time for taking it with me when we attended Catholic mass on Sundays. She asked, "Do you really believe someone is going to terrorize a house of worship?"

I responded, "I hope not. But if someone does, they came to the right place to meet their maker!"

I walked around my assigned Official Government Vehicle (OGV) and evaluated the damage to the rear fender. The newly-seized GMC pickup was confiscated by the Drug Enforcement Administration (DEA) from a major drug trafficker arrested in the Rio Grande Valley.

Thanks to the Federal Civil Forfeiture Law, law enforcement agencies were allowed to seize items obtained from ill-gotten gains considered fruits of a crime. The truck still had the scent of baby powder the previous owner insufficiently applied to mask the odor of the sixty pounds of marijuana. The owner went to prison, the marijuana was destroyed, and I got the pimped out truck that complemented my many undercover roles.

I needed to switch undercover vehicles during this active investigation. There were other confiscated vehicles to choose from in the El Paso DEA inventory that would enhance my appearance as an undercover agent. The black Mercedes would be my temporary OGV until the dust settled after last night.

The suspects saw me in the maroon pickup, and the word spread through the Juarez Drug Cartel that the *gringos* were working in their backyard. The next time, they would make sure I didn't return to the United States alive.

I knew that conducting operations alone in Ciudad Juarez was dangerous but necessary. The DEA had never assigned any agents to work in a city adjacent to "the pass of the north" (El Paso del Norte) for major drug shipments from Mexico into the U.S. I considered the confrontations with the criminals, or bad guys, as a challenging aspect of the drug war. Knowing I was outmanned and outgunned by the drug traffickers, my bravado went further by working in a foreign country I wasn't authorized to be in.

I was not going to back down just because they recognized me and my vehicle following them. I was determined to keep the heat on the drug smugglers. I was on a mission that needed to be completed even if it placed me in danger. The heads of the DEA were counting on me!

The ultimate goal of every law enforcement officer is to avoid serious bodily harm and return home safely. Yesterday's face with death was the second time in as many months.

The first instance occurred when I was parked down the street from a house that belonged to a well-documented drug trafficker in Ciudad Juarez. I planned on conducting surveillance for only an hour and write down license plate numbers of vehicles coming and going from the location.

It was about 9 p.m., and I sat alone in the darkest part of the neighborhood. I turned off the engine of my OGV and rolled down the driver's side window feeling the desert breeze.

It wasn't long before a dark-colored sedan pulled up next to me. I never saw it coming as it approached my location with the lights turned off. The passenger side window was rolled down and the barrel of an AK-47 assault rifle was pointed at my head.

I froze realizing I was a sitting duck with no means of escape. Initially, tunnel vision made me stare into the large, dark hole and not at the human behind the barrel. If there was a defense maneuver for this type of quandary, I wasn't aware of it. Pulling out my pistol would only cause my head to be blown off. I remained calm so as not to startle the gunman.

The driver exited and walked around the front end of their vehicle. He was holding a large caliber pistol. In Spanish, he asked, "What are you doing here?"

I turned my attention to the face of an angry Mexican man and answered, "I was supposed to meet a friend."

"Who's your friend?"

This was no time for a healthy discussion about my intentions. I needed to turn the conversation into my favor because lies would add up to nothing and aggravate the situation. Also, it was hard to create lies with a large caliber rifle barrel pointed at my face.

I asked the man, "Who are you?"

"We are security officers in this area. You need to get out of here now or you're going to have problems!"

I responded, "*Orale* (Okay)!" I was happy to end the brief encounter and accepted the generous offer. I thought to myself, "Hell yeah, I'll leave! I'm damn thrilled these so-called security guards, bearing more than a can of mace and a night stick, didn't want to fuck with me."

I turned my head away from the gun barrel and started the engine of the OGV. I pressed on the gas pedal trying not to peel out.

The AK-47 assault rifle aimed at my face would leave a lasting impression. The armed men didn't see me as a person rather as someone who was trying to take away their livelihood. Coming away from the showdown unharmed, I silently thanked 'the Man above' for sparing my life, again. Somehow I lived to die another day.

My second encounter with death came during the previous night's vehicular chase through the streets of downtown Ciudad Juarez. The high-speed chase was harrowing enough but the gunshots were downright terrifying!

DEA agents from the El Paso and Mexico City Offices coordinated surveillance efforts with a special unit of the Mexican federal police agency known as the *Procuraduria General de la Republica* (PGR). Our intelligence reports claimed the Gulf Cartel, headed by Juan Garcia-Abrego, planned to expand their methamphetamine operations in Ciudad Juarez.

It was believed three men were planning a power move on the Juarez Cartel. Their intentions would have created a bloodbath. Luis Medrano-Garza, Oscar Malherbe, and Jose De La Rosa were high-level members and *secarios,* or hitmen, for the Gulf Cartel.

It got dark quickly as the sun set behind the Franklin Mountains. The daily majestic desert sunset was ignored by the agents who had their sights set on the high-profile killers.

DEA Agent Paul Rodriguez came over the DEA radio, "All units, listen up. A gray Ford pickup is now departing the hideout. There are three men in the pickup. Medrano, *El Amable* and an unidentified man."

A DEA informant assisting in the operation recognized De La Rosa, aka *El Amable,* meaning the kind one. The assassin had earned the nickname by being pleasant and courteous to his victims before killing them. The demented man displayed the perverse traits before attaining gratification in ending another's life.

The other man in the gray pickup was identified as Luis Medrano-Garza, a lieutenant in the organization. He was a hitman who just liked killing people. Both of these ruthless killers were responsible for over sixty documented murders throughout the Republic of Mexico.

"Does anyone have the eye (direct visual contact) on the pickup?" shouted DEA Supervisor Jose Calderon over the radio.

DEA Agent Jake Davis answered, "They're heading westbound at a high rate of speed! I'm on their tail!"

"Whatever you do, don't lose them!" Calderon yelled.

The DEA agents and elite members of the Mexican federal police joined in the chase. Tires spun as police units fishtailed throughout the parking lot of a shopping center while avoiding the large metal speed bumps. The arrest of these men would be considered a significant victory for the DEA in the drug war.

Davis radioed, "The bad guys know we're behind them. The driver is trying to lose me in a residential area behind the *Gigante* (Giant) Shopping Mall."

I used a police maneuver on the suspects, called paralleling, by mirroring their evasive moves on an adjacent street. It was a pursuit tactic similar to the old American western cliché of cutting them off at the pass. I planned to intercept them at the next traffic intersection.

During the chase, a car pulled out from a residential driveway and sideswiped my pickup. It caused me to swerve briefly but I kept control of the steering wheel and continued on. I didn't have time to pull over and assess the damage to the OGV in the midst of something that was a scene out of a Hollywood action movie.

PGR and DEA vehicles were closing in on the gray pickup. Though there had been no joint rehearsals by the two agencies, the raw experience of each agent was exhibited as they converged on the suspects.

The driver of the pickup made several futile attempts to lose us including doubling back towards the crowded shopping area. He was cornered in the *Gigante* Shopping Mall parking lot. The passengers ignored orders to 'freeze' and made a run for it.

El Amable dashed into a residential area. Medrano-Garza ran the other direction inside the bustling shopping mall. The unidentified middle passenger never had a chance to run. He was yanked from the truck, thrown onto the ground and treated like a birthday *piñata* by the Mexican police.

A search of the pickup revealed a cache of AK-47 assault rifles. The suspects had expeditiously jumped out of the truck and never had a chance to fold down the bench seat to retrieve their automatic weapons. Unlucky for them and lucky for us.

PGR Comandante Mendoza, Jake Davis, and I exited our vehicles and ran after *El Amable*. Only a silhouette of the fleeing felon could be seen through the darkness.

There were sounds of gunfire! I wasn't sure where the rounds were coming from. Flashes from the figure alerted all of us that the man might be firing a pistol over his left shoulder to slow his pursuers. Behind me were the Mexican cops returning gunfire. I heard a whizzing sound pass over my head but the adrenalin kept my legs moving forward. We were gaining on the assassin!

As we turned onto another neighborhood street, Comandante Mendoza raised his AK-47 assault rifle in the air and fired several rounds towards the fleeing suspect. Muzzle flashes from the fully automatic rifle illuminated the night, the neighborhood, and the target.

The realization that the bullets were intended for him caused *El Amable* to fall to the ground.

Jake Davis and I were running next to the Comandante. We took a protective position by kneeling behind a parked car. We aligned the fluorescent dots of the sights on our Glock pistols by taking aim at the fallen man.

Breathing heavily, Davis asked, "Is he dead?"

I responded, "I don't think so. I think he's just STD, scared to death!"

Comandante Mendoza ran up to the lying man and kicked him on his side. The man rolled onto his back with his hands in the air, begging not to be shot. Mendoza obliged the request then introduced the assassin to the butt of his AK-47 rifle. *El Amable* was handcuffed and escorted back to the place he began his late night dash.

Meanwhile, Paul had given chase through the shopping mall after Medrano-Garza. Paul was an avid runner so there was little chance the fleeing felon would outrun him.

Paul kept his Glock pistol pointed to the ground as taught in the DEA

Academy. Cadets are taught not to hold the pistol next to their head by pointing the muzzle up in the air as seen on television and movies. There have been situations when police officers were startled and applied pressure to the trigger finger then shooting themselves or a fellow officer in the head with an accidental discharge.

Medrano-Garza turned a corner and Paul lost sight of him. He did not know if Medrano-Garza was armed so he stopped and focused on techniques learned for armed confrontations. He thought, "Hold the Glock with both hands because grip is important. Stand in a crouched position, arms out and slightly bent. Align the flourescent dots on the target for a proper sight alignment."

Using a quick peek technique, he saw Medrano-Garza continue running through the mall's crowded lower corridor. He was moving with relative ease until he knocked down a woman carrying an infant. This made Paul and several bystanders furious at what they witnessed. People started throwing items at the fleeing felon.

Paul holstered his gun under his belt. He needed to sprint faster and find a path to intercept the inconsiderate bastard. He ran to the closest stairway and jumped from the railing onto the assassin's backside.

Both men fell to the pavement. A scuffle ensued with Paul outweighing and outmatching his opponent. Not having his handcuffs with him, he grabbed Medrano-Garza in a chokehold and repeatedly punched the midsection to weaken him.

Paul yelled at his prisoner, "*Calmate, hijo de tu chingada madre* (Calm down, son of a bitch)!" After pummeling then subduing the man, Paul realized he had just nabbed someone considered an untouchable by U.S. federal law enforcement agencies. He dragged the assassin by the collar of his leather jacket to our location.

Medrano-Garza was forced to tell us where another high-level member was hiding. It was more than icing on a cake. Oscar Malherbe was arrested later that evening.

The men admitted planning to create a war with the Juarez Cartel, headed by Amado Carrillo-Fuentes, for control of the Ciudad Juarez-El Paso drug pipeline. They intended on establishing clandestine labs and capitalizing on the new market drug called methamphetamine. It was inexpensive to produce, easy to smuggle, very addictive and highly profitable.

These men didn't realize it but we may have saved their lives. They were looking to initiate an extensive, bloody turf battle with the mighty "Lord of the Skies". The Juarez Cartel was probably expecting them because they knew everything coming into their city. Nobody had ever got close to dethroning Carrillo-Fuentes, let alone intimidate this powerful kingpin.

It was unprecedented for U.S. law enforcement to arrest a high-level member from any Mexican drug cartel. On this night, we arrested three significant members and halted the Gulf Cartel from establishing their methamphetamine routes in Ciudad Juarez. Just as amazing was the way we apprehended them.

It was a Monday and I was on the morning drive to the El Paso DEA office. I reached forward to press play. The powerful and mesmerizing sounds of "Kashmir" by Led Zeppelin filled the cabin of my pickup. The song describes the beauty and mystique of a land that was considered one of the most volatile regions in the world. I could relate to the song because I lived and worked in a similar setting.

Rock and roll music can evoke memories or transport one into another realm. It inspires, motivates, and is therapeutic. Many people consider the sound as being too loud or don't understand the subliminal lyrics. Rock-n-rollers don't try to explain the music because they know "either you get it, or you don't."

I always found a way to relate music to the moment. The interpretation of the words from the operatic to harsh vocalists combined with the electric guitar riffs and the double bass drums of rock music were interconnected with my exploits as an undercover agent in the DEA.

I remember my first rock concert as a freshman in high school. I was overwhelmed with the theatrical performance, thunderous sounds, and spectacular light show of the Electric Light Orchestra. The experience was enhanced with the groovy smell of secondhand smoke that filled the El Paso Coliseum. I was hooked and became an aficionado of classic rock music.

Driving eastbound on Interstate 10 just before reaching the downtown area of El Paso, I looked over the Rio Grande River into the poorest section of Ciudad Juarez, Mexico. Like most *colonias* (rural subdivision) in the Mexican city, it consisted of cardboard shacks, tin sheet roofs and unpaved, dirt roads. The tenants lacked basic utilities and lived in unsanitary conditions.

Their live-for-today mentality will never provide a decent economic future. The most optimistic of Mexicans hope their honest efforts and strong faith in *el Señor* (God) will be enough to survive. An unrealistic perception and naive reliance on hope.

Constrained to constant deprivation of basic amenities, their resilience for suffering and gloom is quite high. This despair results in a reserved attitude. The Mexican poor have a sense of defeatism that keeps them down. Unless the masses express their anger through a coordinated national movement for structural changes in economics, education, and land reform, the status quo will remain the same.

I glanced down to the Mexican side of the river and see a woman using a washboard to scrub the dirt from several items of clothing. She was surrounded by four children who were playfully jumping in and out of the river. The mighty Rio Grande was shallow enough for the kids to wade towards the American side.

A United States Border Patrol vehicle was parked in plain sight on a nearby embankment ready to apprehend any alien invader. The presence was a reminder that the international borderline was evident although invisible. The kids ignored the idle threat and played on both sides of the river.

At night, the *colonia* was pitch black. The only signs of activity were the flames emanating from garbage cans providing warmth and the campfires used to cook the meager meals. The colonia was burrowed south of the Land of Enchantment (motto for the state of New Mexico) and west of the Sun City (motto for the city of El Paso).

Each day, it humbled me to see the extreme poverty that was a stone's throw away from the greatest nation in the world. The imaginary boundary of the shallow river separated the prosperity of a growing economy and the destitute of a third world country slipping backwards.

Americans refuse to look over their backyard fence to see their neighbor suffering from terminal internal economic and social issues. It is easier to ignore the plight of others when it doesn't directly affect us. However, the onus is on the Mexican citizens to take initiative and resolve their internal problems.

Common advice is not to get involved with the domestic disputes of others. Especially in law enforcement, the domestic disturbance is the most dangerous call to respond to. A change of heart by the victim or complainant can result with the police officer being considered as the instigator and having the entire family turn against the officer.

Since high school, I desired to be in law enforcement. My idealistic aspirations of fighting crime drove me towards a Criminal Justice degree from my hometown college, the University of Texas at El Paso.

I made it out of the lower income economic class and was considered a local success by friends and neighbors. There were many opportunities for me to succumb to the pressures of joining the local gangs. Fortunately, my childhood friends desired playing sports instead of engaging in juvenile delinquency. We kept each other in line.

At home, if I acted up, a leather belt was the preferred implement of punishment. However, my mother was quite accurate throwing the most accessible item, her hairbrush. My father didn't need to spank me because his angry stare made his point. We were a close family and my parent's positive reinforcement provided a solid foundation for my ambitions.

In Ysleta High School, I graduated in the Honor Society as number 39 out of approximately 600 students. I was voted Mr. YHS, similar to the "Most Popular Student" recognition, and selected to the All-City Football Team. I didn't seek attention but attained these honors through my polite demeanor and straightforward personality. I was a shy guy who didn't have a girlfriend until my last months of high school.

My confidence grew exponentially when I became a State Trooper. The Texas Department of Public Safety provided my initial experiences in law enforcement. Wearing the red shoulder patch meant I was considered the elite in traffic enforcement. I patrolled the rural roadways in Central and West Texas pursuing speed demons, drunk drivers, and some drug smugglers.

A police officer knows that small favors can go a long way. Liaison with people in the community is important for developing respect and can further investigative leads with cooperative witnesses. Aside from being cordial with others, I changed many flat tires and provided countless rides to stranded motorists. "Courtesy, Service, and Protection" was our motto.

In addition, there are unwritten rules that will make an officer's life better. Never issue a traffic citation to waitresses or cooks at restaurants that you frequent or they will spit in your food. Don't issue a citation to a local vendor that you may need their product or services. Don't issue a citation to the relatives of the local judges because it can alienate you with judicial rulings on criminal matters.

Other rules that can keep an officer safe included not issuing traffic citations during rainy weather because it was dangerous to be standing near the slick roads. Also, don't conduct a search of a suspected felons vehicle without backup because of a higher risk of confrontation.

Most importantly, don't take your work-related problems home to the family. Cops have a high divorce rate for several reasons. Women love a man in uniform and the temptation is always there. Secondly, cops deal with negativity everyday that may be difficult to decompress. Lastly, the power trip can lead to treating their loved ones as subordinates or as offenders.

Texas State Troopers were assigned to patrol the rural roads in the countryside, away from metropolitan areas. With only a limited number of officers assigned to each county, I usually rode solo. On occasion, the small town cops would call me for backup when a dangerous situation needed a closer.

I would arrive at the scene, exit my patrol car with a shotgun in hand, and chamber a buckshot shell loud enough to get everyone's attention. I wanted to make it clear that there was no negotiating with my Remington shotgun. Contrary to the Texas Rangers motto of 'One Riot, One Ranger', my motto was 'One Riot, One Trooper'.

There was a downside to being the king of the road. I saw many mangled and mutilated bodies. Nothing could prepare me for the sight of a horrific traffic fatality. For many police officers, the images of death can never be erased with time.

Like the time I arrived at the scene of an accident where a young man borrowed a friend's motorcycle during a wedding reception. He lost control of the large bike, flipped over twice, and it landed on his head. He failed to put on the helmet that was strapped to the seat. Word got back to the families at the dance hall and they all came dressed in their formal attire to see the Bride's brother lying with his tuxedo full of blood.

Another sickening account involved a student going to a high school football game. He came around a turn too fast, lost control of the pickup and was ejected because he wasn't wearing his seat belt. The truck landed sideways on the boy with his head between his legs, snapping his back. His mother arrived at the scene and became frantic trying to lift the truck off her son. I couldn't calm her down. I couldn't revive her son.

One more story. It was a dark Saturday night on a country road south of San Antonio. A couple pulled over to the shoulder because they were having a lover's quarrel. Somehow it got physical and the woman pulled away from her boyfriend. She entered the path of a pickup traveling about fifty miles per hour. She was hit then entangled under the carriage of the vehicle. Her leg was severed and left about twenty yards behind the rest of her mangled body.

I developed a tolerance seeing human carnage and dealing with the meanness of human beings. After five years as a Texas State Trooper, I decided to enter federal law enforcement. I wanted to take a proactive role in fighting crime instead of being reactive. In addition, the feds provided a higher salary, better retirement benefits, and a larger selection of investigative opportunities.

After submitting applications with various agencies, I was accepted by the U.S. Customs Service Air Interdiction Unit in El Paso. This opportunity provided an introduction to the many facets of employment in the federal government.

As an Air Interdiction Officer, I would fly in the rear section of a Cessna Citation jet utilizing radar and infrared to detect any unauthorized aircraft entering U.S. airspace from the Republic of Mexico. The suspicious aircraft would be intercepted and directed to land at the nearest airstrip for inspection. Enforcement action and investigative techniques would be implemented to inquire about the suspicious flight plan.

As part of my orientation, I learned to fly a Cessna 160 fixed-wing airplane. This familiarization would be helpful if there was an emergency situation and the pilots needed assistance flying the aircraft. The one-year stint in the air was interesting but I wanted something else. I desired to keep my feet on the ground and get closer to the real action.

For most, it is recommended to remember where you came from. Others prefer to forget their upbringing. I knew the streets and felt I could make a difference to stop the growing epidemic of illicit drugs that were destroying American lives. I developed an idealistic sense of personal discipline, pride and obligation to this calling.

I brought this dedication to the Drug Enforcement Administration. I believed in the government's efforts at waging a war on the illegal drug trade. On more than one occasion, I confided in others that my belief in the mission was so strong that if I had been killed, my death would not have been in vain.

Pursuing a career in law enforcement was a challenging part of my life. Attaining my goal of working for the elite in drug enforcement was euphoric. I was determined to perform to the best of my abilities. Along the way, I entered an unconventional territory - a battleground for my sanity and my torment.

Most mornings I was the first agent to arrive in the El Paso DEA office. I made the first pot of coffee so those who came behind me could have the same daily caffeine kick. Keeping it simple, I liked my coffee black. I had been drinking it that way since I was a State Trooper where most 'stop-n-rob' stores provided free, albeit often burnt, coffee. The gratuitous gesture from the store clerk was offered for the presence of a uniformed officer as a deterrent to anyone with any criminal intent.

I sat at my desk to read the daily reports stacked in the in-box. Teletypes and investigative reports were disseminated amongst domestic and foreign DEA offices. Most contained general drug trafficking intelligence or condensed descriptions of sizeable drug seizures and number of arrests.

On occasion, a report would come across our desk from a place like Fargo, North Dakota, describing the confiscation of several ounces of cocaine. It may have been considered a large drug seizure in that region of the U.S. but it only drew smirks of derision and ridicule from the El Paso agents.

The most recent teletype came from the DEA office in Mexico City. DEA Mexico agents took credit for arresting three high-level members of the Juan Garcia-Abrego drug trafficking organization.

The official report was carefully worded claiming the Mexican *federales*, under the direction of the DEA agents from Mexico City, successfully conducted a joint operation to apprehend the assassins in Ciudad Juarez, Mexico.

Headquarters praised the daring supervisors and brave agents from the Mexico City DEA office. The El Paso DEA office was only mentioned as providing intelligence support. There was no need to create problems by disclosing the presence of unauthorized personnel from the El Paso DEA participating in foreign, covert operations.

U.S. agents assigned to domestic offices were not supposed to be working in a foreign territory without diplomatic approval. It was a grievous violation of another country's sovereignty to have a foreigner conducting unauthorized law enforcement operations.

Few joint operations between Mexican cops and U.S. law enforcement ever resulted in the successful apprehension of a wanted drug trafficker or the confiscation of multi-ton quantities of illicit drugs. This operation was an exception.

I didn't expect any official credit for my part in the operation. I wasn't in it for the accolades. Lying low, under the radar, was my style. I liked being anonymous in the front lines of the clandestine war.

The only words of consolation came from my supervisor who jokingly said, "Thanks for not getting killed yesterday. I would hate writing a letter expressing my condolences to your wife."

Chapter 2 – Telephone Line

It had been three years since I received a career-changing telephone call. The college intern walked into the Group One squad bay and said, "There's a guy on the phone who wants to speak to the youngest agent. He won't give his name. You might want to hurry because he sounds awfully nervous."

Considering the receptionist's shy personality, she was not the kind of person who would be joking. I wondered if a veteran agent might be playing a trick on me. I would go along with the prank and answer the anonymous call. Not only was I the youngest agent, I was the only agent in the office this early in the morning.

Pressing the button for Line One, I answered, "Hello, this is Agent Martinez."

The caller asked, "Are you the youngest agent in your office?"

I laughed, "Yes. I'm also the best looking agent. How can I help you?"

There was a pause then, "I don't want to talk to any older agents!"

"Why is that?"

"Because I don't trust any of you guys, especially the older, corrupt ones."

"Well, I haven't been in long enough to be corrupted." I continued, "What makes you think that older agents are corrupt, anyway?"

"I have my reasons."

"C'mon. Have you ever seen or met the corrupt agent?"

"My boss told me that he has a DEA agent working for him. The agent tells him when there is a *dedo* (literally means finger, however it is slang for snitch) in the crew. Also, the agent protects loads coming into El Paso from Juarez."

I asked, "What kind of loads are we talking about?"

No response.

"I've changed my mind. I need to think about this."

I felt the caller's apprehension. I didn't want the conversation to end because this seemed like a legitimate opportunity.

I stated, "Listen to me. I don't know who you are. I'm not tracing or recording this call. If you hang up, nothing is going to change in your life. Whatever you've heard about corrupt DEA agents is bullshit. Every drug trafficking organization claims to have a corrupt cop on the payroll! It's a scare tactic so nobody talks to the cops. I personally know every agent in this office, and I can promise you there is not a single one who is corrupt. Do you understand?"

There have been instances where a U.S. law enforcement officer was arrested for being affiliated with a drug trafficking organization. A corrupt cop is considered a violation of trust to the law enforcement brotherhood and the American people. Cops are held to a higher standard. The American media loves to plaster the crooked cops picture on the front page. Sensationalism sells newspapers and attracts television viewers. Also, it humiliates the accused cop and his family.

The anonymous caller took a deep breath and continued, "I'm not sure if I want talk to you guys after all. I don't know who to trust."

I kept the caller's attention and needed to take it one step further. I had to get the cynical thoughts out of the caller's mind and redirect them to his motivation to provide information. Also, I wanted the caller to feel as if he was in control of the conversation and not being forced to snitch.

I suggested, "Why don't we meet at a location where you feel comfortable. If you don't like me, then you can just get up and be on your way. It will be like nothing ever happened." I let the proposition sink in.

The caller said, "I get off from work at four o'clock. We can meet after that. Let's meet at the Pizza Hut restaurant on the west side of town on Mesa Street."

Growing up on the east side of El Paso, one rarely had a reason to travel to the other side of the Franklin Mountains. I was told the Westside was restricted to the rich, White people. The roads were paved, the homes were newer, and the people were prettier. It wasn't until my junior year in high school before I visited the good side of town. My Ysleta Indians gave the powerhouse Coronado Thunderbirds a tough football game. I wasn't that impressed however I was jealous of their reputation.

Recently, I became familiar with the west side of the city after purchasing a modest home upon joining the DEA. I was living amongst the upper echelon of society and felt I acclimated well. However, my family and childhood friends rarely visited because they considered it as too far of a drive. Old habits were hard to break.

I told the caller, "I'll be wearing a blue shirt and beige pants. Due to our agency rules, I have to take another agent with me. It will be a young agent, like myself. Are you okay with that?"

The caller reluctantly consented.

"By the way, my name is Sal Martinez. You don't have to tell me yours."

"I'd prefer that."

"One more question. What kind of drugs are we talking about?"

"Cocaine. A lot of it." Then the phone went dead.

I reclined in my office chair and thoughts of uncertainty entered my mind, "Would this be the only time I talk to this guy? Will he show up this afternoon? What made him call so early in the morning? Was he an early riser or was he anxious to clear his conscience after a sleepless night?"

The questions kept coming, "Does the anonymous caller really believe that a DEA agent was 'on the take' for a local trafficker? Why would an agent making $60,000 per year want to jeopardize his career for dirty money? Not in the DEA!"

To calm my anxiety that developed because of this call, I reached for the fluid sounds of Fleetwood Mac's, "Rumours". This artistic production was one that rockers needed to have in their album collection. The innovativeness and harmony blended together whereby one had to listen to it in its entirety. I looked at the case files on my desk and realized that there were many other investigative leads to follow up. I didn't want to waste time and get hung up on a phone call filled with innuendo.

The El Paso DEA office received several anonymous calls per day. Most led nowhere because the caller was not deep enough into the drug trafficking organization and could not provide specific names, addresses, or drug distribution details. There were too many questions left unanswered. The ambiguity would leave the agent with nothing solid to follow up on.

Some agents saved the irrelevant documentation in a miscellaneous folder where it was put aside, but not forgotten. Dedicated agents would research and connect it to an active organization. A Report of Investigation, known as a DEA-6, with the vague information would be entered in the internal DEA database called the Narcotics and Dangerous Drug Information System or NADDIS. On the other hand, most agents would simply discard the information into a wastebasket.

The El Paso DEA office was severely understaffed. There were only twenty-two Special Agents and two Intelligence Analysts to handle one of the most active drug transshipment locations in the world. DEA Headquarters hadn't recognized the Southwest border as the front lines of the drug war.

They were concerned with other parts of the U.S. like Florida, California and the Canadian border. Negative publicity from these geographical regions gave the impression that they were being inundated with illicit drugs. Political pressure on the DEA demanded additional agents in those areas leaving the southwest border cities without the needed manpower and support.

Similarly, the city of El Paso had been neglected by politicians at the State Capitol in Austin. The officials were concerned with their own special interest donors and disregarded the needed attention from a distant city. Out of sight, out of mind. El Pasoans have always felt like the comedian Rodney Dangerfield in that, "They get no respect!"

Most of the agents assigned to the El Paso DEA came from other parts of the United States and neither spoke Spanish nor understood the Mexican culture. The agents had diverse backgrounds yet we got along. There might have been an occasional spat between the agents, but there were no grudges held.

There were three Hispanics agents and one Hispanic supervisor assigned to Group One. The other two groups consisted of nineteen non-Hispanic agents. The lack of Hispanics assigned to the office was never an issue, because nobody ever made it one. To prevent animosity, it was easier to ignore the obvious.

The agents all had different skills, but they weren't tied down to limited tasks. With a common goal, each was willing to do whatever was necessary to further the drug war efforts, including the not so glorious job of doing paperwork. When an agent requested assistance for surveillance on a suspect or a stash location, fellow agents were more than accommodating. The chemistry among most agents was just right.

I spent the day at my desk reading case files on untouchable traffickers that contained voluminous amounts of intelligence on their activities. It was apparent that details on drug trafficking organizations came to a dead end when I queried the identities of the decision makers. It was easy to identify the small-timers and some middlemen. But after that, there was a wall of anonymity.

The best way to infiltrate any organization was to 'flip' someone close to the managerial level. It had to be someone willing to give up the life of money and power. It would be going against the precepts of our culture where success is measured by wealth and prestige. Few were willing to forsake that lifestyle.

The DEA mission was enforcing the controlled substances laws and regulations of the United States. The ultimate goal was to dismantle any illicit drug organization by arresting key members and halting the distribution of drugs. It was an idealistic dream for me and, for that matter, every DEA agent. I knew I was in a holy war, with the best outfit to do just that.

I wanted to have a seasoned veteran accompany me to determine if the anonymous caller was legit. However, I would abide by the caller's wish not to meet with an older agent. Another rookie agent accepted the invitation.

Vince Sellers kept his wavy black hair shoulder-length while sporting a thin, seedy mustache. He would regularly wear a black leather jacket and jeans. His looks and demeanor reminded me of the crude comedian named Andrew Dice Clay. Vince emitted an uncaring attitude, as if it was hard for him to give a damn about anything, and his pompous personality alienated people upon introduction.

He was highly opinionated about almost everything and simply had no tact. Occasionally, his words and actions caused him to put his foot in his mouth, but Vince didn't care. Living the single life, dwelling on regret was the furthest thing from his mind. His personal motto was "Everyone's an asshole until proven otherwise!"

I considered my eventual investigative partner as amusing yet dedicated. A friendship based on loyalty that grew with the years. This was how Vince proved otherwise.

At 4:15 p.m., Vince and I sat at a table against the large windows facing the parking lot of the restaurant. We ordered iced tea, and told the waitress we were waiting for a friend before ordering something to eat. We didn't intend on eating but saying this gave the waitress hope she would receive a decent tip.

"Would you fellas like an appetizer?"

I responded, "No thanks."

"Are you sure? You both look hungry."

"Scouts honor." I raised my right hand making the recognized Cub Scouts hand gesture with the three fingers joined.

Vince responded, "Don't believe him. He was kicked out of Cub Scouts."

The waitress asked, "Why?"

"For eating Brownies."

She walked away laughing.

A few minutes later, a nervous looking man in his mid-twenties entered the front door. The man had curly black hair, a medium build, and dark circles around his eyes. He looked around and walked slowly to our table. "Are you Sal?"

"Yeah," I said as I stood up to shake the man's hand. Vince, not known for politeness, remained seated. "This is my partner." They shook hands.

Without hesitation, Vince said, "I didn't catch your name."

"My name is Rudy." The anonymous caller was no longer anonymous.

The waitress appeared and asked Rudy, "Can I get you something to drink?"

"Iced tea, please." No one spoke as she placed the menus on the table.

Rudy looked at each agent, wondering if he had made the right decision. Confessing to two cops about his knowledge of something illegal could only lead to bigger problems. Rudy began, "How can you guys help me if I tell you about people moving drugs?"

I responded, "We need to know the quantity of drugs and your role in the organization."

"I'm not actually involved."

I immediately thought, "Damn, this guy isn't deep enough. He's just someone on the outside looking in." Still, what was his motivation for calling? Was it for monetary reasons or revenge?

I asked, "How would you know about the drugs if you're not involved?"

Rudy answered the question with a question, "Are you sure you aren't recording me?"

I stood up, raised my hands, and said, "You can pat me down if you like."

Rudy shook his head and with a soft voice, "I'm here because my brother is in deep, and I want to get him out of the drug business."

That seemed like a good enough reason to call the police.

The waitress returned with a glass of iced tea and placed it in front of Rudy. "Do y'all need more time to order something to eat?"

The agents looked at Rudy and waited for his response.

"I'm not hungry," he said, as he handed his menu back to the waitress.

"We're okay with the tea, thank you." I said. Both of us handed our menus to the woman.

She walked away disappointed. Living on cash tips meant relying on human generosity. She wasn't optimistic with this table.

Vince asked, "How is your brother involved?"

"He's responsible for finding local drivers for cars loaded with drugs. The cars are driven from El Paso to different cities, depending on the orders he receives. He offers them a thousand dollars to drive the cars."

"Where does he find people willing to take a chance?"

"He looks for clean cut, well-spoken young men. He wants men who don't fit the profile of a drug user and won't be grabbing a cop's attention."

I knew where Rudy was going with the recruitment criteria. Racial profiling is a police tactic used in the past, present and more than likely, the future. It is based on prejudicial views and racial ignorance. Cops will pull over a vehicle driven by a minority more often than by a White person. I did it, and so did most of my brethren in blue.

Rudy continued, "My brother gets a call from someone in the organization who tells him where the loaded cars are parked and where they will be driven. My brother never gets close to the cars. He just watches them from a distance."

"How much is in each car?"

"About a hundred kilos."

"A hundred kilos of cocaine?" I was pleasantly surprised.

"We used to transport weed (slang for marijuana), but there's more money to be made in coke (slang for cocaine)."

I tried to quell my excitement. "What's your brother's name?"

"Dan. Dan Montes."

"Does your brother know you called us?"

"No way! He would be pissed off and disown me."

It was obvious Rudy cared about his brother's welfare. I asked, "Have you talked to him about leaving the business or changing his ways?"

"I've told him that he needs to stop because he's going to get busted. After last night, you guys probably know who he is."

There was no response by us. We looked intently at Rudy waiting for specific details.

"Don't you know about the takedown at the checkpoint in Las Cruces yesterday?"

Rudy was referring to one of several U.S. Border Patrol inspection sites strategically located on major roadways outside of El Paso. Agents at these checkpoints were effectively confiscating significant amounts of illicit drugs leaving the El Paso area destined for other U.S. cities. Although considered sizeable quantities, these seized loads were just a fraction of the total drugs entering the U.S.

The Border Patrol agents are trained to look for nervous behavior from people entering the checkpoint. This subjective and discretionary tactic is considered enough probable cause to initiate a search of a vehicle. Ambiguous mannerisms have been legally sufficient for law enforcement authorities to proceed with further investigative measures. Criminal defense attorneys have found it difficult to disprove the unscientific reasons in court when pursuing an illegal search and seizure argument.

The most feared aspect of the checkpoint is the drug sniffing dog. The canine and his handler normally remain in the secondary inspection area until a vehicle is referred to them for a more thorough inspection. The dogs are sporadically used because they can become ineffective if overused. Like humans, dogs can handle only so much excitement.

I wondered if I had missed reading about the cocaine seizure in one of the teletypes distributed earlier that morning. Actually, the report had not made its way down the chain of command. It was lying on a supervisor's desk pending further investigative action by the El Paso DEA.

I responded, "No, we don't. Tell us about it."

"One of my brother's drivers got busted with ninety kilos. The guy was supposed to take the cocaine to California. For some reason, the Border Patrol pulled him to the side and found the stash in the false compartment located in the trunk. I believe someone dropped a dime (slang for notified the police) on the driver because the driver has made the West Coast run many times before without getting hassled."

"My brother recruits clean-cut, young men who don't look like drug users to drive the loads. He's never had any problems until now."

"Is there someone you believe that turned in the driver?"

"Shit, I don't know what to think! My brother said there is a dirty DEA agent who will find out if someone snitched. The agent has helped them before."

"Has your brother ever met the DEA agent?"

"No. His boss has only talked about the agent."

I knew Rudy was trying to do something good, but he didn't have the details to take it any further. I thought of the best way to obtain specific information. It couldn't hurt to ask. How would Rudy react if asked to gather specific information covertly from his brother?

I wondered if Rudy's apparent desperation to do something good would determine if blood was thicker than water. There are countless reasons someone would want to cooperate with the DEA but this extraordinary situation of brother informing on his brother would require some gentle persuasion.

Trying to be as tactful as possible, I asked, "Would you be able to get some additional details from your brother?"

"What do you mean? You want me to spy on my own brother?"

I continued, "Dan may be in danger. It's important to know where your brother stands with this organization after this drug seizure. We need to know what the people above your brother are going to do."

Rudy's mind was spinning with the consequences of turning on his brother. He knew Dan would be furious and antagonistic with him and the DEA agents. Dan did not like being told what to do by family members or anyone outside of his immediate supervisor in the drug cartel.

Rudy considered the benefits of helping his brother get out of the drug trafficking business outweighing the reluctance to leaving the life of crime. He knew what was best for his headstrong older brother.

"If I do this for you, will you help my brother get out? I mean, you guys can forget about what he's done for the past several years, right?"

"I'm not trying to be funny but coming to us is like a Catholic going into a confessional with a priest. You cleanse your soul for any sins from your past."

Vince looked at me and wanted to laugh at the metaphor.

I clarified the satirical response, "We cannot make any promises until the U.S. Attorney's office agrees with the terms. They make the final decision about immunity and who will be prosecuted. We'll seek approval from the necessary people. So let us take it one step at a time."

Rudy said, "We may not have a lot of time. I'm worried about my brother being punished by his superiors for losing the ninety keys (slang for kilograms). Can you protect him?"

"It is going to be up to him to come talk to us. He will need to be honest about his role in the organization. If he refuses to cooperate or lies to me, I won't help him. Right now, you are doing the talking for him."

Rudy listened and the words sunk in. In fact, he took it one step further for his brother's sake, "What if I tell you something else?"

"Go ahead."

"What if I tell you there is another car loaded with a hundred kilos of coke?"

"Where is it?"

"My brother got scared. He wants to wait awhile before sending another shipment. He wasn't sure if the driver in Las Cruces was going to tell the cops about him or the second car. So he ordered another driver to leave the second car in a shopping center parking lot. He didn't want the driver and the coke in the same place."

"So there were two loads destined for California?"

Rudy put his head down and nodded.

"Rudy, we need a vehicle description and location as soon as possible, before it disappears!"

"Let me talk to my brother. He's hiding out in Juarez and won't talk on the phone. I'll need to find him and then get back to you, tomorrow."

Vince raised his voice, "Wait a minute! The car with a hundred kilos of coke is abandoned in a public parking lot? What if someone steals it?"

Rudy did not respond.

El Paso was averaging nearly one hundred vehicles stolen per week, mostly from shopping center parking lots. After being hot-wired, it takes just fifteen minutes for the cars to reach the safe refuge of Ciudad Juarez. Within hours they were stripped and unrecognizable.

I gave Rudy a piece of paper with my cell phone number. I did this because I was not about to give him a DEA business card. "I hope you call."

I hated vagueness, but there was nothing I could do about it. This, combined with the thought of an unprotected vehicle containing one hundred kilos of cocaine, raised my anxiety level. There was also a desire to ask for details about previous drug shipments, but my focus returned to the second vehicle.

Rudy left the restaurant and walked quickly to his minivan. He sped off, but not before Vince jotted the license plate number on a napkin.

I asked Vince, "What do you think?"

"It sounds legit. Let's see if Rudy takes the initiative to milk his brother for any details. Talk about the lowest form of informant, brother snitching on brother. That's fucked up!" Vince was always blunt.

I said, "If we locate the car, we will probably take it down. It would be nice to follow it to its final destination in California but we can't take the chance of losing it. Worst case scenario, Rudy's brother will be held liable for the lost loads. He will lose his credibility in the organization or likely be killed."

After a moment of silence, I said, "I'll brief the boss. I got the tab." The agents rose from the table and departed the restaurant. I left the waitress a five-dollar tip.

Chapter 3 – A Drop In The Bucket

It was almost midnight when the cell phone rang. My heart rate increased after being startled. I was watching a recording of my favorite comedy series, Seinfeld. I pushed the pause button on the television remote control with my left thumb, put down my glass of milk, and pressed the talk button on the cell phone with my right thumb, "Hello."

"Can we meet in the morning?" It was Rudy.

"We can talk now." I was anxious to get details about the abandoned cocaine shipment.

"The car is safe. The driver took it to his house. He is supposed to keep it there until my brother gets the order to move it. It could be several days. Dan is almost certain the second load of drugs won't be leaving any time soon."

Rudy continued, "My only concern is that my brother said the guy above him is going to call the corrupt DEA. They want to know who was responsible for the loss of drugs in Las Cruces."

"Don't worry about that crap! Do you know the name of the guy talking to your brother?"

"No."

"Let's meet first thing in the morning."

After hanging up, I gazed at a freeze frame of Elaine pushing Kramer.

Like most men, I felt a sense of authority with the remote control in my hand while reclining on my leather throne. The humor of the sitcom was dulled by my nervous anticipation. I turned off the television.

I thought of possible scenarios to seize the drugs without jeopardizing the possibility of future loads. I wanted to be proactive and find a way to take initiative. There are no printed playbooks made available to guide an agent with investigative options. One must rely on past experiences and present-day ingenuity.

I glanced at my collection of books on a shelf. Buddhism and Greek philosophy usually answered my cognitive questions. Although I read for theoretical reasons, I remained grounded as a Catholic because I admired the fundamental doctrines and rich traditions. Aside from the Bible, "Of the Imitation of Christ" eased my soul when feeling dispirited.

Eager for guidance, I flipped through the pages of "The Art of War". Sun Tzu said, "If the enemy opens the door, you must race in." This meant employing a spy. Another quote was, "Sagacious generals who are able to get spies will invariably attain great achievements." Rudy would need to be my spy.

The next morning, Vince and I met Rudy at the Hamburger Inn restaurant in central El Paso to discuss our next move. We talked over a cup of coffee and the best bowl of menudo in town. This iconic eatery was frequented by many El Pasoans during a late night trek for the ultimate hangover remedy.

Earlier that morning, I had read the preliminary report regarding the cocaine seizure in Las Cruces. The driver had sung like a canary and pointed the blame on his immediate manager. Agents from the Las Cruces DEA office were en route to El Paso with their sights set on a trafficker named Dan Montes. I made a phone call and convinced them to stand down for a couple of days.

I asked Rudy, "Do you know where the vehicle is located?"

"Yes. It's not going anywhere for awhile."

"Good. Now, tell me more about your brother."

Rudy said, "He's been caught up in the life of money, women, and power. There is nothing else he can do for a living. Dan has said he would rather be arrested or killed before becoming a 'regular Joe' with a lame ass job." Dan Montes didn't realize how close he was to his naive aspirations.

Rudy continued, "The drugs are hidden in the cars by people we don't know about, and they don't know anything about my brother. You have two separate groups. One conceals the drugs and the other is responsible for the transportation."

"After the car is loaded, Dan is told where it is parked. The suppliers watch the car until one of my brother's drivers shows up. My brother then takes his driver to retrieve the car. The keys are always left in the ashtray."

Vince ranted, "You're saying a million dollars worth of drugs is in an unlocked vehicle! In an open parking lot, in the middle of the auto theft capital of the United States. Accessible for anyone to open the handle of the car and find the keys in the ashtray. Are you shitting me?"

Rudy ignored the tirade, "My brother pockets $5,000 for each car he contracts. Dan pays the driver up to $2,000 upon delivery. The driver takes the drugs to cities like Houston, Chicago or Riverside, California. Dan follows the car until it passes through the riskiest part of the journey."

I responded, "The U.S. Border Patrol checkpoint."

Rudy continued, "Dan runs interference for the drug vehicles. He sets up near the checkpoint while the driver remains at a roadside park or truck stop. He knows when the Border Patrol will close the checkpoint due to shift change or limited manpower. During this time, the loaded vehicle will pass safely through the unmanned location."

Vince volunteered a personal observation, "If your brother put as much time and effort into a legitimate career, he would be very successful."

Rudy defended his brother, "Having a nine-to-five job is boring. Some people like the lure of money and power. We gotta do what we gotta do. Growing up poor, we didn't have a silver spoon in our mouth like you!"

I returned to the issue at hand, "Tell me where the second vehicle is located."

"Jason Sanchez lives in a duplex in a poor part of El Paso, near the downtown area. His instructions were to secure the older model Ford Taurus in his driveway until he got the order to drive the load. There is a $2,000 payment waiting for him after he drops off the car at a motel in Riverside, California."

"What is your brother going to do?"

"He is going to stay in Juarez for a couple of days. He's worried the cops are looking for him."

The meeting adjourned with Rudy agreeing to persuade his brother to meet with us. Vince and I returned to the DEA office to brief the boss.

The Group One supervisor, Jose Calderon, had been assigned to the El Paso DEA office upon his promotion to the supervisory level. Although a *boriqua*, born in Puerto Rico and raised in New York, he had a good sense of the Mexican culture. His resume included a three-year stint at the U.S.

Embassy in Mexico City.

Short in stature, dark complexion and curly black hair gave him a Mestizo appearance. His outward calmness and efficacious manner made him very accessible. Though occasionally tentative in his decision making, he never tried to compensate for his size with a Napoleonic attitude.

A good supervisor is measured by his ability to delegate responsibilities. Calderon demanded the best from his agents and those who didn't make the grade were transferred to another group. Of the three groups in the El Paso office, Group One was considered to have the most compassionate and hands-off leader.

After the briefing, Calderon ordered all his agents to drop what they were doing. Like his youngest agent, he was equally anxious to set up surveillance on the Ford Taurus. Calderon announced, "We can't wait any longer to establish surveillance on the car. I don't care if you scheduled a lunch date with your wife or girlfriend, or both. Stop what you're doing and prepare to spend the next several days living in your OGV's."

All Group One agents were briefed about the surveillance. The vehicle's description and license plate number were provided to agents assisting in the operation. An enlarged black and white photocopy of Sanchez's Texas driver's license was distributed to each agent. The address was provided, and everyone headed that way without hesitation.

One of the most important aspects of a DEA agent's job is effective surveillance. Communication and teamwork are critical. It is necessary to have one agent, known as the surveillance coordinator, to position all participating agents in the most strategic location.

Calderon assigned senior agent Paul Rodriguez as surveillance coordinator. Paul had returned to his hometown of El Paso several months earlier after a three-year stint in Guadalajara, Mexico. He was a seasoned veteran who worked for the DEA on both sides of the border. The return to his hometown was made to ease his frustration with the Mexican cops and American bureaucrats pretending to be working together in the war on drugs.

Surveillance begins when an agent, known as 'the eye', gets in position for a direct line of sight with the person or vehicle, known as 'the target'. The agent will be the first to see when the target is moving and notify the other agents. The eye must remain focused because any form of distraction could result losing sight of the target.

The rest of the perimeter agents are strategically located in the vicinity. They must evaluate their surroundings as to the available routes of departure by the suspects. Just as important as the accessibility to pursue the suspects, is finding the most direct avenue to protect another agent if trouble arises.

Once the eye notifies the perimeter agents of the target's direction of travel, each agent must be ready to become the initial pursuit vehicle behind the target known as 'the takeaway'. The other agents fall in behind, periodically alternating to become the eye. These actions ensure that a surveillance vehicle is not constantly behind the target causing the agent to be recognized or 'burned' by the suspect.

Contrary to Hollywood movies, one should not follow directly behind the suspect without any cover. It is best to stay several vehicles behind so as not to be in a direct line of sight. Bad guys looking in the rearview mirror may recognize a suspicious vehicle if they see it more than once in a short period of time.

The day went by with only one sighting of Sanchez. He had exited his house, walked to the back of the car, and adjusted the right taillight cover. Seeing the suspect assured the agents they were at the right place.

The sun settled behind the Franklin Mountains, and the neighborhood street transposed into a lethargic scene. This low-income neighborhood, like so many in El Paso, consisted of modest homes, older model cars and inactivity. The few inhabitants that came out of their homes were unaware of the DEA presence. This surveillance was just like the neighborhood, uneventful.

In a parking lot, several blocks away from the target location, Paul requested a meeting with Vince and me. He pulled up next to me, facing the opposite direction so we could talk without getting out of our vehicles. Vince arrived and exited his vehicle to stretch his legs.

Exhibiting paternal concern, Paul asked the younger agents, "Did you bring a change of clothing? Just in case we do an all-nighter into tomorrow." Both men nodded.

Vince said, "Yeah, I learned quickly to keep an extra set of clothes and toiletries for lengthy operations like this one. I have a feeling we'll be here for a few days." Simultaneously, we all took a deep breath to release the anxiety of anticipating the worst.

I asked, "Isn't it amazing how there are no children playing in the street. It's a beautiful afternoon, so where are the kids? Growing up, we played outside until the sun went down. We didn't want the sun to go down until midnight!"

Paul answered, "Kids today are preoccupied with television and computer games. This past Christmas morning, I went for a jog, and there wasn't a single kid in my neighborhood outside tossing a new football, riding a bike, or skateboarding. Kids don't play the games we used to play."

I continued, "I remember playing *La quemada* (the burn) where a handball was used to roll into dug-out holes in the dirt. If the ball landed in your hole, you had to run after the others and hit them with the ball before they made it to the safety zone."

Paul added, "It was similar to another game called *Los frijoles estan quemando* (the beans are burning). It was like hide-and-seek but with a leather belt that would be hidden in the bushes or trees. If you were the lucky one to find the belt, you would swat the others before they made it to the safety zone."

Vince said, "Damn, you Mesicans played some violent shit!" We laughed and then there was a pause for further reflections from the good old days.

An unknown agent made a humming sound over the DEA radio, drawing wry chuckles from the other agents. The humming was a sarcastic jab that the surveillance appeared to be a waste of time, or a hummer. The El Paso agents had recently experienced numerous hurry-and-wait surveillances that resulted in no drug seizures or arrests being made. Confident about the possibility of confiscating one hundred kilos of cocaine, I didn't let their pessimism dampen my hopes.

DEA agents know that patience is required during the hours of inactivity. One usually read a paperback, returned telephone calls, or listened to the radio. It was best to find a shaded area under a tree. The engine was turned off to prevent the vehicle from overheating, and the windows were rolled down to stay cool.

Intuitiveness is necessary when looking for an inconspicuous yet strategic location to park in his or her area of responsibility. Agents would occasionally switch locations for a change of scenery and to prevent neighbors from reporting a suspicious vehicle on their street. For safety reasons, an agent should have an all around, clear view of his immediate surroundings.

Agent Jake Davis did not adhere to this last rule. He parked his OGV on a vacant lot unaware of the entrance to an alley on his right rear blind spot. Three homeboys, or locals, noticed the out of place sedan occupied by a Caucasian in their *barrio*. Reclining back in the driver's seat, Jake never saw the kids sneak up on him.

They surrounded the car, jumped on the bumpers, and wildly rocked the vehicle. They chanted, "*Marano! Marano! Marano!* (pig)" Startled from his nap, Jake thought he was being attacked and overreacted by getting on the DEA radio and asking for backup.

After a minute of provocation, the assailants ran away cursing at the outsider and flashing their territorial gang signs.

After the comic relief, the agents discussed a meal rotation for those who did not bring their sack lunch to work. A list of drive thru restaurants in the vicinity was broadcast over the DEA radio. Eating at fast-food restaurants was an occupational hazard for cops especially when there was no time for a sit-down meal.

It was about eight o'clock when the unexpected occurred. Jason Sanchez got into the Ford Taurus and drove away from his residence. Vince was the eye and shouted on the DEA radio, "The target is headed westbound on Alameda Avenue! Take away (closest surveillance agent), do you copy?"

Jake Davis was in position and fell behind the Ford Taurus. He acknowledged, "I got visual!" The other agents, caught off-guard, scrambled to catch up.

Sanchez drove five blocks, and made two left turns before stopping at a neighborhood convenience store. As he walked into the store, Sanchez grabbed his wallet from his rear pant pocket and appeared to be counting dollar bills.

"What the hell is this guy doing driving the car?" Davis asked his fellow agents over the radio. There was no answer. All the agents were just as surprised.

Meanwhile, I was on my cell phone talking to a dispatcher for the El Paso Police Department. I requested immediate assistance from a marked patrol unit. I believed this would be a great opportunity to conduct a traffic stop on the vehicle. The blame would be directed at Sanchez for foolishly driving the car and being stopped for a traffic violation. This would deflect any culpability from Dan Montes by the owners of the cocaine.

It took five minutes for a 'black and white' to show up. I introduced myself to the two uniformed officers and instructed them to stop the Ford Taurus immediately after it was seen departing from the convenience store.

Probable cause would need to be made up by the officers. Cops do it all the time. If a cop wants to stop someone, he will find a reason.

On cue, Davis said over the radio, "For your information, the right taillight is out on the target vehicle." Earlier, Sanchez did not make the time to fix the problem.

I smiled and told the officers, "There's your probable cause for the stop, boys." Parked one block away from the convenience store, the uniformed officers waited for 'the eye' to call out the direction of travel. They had less than five blocks to execute the traffic stop before Sanchez made it back to his driveway or the safety zone, just like the game of *La Quemada*.

Sanchez walked out of the store and placed a bag of groceries on the front passenger seat. He entered the Taurus and sat there for a few minutes.

Jake announced, "I think he's looking around. He may be scanning for cops. Everybody hold your position."

Sanchez turned on the vehicle lights, applied the turn signal, and proceeded to drive very cautiously. It was two blocks later when he noticed a police car with its emergency lights flashing in his rearview mirror. He slowed down and pulled over to the right side of the road to let it pass. But the police car didn't pass.

"Shit, they're stopping me!" His mind spun frantically, wondering what he had done wrong and disbelieving his terrible fate. He deliberated, "Should I try to outrun them? Do I abandon the car and run into the *barrio*?"

He shifted the lever to park and hoped the cops would just let him go.

The uniformed officer approached the driver's side window. He informed Sanchez that he had a defective taillight and asked him for his driver's license and proof of liability auto insurance.

"My taillight?"

Sanchez reached into the glove compartment. He shuffled through loose pieces of paperwork before producing the insurance form.

The officer noticed the name on the insurance was not Jason Sanchez. He asked, "Who does the car belong to?"

"It's a friend of mine. I was helping him with some mechanical work."

"Why are you so nervous?"

"I'm not nervous. Isn't it normal to be a little shook up when the cops pull you over?"

The officer asked Sanchez if they could conduct a search inside the Ford Taurus.

"Why?"

The officer asked, "Do you have something to hide?"

"No."

"Well then, what is wrong with me looking inside your car?" Police officers like to turn the table and play the guilty conscience game. This puts the violator on the defense. Most people don't want to disrespect the police officer so they give permission to search, even when there is something illegal in the vehicle.

"Go ahead then." He was confident that two traffic cops wouldn't locate the cocaine in the hidden compartment.

It took nearly fifteen minutes. Myself and the other agents were getting anxious wondering why the uniformed officers were taking so long to discover the drugs. One of the officers returned to the patrol unit and used the portable radio, "Agent Martinez, we can't see any sign of welding or loose screws which might indicate a false compartment. What do you want us to do?"

I replied, "I just got off the cell phone with your dispatcher. A canine unit is in the area. Make Sanchez believe a fellow officer called you on the police radio. Tell him the police department has a new canine that needs introductory training and it happened to be in the vicinity."

Within ten minutes, the canine unit arrived with an energetic German shepherd riding in the caged back seat. The canine handler grabbed the leash and walked the dog around the Ford Taurus. The dog jumped into the car's front seat, but found nothing.

Outside again, the dog was slowly led counter clockwise around the car. The dog stopped near at car's rear bumper, sniffed intently and jumped into the trunk. It was empty except for a loose spare tire. The dog's handler asked the other officers, "Isn't there supposed to be a compartment for the spare tire?" Probable cause.

The officer guided his dog around the rest of the car and then said, "The dog has indicated a 'positive hit' in the trunk area."

Sanchez needed to sit on the curb as his legs became weak.

The uniformed officers told Sanchez the Ford Taurus would be driven by one of the officers to the El Paso Police Department downtown station for further inspection. Sanchez was to be detained in a holding cell pending the outcome of the inspection. Instead, the Ford Taurus was driven to the third floor of the parking garage of the Federal Building where the DEA agents parked their OGV's. It was a secure location with ample space to dismantle a passenger vehicle.

The Federal Building was adjacent to the El Paso Police Department's Downtown substation, the El Paso County Detention Facility, and the U.S. Federal Courthouse. The proximity of the buildings made it convenient for federal agents to process, incarcerate, and escort the defendants to judicial hearings.

After admiring the concealment method, it took forty minutes to reveal the first cocaine bundle neatly packed in a masterfully constructed compartment. It required several agents to dismantle the panels in the trunk using screwdrivers, hammers, and a crowbar.

One hundred packages of cocaine were retrieved. Each bundle was wrapped with cellophane over a moisture-proof elasticized rubber material displaying an emblem of a scorpion. The agents were familiar with the emblem and its Mexican owner.

Drug cartels identify their specific product with certain emblems or markings. Just like any consumer product found on a supermarket shelf, the consumer also needed to know the distributor and quality of their purchase.

It was time to further deceive Sanchez. He couldn't get any hint that he had been made by the DEA before the traffic stop. A police officer escorted Sanchez across the street to the DEA office on the seventh floor of the Federal Building. Vince and I were waiting for him in the interview room.

"Mr. Sanchez, my name is Sal Martinez and this is my partner, Agent Sellers. I am going to read your Miranda rights. It is a formality that needs to be done before we ask you any questions." Sanchez put his head down, took a deep breath and started to sob.

After reading the statutory rights, I said, "The El Paso Police found one hundred kilograms of coke in your car."

"Cocaine?"

"You have two choices. You can go to prison for a very long time. Or you can cooperate with us, and we'll go easy on you. Let me warn you. If I feel you are lying and wasting our time, this interview will stop and the deal is off. Do you understand?" Sanchez nodded as he looked up with tear-filled eyes.

Many defendants believe their cooperation with arresting agents is in their best interest. The reality is that the information provided through cooperation will likely be used as incriminating evidence against the same defendant. The self-incriminating statements are used as leverage to dissuade a defendant from later changing his story. More importantly, the information fills in the gaps of a porous investigation.

The initial interview is where the game of tag begins. Shifting the blame on someone higher in the drug trafficking organization takes the heat off of the person who is 'it'. Agents encourage the defendants to be as detailed as possible as their cooperation may lead to non-prosecution or prevent a lengthy prison time.

"I know you're not the owner of the coke, so where did you get it?" I knew the answers before asking the questions. It was a matter of corroborating what Rudy Montes had told me.

"I was going to be paid some money to drive the car to California. I didn't know how much was hidden in the car." His eyes shifted left to right thinking of what to say next. Switching to any angry tone, Sanchez exclaimed, "They told me I was transporting marijuana! Those fuckers were only paying me two thousand bucks!"

Sanchez was more upset about the deception from Dan Montes than getting busted by the DEA. He was transporting over two million dollars of merchandise yet receiving less than one percent of the value of the cargo.

The interview did not last very long. He confessed and blamed everything on Dan Montes. There wasn't much more he could provide to what was already known by us. Sanchez was escorted to the El Paso Sheriff's Office Detention Center where he was booked. He wouldn't feel freedom for several years.

The cocaine was transported to the El Paso DEA drug depository for safekeeping. It would remain there until the Assistant U.S. Attorney assigned to the criminal investigation said it could be disposed of properly.

It was three o'clock in the morning when Sanchez' wife called Dan Montes on his cell phone. She was crying hysterically, explaining that her husband had gone to the store for groceries and was stopped for a broken taillight. Now he was in jail!

Montes became outraged. He expressed disbelief that Sanchez foolishly drove the car to run a stupid errand. Sanchez' wife defended her husband saying, "Our personal car didn't have any gas in it. We needed to buy milk for our kids."

Montes hung up on the woman. He didn't care about no stinking kids. He had to explain the loss of nearly two hundred kilos of cocaine. He wondered, "Would his superiors believe that the cause for these two cocaine seizures was unrelated? Would they doubt him, ignoring his proven loyalty to the cartel? Would they kill him?" He couldn't go back to sleep. He needed a strong drink and a quick decision. The three shots of *Tres Generaciones Tequila* didn't ease his anguish.

The majority of the cocaine in Ciudad Juarez and El Paso was nearly one hundred percent pure. It was almost never diluted, or stepped on, by the Mexican cartels. The wholesale price for one kilogram of cocaine in the El Paso area was approximately $10,000. It was valued at least twice this amount in most other U.S. cities.

Dan Montes was still accountable for the loss of nearly $2 million dollars of the wholesale product. He had a reason to fear for his life. The drug cartels were not financially devastated with the loss of some of their shipments. However, any loss of profit resulted in somebody being held accountable.

Throughout the next morning, Group One agents were busy completing standardized paperwork from the cocaine seizure and arrest. The numerous reports and procedures required a team effort. The surveillance and arrest reports were based on original surveillance notes collected from each agent. These reports needed to coincide chronologically in case the agents were required to testify in a court of law.

As customary, we needed to corroborate our statements and details. No agent wanted to be discredited by a despicable criminal lawyer. We knew only a sharp defense attorney could expose any discrepancies during cross-examination in a criminal trial.

Drug and non-drug evidence reports described the evidentiary items seized. It was critical to list every person who had possession of a piece of evidence from the moment of its collection to its introduction at the trial. Documenting the chain of custody for every piece of evidence is imperative to prevent any tampering or tainting of its authenticity.

Non-drug exhibits were physical items used in furtherance of a crime. In this case, handwritten notations made by Sanchez on a piece of paper, telephone numbers of co-conspirators, and an address where the drugs were to be delivered. The exhibits were assigned a number, photographed, and secured by the evidence custodian in the DEA drug depository.

It was after lunch before I had a chance to return his call. Sounding like a jealous lover, Rudy asked, "Why did you take so long to call me? I couldn't sleep last night!"

"Take it easy. Everything went smooth. We made it look like Jason screwed up so there shouldn't be any heat on your brother."

"My brother is freaking out! He doesn't know if he should stay in Juarez to deal with his boss or come to El Paso and take his chances of getting arrested."

"Do you know where he stays in Juarez?"

"He's got a girlfriend he stays with sometimes, but I don't know where she lives."

As a DEA agent, I wanted Dan to remain in Juarez so that the investigation could continue. It would be interesting to learn how the owners of the cocaine would react. Even if the repercussions meant painful punitive measures. I just hoped death wouldn't be the option.

Moralistically, I knew it would be safer for Dan to return to El Paso. To clear my conscience, I concluded that the deadly risk of being in 'the game' was on Dan Montes.

"Rudy, make sure you keep in touch with your brother throughout the day. Try to keep up with his whereabouts. Let him know that you are there for him."

"Okay. Can I say something?"

"Of course."

Rudy ignored his anxiety for a moment by using some humor, "You guys need to drive different cars."

"What are you talking about?"

"I drove by Jason Sanchez' house yesterday, and picked out your narc vehicles very easily. Your cars don't blend in with neighborhoods like the one you were at. Detail waxed cars with tinted windows and an antenna on the trunk are dead giveaways!"

"Rudy, thank you for your input. I will place an anonymous note in the DEA suggestion box tomorrow."

"You think I am joking? Ask the White agent who had the kids jumping on his car if he would agree with me?" Rudy broke out in laughter. "I wished I had taken a picture of that."

I ended the conversation, "Get some shuteye and call me if you hear from your brother."

Chapter 4 – Get a Rope!

I walked into Calderon's office to submit several DEA reports for supervisory approval.

He smiled, "Well Mr. Martinez, it looks like you got your cherry busted." Calderon had been a supervisor as long as I had been an agent, so this was a new experience for both of us. In fact, this episode was new to most of the agents, as last night's one hundred kilogram haul was the largest seizure in the El Paso DEA office in several years. It made him proud to see his youngest agent begin his career with a sizeable confiscation of illicit drugs. He continued, "Do you anticipate anything happening in this case within the next day or two?"

Sipping on a lukewarm cup of coffee, I responded, "My primary concern is Dan Montes. If he doesn't get killed, I'd like to allow him to remain on the street before we pick him up. He may lead us to other players or additional drug loads. As for now, he is considered an unwitting informant since we haven't approached him to cooperate. We will rely on the debriefings from his brother, Rudy. I anticipate this case will keep us busy for awhile."

"Okay. I was thinking of assigning a senior agent to help you with this investigation."

"That's not necessary. Vince and I can run with this. You will be the first to know if there is something we're not sure of."

On cue, Vince entered the supervisor's office with an energy drink in hand. He sat down next to me without saying a word. Everyone in Group One got used to his unpolished behavior. He was a man of few words, little manners, yet always understood.

Calderon glanced at Vince, smiled, and returned to me, "Now that your partner is here, prepare for a drive to Pecos. We just received a call from the Border Patrol checkpoint in Sierra Blanca. They arrested one man smuggling over a fifty pounds of marijuana."

Vince blurted, "This collateral duty blows! I don't understand why the Border Patrol agents can't take care of their own business. We waste a whole day cleaning up their mess."

The Supervisor continued, with a chuckle, "Besides kicking ass and taking names, there are other duties that need your attention. It's your turn on the rotation list to respond to the checkpoint. Secure the dope, transport the hoodlum, and enjoy the scenic drive to 'Hickville', derogatory slang for people from a rural area.

His agents were in no mood to appreciate the poor attempt at humor. We had been on other checkpoint runs and knew the routine. We shook our heads and walked out of the office.

Border Patrol agents were not authorized to judicially process certain law violators, including drug traffickers. They detained the violator and then transferred the drugs and the defendants to another law enforcement agency for judicial proceedings.

The DEA was contacted for federal prosecution if the drugs meet the specific threshold amounts: more than fifty pounds of marijuana, one kilogram of cocaine, or one ounce of heroin. For anything less, a state law enforcement agency would be contacted to pursue state criminal prosecution.

Border Patrol agents along the international border discover hundreds of pounds of marijuana almost daily. Marijuana is so abundant along the border that the agents often find it abandoned along the Rio Grande River. Electronic surveillance, such as motion detectors and infrared cameras, were strategically placed along the U.S. side of the river. When human movement was detected, Border Patrol agents were dispatched to the location to intercept. Rather than being arrested, the 'mule' discards the contraband and flees back across the river into Mexico.

Most checkpoint cases fit the same scenario. The drugs are concealed within a false compartment in a vehicle's floorboard, truck bed, or dashboard. The ingenuity for creating a false compartment to conceal drugs is limitless. On the other hand, some smugglers do not make much of an effort to hide their illicit cargo. Thus the adage, "Only the dumb ones are caught!"

Mules came in every shape, size and age. Elderly, high school students, mothers cuddling babies, etc. Their primary motivation is making money at most any risk. All they have to do is avoid detection from law enforcement authorities by crossing the river, passing a checkpoint, or driving a vehicle.

They are disposable to the Mexican drug cartels because there is always another smuggler waiting to replace them. Cartels value their illicit drug more than they care about the welfare of their human assets.

Recently, a passenger in a commercial bus was arrested for transporting two kilos of cocaine. Foolishly, he wrote his true name on the identification tag attached to the tote bag. He claimed that it was his favorite travel bag and feared someone would steal it.

Jurisdictional guidelines required federal prosecution from any drug case at the checkpoint in Sierra Blanca to be held in Pecos, Texas. According to U.S. law, the defendants had to be read their Miranda rights by a magistrate judge soon after the time of arrest.

There was little time for the DEA agents to prepare for the arduous journey. We had to drop what we were doing, secure the seized illicit drugs, and prepare the required forms. The worst part was the four-hour drive from El Paso to "The Birthplace of the First Rodeo".

There was one consolation for the weary agents. Upon our arrival, the small-town people treated the out-of-towners with the utmost hospitality. They were happy to see new faces in their mundane community. As for the lawbreakers, the federal judge relished the opportunity to express his anti-crime opinions and administer the renowned 'West Texas Justice'. Before some judicial hearings, the judge would shout to the bailiff, "Bring in the guilty bastards!"

Once the defendant was read his statutory rights and advised of the criminal violation, we were anxious to return home. We tactfully refused the invitations to stick around for dinner. Our minds were fixated on the long trek through the desert back to El Paso.

The isolation was augmented with no clear reception from any American radio stations. Only Mexican radio stations with higher wattage could be heard. Vince didn't care. He didn't like to listen to any music. In his head, music sucked like everything else.

To stay awake, I opted to initiate a discussion with Vince about something controversial. There was nothing wrong with a healthy, intellectual conversation about a current topic. I loved to hear the opinions from my partner's demented mind. As for others, I avoided two topics – politics and religion. It killed me to realize how ignorant people could be.

I began, "Someone asked me about the legalization of marijuana. I told them it is not morally acceptable to have a mind-altering drug made easily available for public consumption. What do you think?"

"I agree."

I continued, "Imagine walking into a convenience store and buying your favorite wacky weed. The selection would be similar to buying tobacco or alcohol. Sure, anyone can buy weed on the street. But it just doesn't seem moral to legalize it."

Vince responded, "People don't know when to say when. They abuse alcohol, pharmaceutical drugs, and any other substance they can get high with. If people would be responsible and know their limitations, then legalization would be easier to justify."

"My biggest problem is that people in certain occupations would get stoned, and endanger the safety of the public. For instance, a bus driver could be tripping out and plow into other vehicles on the road. Irresponsible usage will only kill innocent people, just like alcohol does for those driving drunk."

"People believe 'weed' is similar to alcohol. I don't agree. Drinking one beer is not equivalent to smoking one joint. The immediate effect of smoking marijuana is much stronger than that from liquor or beer."

I added, "What about the long-term effects of getting stoned? I know some of my homeboys who puffed everyday and they have no ambitions to succeed. They just live to get high. Their conversational skills are limited, and I get no intellectual stimulation from them."

"Instead of promoting the Just Say No campaign, the motto should be Just Stay Home. Pot smokers would be encouraged to stay home, puff on a doobie, and innocent people wouldn't be at risk."

"As for saving taxpayer dollars on the drug war, our efforts should be focused on harder drugs like cocaine, heroin and meth. It would save a lot of wasted time for law enforcement, the criminal courts and the prison system."

"Less paperwork for us, too."

Vince and I began to develop a tight relationship through personal and business experiences. We would spend a lot of time together in the years to come. Only something disastrous could change all of that.

Chapter 5 – Kill Them With Your Kindness

The following day, I walked through the rear entrance of the Federal Building and used the service elevator to the top floor shared by the DEA and the FBI. Ironically, the two agencies were forced to cohabitate during their training academies in Quantico, Virginia. That is where the ongoing sibling rivalry began. All the other federal agencies were located on the floors below because they were considered inferior to the DEA and FBI.

Most tenants were cordial with each other except for the 'feebs'. FBI agents have been personified as straightforward and by the book. But I didn't care for the coat-and-tie geeks whose internal culture of arrogance was built by their cross-dressing founder, J. Edgar Hoover.

Instead of focusing on matters of national security, the FBI has assigned agents to investigative areas already empowered by more qualified agencies such as the Alcohol, Tobacco and Firearms (ATF), the Internal Revenue Service (IRS), and the DEA. The egos, distrust, and turf wars ensure problems will persist among the law enforcement agencies in the federal bureaucracy. Ask any cop who has worked with the FBI and they will describe a one-way relationship.

History had shown that behind the facade of respectability was an organization that manipulated criminal violations against many unsuspecting Americans. U.S. citizens who expressed political views that were interpreted as immoral by the FBI were pursued with vigor. Yet, the agency continues to grow and expand its powers with an unlimited overreach.

All federal agencies must gratify an unjustifiable desire to increase their span of control. At the end of each fiscal year in October, budget increases are requested and approved to upgrade equipment, improve operational programs, and increase manpower. Even when there is a surplus from the previous year's budget, it must be spent on anything before additional money is requested from legislators.

Creative writing is not essential when using a pen that is mightier than the sword. Office furniture, office equipment, personnel gear, etc., are requested and purchased even though they are not needed. All leftover money must be spent to mislead Congress and American taxpayers that a larger budget is necessary to function effectively in the upcoming fiscal year.

Agency heads know that asking for less will only relinquish the authority it has accrued. Downsizing in the federal government is a bad word and exposes the poor leadership of those who are unable to attain more wealth.

I pressed my code into a wall control panel and entered the DEA office. I walked into the reception area and saw the young college intern with a book open on her desk. She balanced forty hours as a receptionist with the DEA and sixteen hours of higher education at UTEP on a weekly basis.

"Hi Elisa. How are things at my alma mater?"

"Fine. I'm studying for finals."

"Good. Knowledge is power. Aside from formal education, I suggest you talk to as many people in a career field that interests you, and an opportunity will arise when you least expect it. Some people call it playing politics, but I call it networking."

She nodded, "Okay."

I offered, "Here is some advice that is sad but true. When it comes to finding employment, it is not what you know but who you know."

She replied, "That sucks."

"Also, don't major in Criminal Justice. There is no money to be made in law enforcement!"

"Can I ask you a couple of questions?"

"Of course." I pulled up a chair next to the young woman. I was certain none of my fellow agents had made the time to sit and talk to the shy subordinate.

She asked the most common question a police officer gets. "Have you ever shot anybody?"

"I have been through three different police academies. With my firearms training, I am confident that I can shoot and kill someone. As for your question, no I haven't. I pray that I don't ever have to do that."

She had a look of disappointment. I could see she wanted to hear something more exciting. I obliged, "I've drawn my weapon many times and was ready to pull the trigger. On one occasion, I came close to killing someone during a hostage situation. A man was threatening to kill his infant child. He had a knife to the kid's throat when he stepped outside his front door. I had the sights of my Ruger rifle aimed at the man's head. Any indication of moving the knife would have led me to blow his head off. Thankfully, the man passed his child to a hostage negotiator from the El Paso Police Department and nobody was hurt."

"What about firing warning shots up in the air?"

"In law enforcement, there is no such thing as a warning shot. If a police officer draws his weapon and fires a round, it must be meant to kill."

Elisa added, "That means you don't shoot to wound them either."

"Most cops would love to shoot a bad guy and be a hero. However, most go their entire law enforcement career without ever shooting their gun at someone. The only time I shot at someone was during a high-speed chase."

"Please tell me what happened!"

"When I was a rookie State Trooper, my senior partner and I got into a vehicle chase with a guy who had stolen a pickup after burglarizing a home outside of San Antonio. My partner drove the patrol unit while I rode shotgun."

"Shotgun?"

"I guess the term originated during the old western days. The front seat passenger riding next to the horse carriage driver carried a shotgun to protect them from bandits. Anyway, we reached speeds over 120 miles per hour on a two-lane road outside of Floresville, Texas. There was a sense of disbelief. Throughout the chase, I actually felt like I was in a Hollywood production."

"My partner tried a spin out technique. Our patrol unit was positioned close enough to bump the left rear of the stolen vehicle. This should have caused the truck to spin out of control and come to a stop. But the bad guy was determined to outrun us."

"Were there other cars on the road?"

"Yes. The guy actually played 'chicken' with oncoming traffic by driving directly at them and making them swerve off the road. He was going to kill someone. So, I rolled down the front passenger window and stretched out enough to extend my shotgun. With the wind in my face, I fired two rounds into the tires of the pickup. The rear tire blew out, and the punk lost control. After coming to rest on the bar ditch, I jumped out of my patrol unit and chambered another round in the shotgun. I was hoping he would reach for anything so I could blow his head off."

"Did he try to run?"

"My partner and I never gave him a chance. We yanked him out through the half-opened driver's side window and proceeded to give him an attitude adjustment."

Elisa asked, "You beat him up?"

"To be honest, we punished that punk. It was the true definition of police brutality. He felt the wrath of many upset police officers that morning. Let's just say we were fortunate there wasn't anybody videotaping the 'intervention.'"

"Why did you have to do that to him?"

"The general public doesn't understand that cops can get scared and angry at the same time. After driving at high speeds and endangering other people's lives, a cop just can't shut off his emotions. It's only human nature to release the frustration on the perp, short for perpetrator, until the adrenalin subsides."

"What was the criminal charged with?"

"He was charged with burglary, auto theft, aggravated assault on a peace officer, and some misdemeanor violations."

"Wow, that was exciting! Was that the fastest you've driven?"

"No. Shortly after that chase, I was assigned a souped up Ford Mustang with a five-speed stick shift. It was a Christmas day when a Wilson County deputy came over the radio and said he was being shot at. I was his only backup because there were no other officers on duty. I was twenty minutes away so I maxed out at 151 miles per hour in my patrol unit."

"Weren't you scared?"

"My only thought was to get to the scene 'asap' to help a fellow officer.

My adrenalin was on overdrive. As I approached a major intersection in Floresville, I lost control of my patrol unit and hit a speed limit sign in the median. I got out of the car, quickly inspected the damage to the vehicle then continued on to help my brother in blue. As I was reaching the officer's location, he came over the radio and announced it was a misunderstanding."

"What did he mean?"

"He said it was two boys shooting beer bottles near his house. He thought they were shooting at him. I was furious! I wanted to strangle the fat deputy for causing me a lot of paperwork over my wrecked patrol unit."

"Wow! Aren't you afraid of being shot?"

"I try not to think about it. When I was wearing a police uniform, everyone knew I was a cop. Now, as an undercover agent, I actually feel safer. The only thing I fear now is kryptonite."

"You are too silly. Now, let's go back to why you wanted to be a cop."

"I used to watch the television series called "Miami Vice". It sparked a desire to fight the good fight by arresting bad guys. I get upset when I see thugs making easy money, living like the rich and shameless, while people like you and me are working hard to pay bills. By the way, do you have bills to pay?"

"Of course."

"Would you please give it back because he's looking for it?"

Confused, Elisa responded, "I don't get it."

I smiled and cupped my hand over my head as to insinuate a hairpiece, "Bill's toupee!"

This forced a sympathetic teehee from Elisa, "Oh, I get it."

I enjoyed sharing light humor with the support staff even if it meant telling corny jokes. I saved the inappropriate jokes for my fellow agents.

Needing my daily caffeine fix, I walked to my desk and retrieved my personalized DEA Academy ceramic mug with a replica of a Special Agent badge engraving.

I went into the break room in search of the Holy Grail. Next to the coffee maker was an empty coffee can made available for donations from visitors. Although the DEA office received ample visitors, there never seemed to be more than a few coins rattling in the can. I thought, "Cheap bastards!" It was after four o'clock, and the coffee pot was turned off. I filled my mug with the leftover tepid coffee, took a sip and thought of my days of drinking stale coffee while with the Texas Highway Patrol. This produced another craving.

The one bad habit I picked up while a State Trooper was chewing tobacco. Riding alone for eight-hour shifts on desolate Texas highways were usually uneventful. To pass away the time, I succumbed to the peer pressure from my senior partner. I disliked the monotony of chewing gum or sucking on hard candy. Worse, those things caused cavities!

I opened my desk drawer, pulled out a bag of Levi Garrett chewing tobacco, stuck a wad in my mouth, and spit into a Styrofoam cup with a napkin stuffed inside.

I felt someone was staring at me. My sixth sense was correct.

Vince said, "You gross fuck! Why don't you just order your false teeth now?"

As I sealed the bag of chewing tobacco, I responded, "Everyone has a vice."

"Why do you put that crap in your mouth?"

I answered proudly, "It's a requirement if you're from Texas."

"But you're from Mexico!" Vince said sarcastically.

I stood up and walked towards Vince. "No, I'm a Texican! Let me enlighten you, *gringo*. Both my grandparents and parents were born in El Paso, after my great-grandparents came to the U.S. legally. I was born and raised in El Paso, not Mexico. It sucks that we have to identify our heritage to your self-proclaimed supreme race as Mexican-American. I don't hear others saying German-American, Irish-American or wherever your inbred ancestors came from."

"Ease up, *hombre*."

I continued, "Caucasians stereotype me as a Mesican while native

Mexicans consider me a *gringo* because I was born on this side of the Rio Grande. Instead of battling with the dual identity, I simply consider myself a Texican."

Vince continued with his brand of sarcastic humor, "Excuse me! I thought you all were considered wetbacks."

"I'm more American than you are! I may be considered a wetback because my ancestors crossed a river, but you are fucking soaked since your ancestors crossed an ocean!"

"This is our country. We took it fair and square!"

"Bullshit! This country was originally occupied by Native Americans before White people came in and stole their land. The conquest and racism continued when Blacks were enslaved, Japanese were rounded up, and then having Mexicans deported."

Vince smiled, "This is our land now. So, go back home!"

I reached for my Iron Maiden compact disc and played "Run To The Hills". The lyrics describe the cruelty committed by the White Man on the so-called savage, untameable Indians. I ended the debate with, "The only true Americans are Native Americans, and I don't see any feathers on your head! However, you are one 'cool arrow'." I was subliminally calling him *culero*, meaning asshole in Spanish.

Vince figured out the play on words and responded, "*Tu eres culero* (You are an asshole)!"

I laughed and changed the subject, "Start clearing your desk because 5:01 p.m. is our estimated time of departure from here. Ask Jose and Paul if they want to join us for 'choir practice' at the L & J's Bar."

L & J's Bar was a watering hole frequented by local professionals and off-duty cops. It was deemed the Hispanic version of the sitcom Cheers because everyone knew each other's name. It was a safe haven for the DEA agents as the regular patrons would warn us of any unfamiliar customers amongst them.

Calderon, Paul, Vince, and I were the self-confessed after-work social drinkers of the El Paso DEA office. Some of the other agents were envious of our camaraderie, but it never created animosity. It was an open invitation that was rarely accepted by the others.

En route to the bar, the married agents made a courtesy call to their spouses. The wives heard, "It's a work-related meeting," or "The boss is going to be there." The agents assured them that it would only be a couple of drinks, then home for a late dinner. The calls were considered as notification, however, the men were really asking for permission.

Being single, Vince took the opportunity to rub it in, "You guys are pussy whipped! I don't know if I want to be seen with such wusses!"

I asked, "Are you calling me a pussy?"

"Absolutely!"

"Well, you are what you eat. Dick!"

A bucket of bottled beer was ordered before we settled into our corner of the bar. We raised and tapped our bottles, and I said, "Life, liberty and the pursuit of 'Happy Hour.'"

Calderon did most of the talking during the business meeting. He wanted to make certain his agents were on the same page regarding the on-going investigation.

After a few beers, the topic of conversation turned from work to pleasure. Vince pointed to the attractive blonde waitress, "There's my future ex wife!"

I responded. "I'm going to ask her if she wants to see my BMW."

"Your what?"

"Big Mexican Wiener!"

All the patrons heard a burst of laughter.

I went further and called the waitress over to our table, "Excuse me, do you have any Mexican in you?"

"No."

"Do you want some?"

Her jaw dropped, and Vince nearly spit a mouthful of beer. She was a good sport, knowing we were harmless. She also knew we were good tippers.

Vince said, "You know I would like nothing better than to be your trophy husband."

I added, "Don't believe him. He can only give you the best two minutes of his life."

I got up and made my way to the jukebox. I slipped a five-dollar bill into the machine and selected several songs from the "Essence of Billy Holiday". The ghostly, dispirited lyrics exemplified the persecution African-Americans, especially Black women, have had to deal with in America. The chilling tunes did not detract the DEA agents from their beer fest. The music led us into a discussion about police officers making traffic stops based on racial profiling.

Vince began, "Cops have the right to stop and question someone who doesn't belong in the neighborhood."

"Bullshit!" responded Paul, "If I am cruising through a predominately White section of the city in my low-rider, why does that make me a target?"

"You look out of the ordinary, therefore, the police can use their authority of reasonable suspicion."

I added, "Racial profiling by cops has always been used, and it will continue to be used as an investigative tool. Lets face it - racism, prejudice, and discrimination are part of our society. Police officers have the same opinions as anyone else."

Paul said, "No shit! It will take generations before people change their views in White America."

I said, "It is learned behavior from family members and friends. Growing up and listening to other's racial stereotypes has a permanent impact."

I challenged Vince, "How many Black friends did you grow up with?"

"None. We only had one Black family in our neighborhood but they never did anything with us."

Paul said, "So did we. I played sports with the boys, but we never hung out together."

I said, "Same here. In fact, I only hung out with one White dude in my neighborhood. The other White kids never invited me or my parents to their homes for any social functions."

Calderon said, "Blacks, followed by Latinos, are more likely to be targeted for arrest and victims of excessive force by cops. Look at the prison population. Most of the them are there because of biased arrest tactics and an unfair judicial system."

Paul asked, "So are we in agreement that many people stopped and arrested by the police is due to racial profiling? And, should we believe the suspects were guilty of doing something illegal?"

Vince answered, "Hell yeah! Throw them into jail with no bail bond and toss away the key. Let them rot in there forever!"

I said, "Calm down, Top Cop! I admit I used to profile my own 'peeps'. As a State Trooper, I pulled over Mexicans who caught my attention because they got nervous when they saw me or because they were in an area they did not belong. I knew those homies were up to no good so I jacked with them. Sometimes, they were guilty."

Vince said, "There you go. Racism used against your own people. Justified discrimination!"

The conversation changed themes several times including the war stories of our law enforcement experiences. Cops like to boast of their work experiences with anyone who will listen.

I told them of the time I was a rookie State Trooper in Floresville. On a Monday morning at approximately 10 a.m., motorists reported a vehicle swerving on a major highway headed towards San Antonio. The driver was pulled over by an off-duty officer.

I arrived to see several vehicles surrounding the suspected drunk driver. Witnesses claimed the man was swerving all over the road. The officer produced a vodka bottle found on the front seat.

I walked up to the suspect and realized it was the local parish priest. He smelled a slight odor of liquor on his breath. "Father, are you okay?"

"Yes, my son."

I wanted to get the priest out of his predicament. Not following protocol, I did not ask the priest to perform any of the required sobriety tests on the highway. "Do you have any health issues that need medical attention?"

"No. Do what you must, my son."

With so many witnesses, I had no choice but to arrest the priest. Going against department policy, I handcuffed the prisoner with his hands to the front and sat him in the front passenger seat. I was overcome with tremendous guilt when the priest put his handcuffed hands together and muttered several prayers during the trip to the jail. I knew I was going to hell.

It was several weeks before I attended another Catholic mass. It was lead by a visiting priest. Parishioners looked at me with disgust for arresting their spiritual leader. One eucharist minister turned away from me as I reached for the holy wine during communion. The children of God were not happy with the heathen in their congregation.

I never told anyone that the man of the cloth had numerous receipts strewn on the floorboard of his vehicle from seedy motels located on the southside of San Antonio. Even the priest had manly vices. Most professional businesses would terminate an employee for committing a criminal offense. Not the Church. The priest was transferred to another parish to hide him from those who knew about his flaws.

Others heard of the rookie State Trooper assigned to their small town. I wasn't playing by their rules. I didn't suck up to elected officials, engage in daily gossip, or ignore the traffic violations committed by spoiled children from those connected to influential people.

With no local family ties, the new kid in town caused political waves by pursuing criminal charges on the Sheriff's son, the Mayor's sister, and other dignitaries who hid behind political immunity from prosecution. They had committed serious traffic violations, like intoxicated manslaughter, and I wanted them to pay for their crimes.

I continued with the better of the stories. Late one Saturday night, I had stopped a man for speeding and driving without headlights on. The driver claimed he was trying to make it home before sundown since his headlights weren't working. I enlightened him that the sun had gone down several hours ago.

The driver was obviously intoxicated. I administered the simplest of sobriety tests and asked him to recite the alphabet. The driver could not get past the letter D, twice. As I advised the young man that he was going to be placed under arrest, the man began pulling down his pants.

My initial thought was that the drunk was reaching for a weapon. I pulled out my sidearm from its holster and pointed it down next to my right thigh.

The man exclaimed, "I've gotta take a shit, right now!"

I literally scared the shit out of this guy. I tried not to laugh. I holstered my pistol and instructed the man to get off the roadway, away from the view of passing motorists.

With his pants below his knees, the drunk waddled to a nearby barbed-wire fence and proceeded to defecate.

I retrieved paper towels from the glove compartment in my patrol unit and walked towards the man. However, the man was finished and pulled up his pants.

"Wait!" I said, "Here is some paper towels to wipe your ass!"

"I already did."

"With what?"

"My underwear."

"What did you do with your underwear?"

"I put them back on."

I transported the smelly drunk to the jail as fast as possible and with the windows rolled down. It took several days and a full can of Lysol to eliminate the foul odor in the patrol car.

The conversation changed when Vince saw two El Paso FBI agents enter the bar. He mumbled, "Here comes a couple of dicks with ears!" He then waited until they were close and said, "How's your wife and my kids?"

The agent had no idea that Vince actually had had an affair with the FBI agent's wife. They had a rendezvous when she was on a 'girls night out'. Vince met the woman at a bar then drove her in his OGV and banged her behind a dumpster. The two never saw each other again.

Embarrassed, the FBI agents tried to avoid sitting near the DEA agents, but the bar was filled to capacity. They leaned on the only bar stool available, next to Vince.

I leaned over and asked, "Hey, *Mamando* (slang for Sucker)! Do you know how to seat four FBI agents on one bar stool?"

"Stop calling me that! My name is Armando!"

Vince answered the riddle, "Turn the stool upside down!" The DEA agents laughed.

"I think you guys have been snorting the drugs you've been seizing." Armando was known as a back stabbing, 'how-ya-doin' phony who pumped up his ego up at the expense of others. He sought the boss' recognition by trashing fellow employees, then, two-faced, would trash the boss to the others.

He was part of the fifty-man El Paso FBI drug division, which had made no significant arrests or drug seizures in recent years. They were extremely jealous of the current El Paso DEA successes.

Their biggest problem was that they were not in touch with the local drug scene as exemplified by Armando's off-duty attire. It consisted of a Hawaiian shirt, tight pressed blue jeans, and cowboy boots. Meanwhile, his coworker was dressed like a yuppy.

Armando said, "By the way, I don't appreciate whichever one of you is putting my business cards in the bathrooms of bars and strip joints throughout the city."

I was guilty of grabbing a handful of the FBI agent's cards and distributing them whenever I had a chance. I had been doing it for several months.

Looking at Armando's boots, I asked, "Do they make those for men?"

Armando replied, "I'm relieved this will be the last time I have to listen to you. I'm transferring to Quantico as an instructor."

Vince said, "I heard the FBI was expanding their mattress tag sting operations."

Unrelenting, I added, "After you leave, we'll have a 'glad you're gone party."

A table became vacant across the bar. The FBI agents grabbed their ice waters and darted towards the oasis.

Paul said, "I can't stand those pencil dicks. I don't trust anyone who doesn't drink a beer."

Calderon had been sitting quietly, smirking as his agents verbally tore the feebs a new asshole. "I sense a theme here. You guys don't care much for our sister agency, do you?"

"Incest is best!" I retorted.

Paul added, "FBI stands for fucking bunch of idiots."

After several buckets of beer, all but Vince left the bar before midnight. The blonde waitress was ending her shift and accepted his invitation to talk about life under the full moon. They met outside in the parking area and sat on the trunk of his OGV sharing a six-pack of beer.

Located across the street from the bar was the historic Concordia cemetery. Since the early 1800's, prominent politicians, pioneers and old Western heroes, such as John Wesley Hardy, were buried there. During the daylight hours, tourists stroll through vast burial grounds revering the famous headstones.

Vince playfully dared the waitress to take a walk through the unlit cemetery. He assured her, "Trust me, I work for the government."

As they walked hand in hand on the sacred grounds, Vince mischievously scared her. She turned and hugged him out of fear. He then made his move and there was no resistance.

They kissed and maneuvered their bodies to a comfort zone in the darkness. The passion was enhanced by the eroticism of having sex in a cemetery. As Vince held the waitress' legs over his shoulders, he glanced down to see that he was using J.J. Johnson's flat headstone for leverage.

Conscientiously, he apologized to the spiritual world for disrespecting Mr. Johnson. Selfishly, he thanked the Johnson family for accommodating the salacious fantasy.

Chapter 6 – The Heroin Queen

Yvette Gonzalez was a local girl from the barrio who had been a DEA Special Agent for the past six years. At 5'2", 110 pounds, mid-thirties, and long black hair, she displayed a stern personality and relied on her foul mouth as a defense mechanism from others. She was quite at ease talking with the female support staff by allowing her amiable demeanor to show. But she quickly transformed into a hard-shelled woman when it came to talking to any man. Some thought of her as a bitch on a permanent period, but I knew what my 'Home Girl' was really about.

Law enforcement agencies are afflicted with a long-established chauvinism, making it difficult for women to promote. Women need to make up for their lack of physical abilities by working harder to prove that they can achieve what men can. They withstand more sexual harassment and sexually-oriented jokes but don't complain to male supervisors to prevent alienation.

The mother of two was not intimidated by the male dominated profession. Yvette never saw herself doing anything else, and she pursued her career with dedication. Known as the Heroin Queen, she had successfully negotiated and consummated many undercover deals with street wise traffickers. The men she arrested were shocked and embarrassed to learn they were set up by a female narc.

Yvette's success began with her fluency of a unique border lingo called Spanglish. This *barrio* dialect is very prevalent in the El Paso area. Simple words like yes and no are *simon* and *chale* respectively. Nouns include terms such as *la troca* (truck), *la ranfla* (car) and *lonche* (lunch).

There is not an accurate English translation for the regional street slang, idioms or jokes, especially those with sexual innuendo. Much of this street lingo was passed from older to younger generations in *El Chuco*, affectionate nickname for the city of El Paso.

Yvette opened up to me, "I am glad the *babozos* (clowns) at Headquarters sent another Hispanic to our office. I've been wanting to pass the baton for my undercover deals. There aren't many agents who can be successful if they don't speak the language."

It was a Monday morning when Yvette asked me to join her in the informant debriefing room. "*Mijo* (son), I have Stinky in the debriefing room. He says there's a *pendejo* (dumbass) that has twenty ounces of shit to sell." Yvette had a unique way with words and I loved it.

His lack of personal hygiene and unfamiliarity with a deodorant stick had earned him the nickname Stinky by DEA agents. Yvette and Stinky had teamed up on several successful drug busts in past years, seizing more black tar heroin than all the other El Paso law enforcement agencies combined.

Born and raised in the slums of Ciudad Juarez, he was illiterate and had difficulty verbalizing a complete sentence. He signed his name on DEA informant paid receipts with the letter X because he had never learned to write. There weren't many job opportunities that would pay him like that of being a DEA informant. Although he had been paid almost $10,000 by the DEA in the past ten months for arranging two buy/busts, he was low on cash and needed more.

I grabbed my mug of coffee, took a deep breath of air, and entered the debriefing room. I greeted the informant, but avoided shaking his hand, "*Que pasa, vato* (What's happening, guy)?"

Stinky related, "I met this *vato* over the weekend at a bar who told me he had a fist sized amount of heroin. He said it was twenty ounces and was asking $1,800 an ounce. I told him I knew someone who would be willing to pay that amount."

"Damn, that price is too high per ounce, especially for a bulk purchase."

"Sorry, I just wanted to keep his interest."

"Who does this guy run with?"

"People from Juarez. He says he can deliver it within an hour after you meet him and talk about price."

"What did you tell him about the buyer?"

"Yvette said you would be doing this job with me. I told him we've done a lot of deals and have partied hard all over El Paso. I mentioned that you have paid up to $2,000 per ounce because money is never a problem."

"Shit, you say too much! You've got to stop negotiating for us. I sure as hell don't want to get caught in a lie during the first meeting."

Stinky put his head down like a scolded child. He had been warned before about painting a pretty picture regarding his financier. However, he was confident his deceptiveness would successfully lure any potential drug dealer.

I asked, "What's the guy's name?"

"Pedro."

"Pedro what?"

"I don't know."

"Where is he from?"

"I don't know."

Extracting details from uneducated informants like Stinky required patience. Yvette and I stepped out of the room. She asked, "Can you do the undercover on this deal?"

"No problem. *Este pestozo* (This stinker) has a good record when it comes to setting up deals. Let's arrange an introduction this afternoon, and I'll see if the dealer is legit. Let's run it by the boss for approval."

I returned and instructed the informant to set up a meeting with the heroin dealer. "Do not tell him anything else about me. Don't negotiate the price! Push him to have the heroin ready, because I do not like to wait around with cash in my hand. Let's meet in a public place not far from here."

Stinky nodded his head. The informant was escorted to the rear exit of the DEA office. The door leading into debriefing room was left wide open to let the area air out of the lingering body odor.

A vague physical description of the heroin dealer was all the DEA agents had. Agents detested working on cases involving targets of investigation with the First Name Unknown (FNU) or Last Name Unknown (LNU). A criminal history inquiry could not be conducted without specific personal identifiers. It was unknown if the dealer had a violent history or any prior firearm charges. This made it a riskier proposition for the DEA supervisor to approve.

U.S. law enforcement agencies rely heavily on informants. It is rare for any investigation to be conducted without at least one informant's input. Behind every successful agent is an effective informant.

It is critical that law enforcement agents keep the informant's identity secret. If the bad guys discover the true identity, it could mean death for the informant. In official documents, the informants are referred to by a designated agency number or as a Confidential Informant (CI), Confidential Source (CS), or Operative. Unofficially, agents simply refer to them as snitch, charlie, or rat.

The primary motivation for most informants is financial reward. I paid tens of thousands of dollars to several of my assigned informants. They can make a decent living by devoting their time to the underworld and setting people up. Stinky did just that.

For others, they are trying to work off a beef. They might have been arrested for a criminal offense and given an opportunity to set up others. They are forced to play a game of tag. Their effectiveness will affect the outcome of their own pending criminal activities including a rejection of prosecution by the U.S Attorney's Office. This meant the Defendant-Informant could have committed a more serious crime than the people he set up!

In the DEA, each established informant is under the supervision of a specific agent. The agent is responsible for directing the informant to perform specific activities and gather drug-related information. Those who are insubordinate or commit other crimes are black-balled, meaning excommunicated by the DEA.

The Informant Conduct Agreement form explains the rules an informant must follow while working for the DEA. Every paid informant was required to sign the form with the understanding of abiding by the requirements. The list of rules can be summarized as behavioral guidelines, that is, don't do anything illegal and if you do, confess to your controlling DEA agent about the misdeed.

While informants have no official status as an employee, the DEA prohibits the informant from violating any law and separates the DEA from any responsibility. However, the deeper the informant is involved with any illicit activity, the better it is for productive enforcement efforts.

Informants are forewarned that they may need to testify in a court of law. This is something informants, controlling agents, and prosecuting attorneys do not want. It will only open the door for the defense attorney to scrutinize the background and motives of the informant.

Prosecutors do not want the jury to learn of the monetary incentive of their key witness. Law enforcement agencies have been instructed to withhold payments until after the trial. The informant knows he will be financially rewarded, sometimes with exorbitant amounts of money if he says the right things for the prosecution on the witness stand.

If a jury realizes the type of person the informant is, it could lead to an acquittal of the defendant. A good defense attorney could attack the credibility of an informant and their nefarious lifestyle. The deceitfulness of the informant could be exposed and detract from the defendant's criminal allegations.

If an informant must testify, prosecutors divert attention from their criminal record and emphasize that he is testifying for the good guys. Prosecutors rely on the mindset of juries, that is, "Whatever the prosecution and the informant say must be the truth. Our government wouldn't lie to us."

I nearly completed a pre-formatted operational plan. The checklist included identifiers of the Pedro LNU and possible scenarios. Next to each participating agent's name was his radio call number and cell phone number. All that was needed to finalize the one-page form was the time and location of the undercover meeting, known as the meet location. The last line on the page was a critical question, "Were other law enforcement agencies notified?" This was a necessary precaution to prevent two police agencies from working against each other.

Several weeks before, the DEA agents had been preparing to apprehend a drug dealer based on an informant's allegation. Simultaneously, an informant from the El Paso Sheriff's Office Narcotics Unit claimed he had someone bringing a large amount of cash to purchase drugs. Both agencies showed up to a prearranged location for an anticipated buy/bust operation.

The lack of communication and potential standoff could have turned deadly if it were not for Paul recognizing one of the sheriff's deputies parked in the vicinity of the meet location. Members of both agencies were embarrassed about the failure to delegate someone to make a courtesy call to each other.

It was nearly 1 p.m., when Stinky called, "He has the stuff. I just saw it."

"How much does he have?" I asked calmly trying not to seem anxious.

"He showed me a sample. It looked like two ounces."

"Where's the rest?"

"He said it's nearby."

"Is he alone?"

"He came with three other guys."

"Shit, three guys? Any weapons?"

"I didn't see any."

"What do they look like, and what are they wearing?"

Stinky provided vague physical and clothing descriptions. One of them drove an old, blue pickup with *Frontera Chihuahua* (Mexican State of Chihuahua) license plates. This was a dead end when it came to identifying suspects. It was almost impossible to obtain background information of vehicle ownership from the Mexican databases.

I finished, "Let's meet at the Fox Plaza Shopping Center. I'll be there in thirty minutes. Tell him I don't have time to bullshit around!"

I gathered the participating DEA agents in the Group One squad bay to brief them on the background of the case and to discuss possible scenarios of the 'buy/bust' operation. I provided them with a copy of the operational plan for the undercover meeting. Several questions were asked regarding the four unidentified suspects known as FNU LNU. The unknown heightened the agents' anxiety and warned them to expect the unexpected.

Jose Calderon stressed the importance of the undercover agent's safety. "You must not get too complicated with the bust signal. And, if you feel threatened by the bad guys, a danger signal is just as important. There must be no question by the agents on surveillance that a signal was given. Yvette, stay close in the undercover car with direct sight of Sal when he meets with the dealer."

I announced, "If I feel my life is in danger, I will simply raise both of my hands in the air. As for the bust signal, after I see the heroin, I will remove my red bandana from my pant pocket and wipe my forehead."

Calderon concluded, "I want Paul to be the surveillance coordinator on this operation." Paul was familiar with the area. All the surveillance agents departed the Federal Building in their own designated OGV's.

Yvette and I rode together. The plan was for Yvette to drop me off and park at a safe distance. We discussed scenarios to make sure we were in synch with the undercover operation.

I related a similar undercover operation where one simple mistake almost led to a gunfight. "I assisted Group Two as an undercover agent for a cocaine deal. Their informant set up a meeting between me and the 'bad guy' at a location I didn't like."

Yvette asked, "What happened?"

"The informant said the guy would be waiting for me outside a sandwich shop on the west side of town."

"When I get to the parking lot, nobody is there. In fact, the restaurant was closed and there were no vehicles around. Foolishly, I still entered the parking area, shifted my OGV into park and turned off the ignition."

"So what's the big deal?"

"I sat there like a sitting duck with several thousands of dollars of DEA flash money laying in the front passenger seat."

Flash money is a specific amount of money wrapped in bundles and placed in a tote bag. The undercover agent displays the bundles of cash in a quick-peek method to the drug seller. Showing the actual currency furthers the drug negotiations by enhancing the credibility of the buyer. The drug seller is not allowed to touch the money.

"Did I tell you I also rolled the windows down so I could get some fresh air?"

"Damn!"

"The bad guy was standing behind the building. I never saw him but he had a clear view of me."

"So what happened?"

"I saw some movement in my rearview mirror. I turned and saw him walking towards the passenger side window. I pulled out my Glock and had it aimed towards the window. He walked slow enough for me to turn on the ignition of the OGV before he got too close."

"Did you still negotiate with the guy?"

"After I chewed his butt out, we acted like nothing ever happened. After an hour of discussion, he came up with two kilos of coke. However, I charged him with Conspiracy to sell ten kilograms of cocaine. He will be spending several years in prison thinking about acting like a high roller in this game."

Although the defendant produced only two kilograms of cocaine, the U.S. Attorney charged him with intent to distribute ten kilograms. The Conspiracy criminal charge punishes defendants just for simply talking about a crime.

"He went to prison because he bragged about something he couldn't produce? *Chingado* (Damn), that's messed up."

I emphasized, "There are two mottos to this story. First, mean what you say and say what you mean. Second, do not turn off your engine or place your OGV in park when meeting a bad guy. Keep the gear in Drive and be ready to haul ass."

"Good advice."

"As for this meeting with Stinky, if the shit hits the fan, get out of the area and let our surveillance units move in." I was overly protective of my female partner. I didn't want Yvette to get hurt if a gunfight erupted.

She replied, "I know what I'm supposed to do, *Loco*! I'm not a *pendeja* (dumb female) like most men think I am."

Easing the tension, I said jokingly, "I agree with you. Men are inconsiderate pigs! I don't know how women put up with the need for men in their lives. If I were a woman, I'd be a lesbian."

"*Callate* (Shut up)!"

The Fox Plaza Shopping Center consisted of approximately twenty street level retail stores. The parking lot was usually vacant after other larger, trendier shopping malls opened for business around the city.

The DEA agents were doing the customary reconnaissance at the meet location prior to the arrival of the undercover agent. Agents looked for suspicious persons who might be conducting counter-surveillance. One distinguishing feature is someone sitting in a vehicle, backed into a parking space, positioned for an expeditious departure. In actuality, the agents were looking for anyone who was acting like them.

Paul saw the old, blue pickup described by Stinky parked in front of the Jack in the Box restaurant. He drove through the parking lot once more and instructed Jake Davis to find a location with a direct line of sight of the truck.

Jake announced over the DEA radio that he could see the informant standing in front of the pickup, talking to a Mexican male wearing a multi-colored shirt. Agents identified the suspects of the surveillance by the color of their clothing or an obvious physical feature of the suspect.

Jake said, "I have the CI standing next to the suspect. Let's call the suspect 'Missing Link' because he is one ugly SOB!"

Yvette and I laughed.

Vince identified two males sitting on a curb on the other side of the restaurant. They were both wearing white t-shirts. There was still one suspect unaccounted for by the DEA agents.

Before the undercover agent is permitted to enter the meet location, the surveillance coordinator must feel confident that the area is considered safe. Paul called me on the cell phone, "We haven't located the fourth player. What do you think?"

I answered, "We can't keep the dealer waiting too long. I'm packing (carrying my pistol) and feel safe. Let's do this."

Paul picked up the DEA radio and requested a status of the surveillance agents. All were in position. Paul instructed Yvette to drive into the parking area.

Although there were plenty of parking spaces available close to the restaurant, we parked several rows away from the blue pickup. Yvette remained in the OGV after I exited.

Working undercover requires the art of persuasion, that is, convincing the bad guy you are not a cop and you are someone who can consummate a drug transaction. I was comfortable playing the undercover role. My confidence grew each time I was asked to be the undercover agent by fellow agents.

Upon my arrival to the El Paso DEA office, I became the go-to guy for undercover operations. Being Hispanic and familiar with the local street lingo, I was responsible for countless arrests and drug seizures. I helped other agents successfully complete their investigations. They appreciated my zealousness and respected my fearlessness.

Mexican drug traffickers were reluctant to meet a White guy or a female for a drug deal. There was a blatant distrust of White people and a sexist attitude towards women. Even in the underworld, racism and sexism were prevalent.

I knew exhibiting a specific physical appearance was necessary to give the criminals the impression I was one of them. I grew a goatee, let my curly hair grow almost shoulder-length, and wore various earrings to complete the guise. Selecting the appropriate attire became essential for any last-minute requests from other DEA agents to perform in an undercover role. I was willing to sacrifice name brand clothing for less expensive, more appropriate apparel. But I always wore a loose shirt to conceal a Glock pistol tucked under my belt.

The final touch was my assigned undercover vehicle. The GMC Sierra pickup had a customized paint job, chrome running boards, and chrome rims that ran low to the ground. When driving it around town, many Blacks and Hispanics complimented me on my flashy truck. I heard comments like, "*Ese* (hey you), that is one sweet and low ride you got there!" On the other hand, 'shit kickers' (slang for cowboys) questioned my taste with a sarcastic, Southern accent, "Damn, why'd you do that crap to your truck?"

The CI walked briskly towards me. Stinky said, "*El vato esta listo* (The guy is ready). He may be asking for $1,800 per ounce."

My adrenalin and senses were heightened including the sense of smell. Stinky emitted a foul odor worse than ever before! I looked over my shoulder and saw 'Missing Link' standing behind the restaurant. I scanned the area and saw the two men sitting on a curb. It was unknown if they were packing heat. I felt safe as long as they remained at a distance.

Stinky escorted me to meet 'Missing Link'. The heroin dealer wore soiled blue jeans, a wrinkled button-up shirt and a five dollar pair of counterfeit Nike sneakers that were *Hecho in Mexico* (Made in Mexico).

I reached out with a homeboy handshake, "*Que onda* (What's happening)?"

'Missing Link' mumbled something. Formalities were not a prerequisite during a criminal transaction. In fact, they would be considered suspicious. You don't want to come across as being too friendly or too refined.

I asked Stinky to leave the two of us alone. This tactic was used to minimize the informant's participation in the negotiations and prevent him from having to testify about our discussions in a court of law.

I began, "I'm looking for *chiva*, and I need it today." *Chiva* is local slang for black tar heroin. "My plane leaves this afternoon for Dallas, and my people expect me to bring them something."

"These things don't just happen right away, *ese*. I don't even know who you are. You might be a cop."

I pointed to Stinky and said, "We have made a lot of money together. We don't like to fuck around. If you can't take care of this small-time shit, then I'm walking away." I wanted to challenge the man and provoke his ego.

"*Calmate* (Calm down)! I just want to know who I'm dealing with."

"I understand, but I haven't been able to find any good shit in the last couple of days. *Los negros* (the Blacks) in Dallas love our local *chiva*, and I don't want to go back empty-handed."

"How come I've never heard of you?"

Quick thinking is necessary during undercover negotiations. The cross examination by traffickers was intended for familiarization of the potential client and to pick up on any suspicious language or mannerisms.

I responded, "I usually get my product in the eastside of El Paso. Last night, my usual contact was arrested for roughing up his *ruca* (spouse or girlfriend). I despise wife beaters!"

"Was he your only connection here in *El Chuco*?"

"I don't trust too many people. Now, I'm going to be looking for another connection."

'Missing Link' thought for a minute, "I'll sell you two ounces for $3,600. If your people like it, then I can get them some more of the same."

"Unfortunately, I don't have the time to try samples. I'm expected to bring back enough for my regular clients."

He was battling an inherent skepticism of not trusting me versus the possibility of making thousands of dollars in an instant. Taking a deep breath, 'Missing Link' said, "I have twenty pieces at $1,800 each." Pieces was slang for ounce.

"*Chingado*! That's too much for each piece!" Buying bulk amounts should afford the customer a lower net price for any product.

'Missing Link' did not respond. He stared, expressionless, at the desperate customer. It was a take it or leave it proposition.

One cannot be too anxious to complete the deal because it is a giveaway of being a cop. Part of the undercover game was to patiently negotiate the price while allowing the bad guy to get greedy. I desired to arrest the suspect as much as he wanted to make a lot of *lana* (money).

I could see that the dealer was thinking of the possibilities. $36,000 would be enough to keep him and his amigos in a drunken stupor for days. 'Missing Link' saw himself getting the VIP treatment from the *señoritas* at the *zona rosa* (red light district) in Ciudad Juarez.

I countered by claiming there was one other seller who was on standby with a competitive offer. The dealer didn't give a shit about the shallow threat. He knew he had a desperate buyer for his product and was going to hold his ground.

I shook my head and looked behind me pretending to be disgusted. I could see Yvette sitting in the driver's seat of my OGV. 'Missing Link' noticed her, too.

I said, "My *ruca* is holding the cash." DEA agents know it is never a safe tactic to have the 'buy money' and the agent together. It would be too tempting for a rip-off and very risky for a hostage situation.

Yvette maintained possession of the currency in a gym tote bag. Each bill of the $20,000 in official government funds had been photocopied at the DEA office. In the rare event the money is transferred to a drug dealer during a negotiations and later retrieved, the serial numbers would corroborate the cash as evidence for criminal prosecution. On this day, I had no intention of passing the dead presidents.

In full alert mode, I saw a man slowly maneuvering through parked cars coming in my direction. The two men, who were sitting on the curb, stood up and strolled behind the burger joint. I lowered my right elbow to my waistband, nudged the pistol handle, and reassured myself that the Glock was there.

I was now feeling uneasy as I was outnumbered. Not liking the odds, I felt a need to end the negotiations as soon as possible.

"Listen," I demanded, "I'm leaving if we don't work something out now. The price is too high."

'Missing Link' countered, "*Bueno* (Okay), I'll take $1,600 per piece (ounce), but I want to see the money first." This is the next stage of drug negotiations, that is, "You show me yours, and then I'll show you mine."

"I have the money so don't worry about that. My concern is the quality of the product. I can't afford to piss off my people with bad shit."

"Let me see the money!"

I turned to Yvette and waved her in. She shifted the car into gear and drove quickly to my location. She pulled up and kept the engine running. I reached through the rolled down passenger window and grabbed the unzipped tote bag lying on the front seat. I opened the bag and flashed the scattered bundles of U.S. currency.

With eyes wide open, 'Missing Link' asked to grab a bundle of the money.

"*Chale!*" (slang for no) I said. I tossed the tote bag onto the front passenger seat. Without saying a word, Yvette sped away to a different location in the parking lot remaining in direct sight of me.

The drug dealer was confident the money in the tote bag would be his and said, "Follow me to my truck."

Thoughts of the unexpected raced through my mind. Walking around the building, I evaluated various rip-off scenarios and ways to react.

'Missing Link' opened the passenger door of the truck and pointed at a twelve-pack carton of Budweiser beer on the floorboard. Hidden under the empty beer cans was a fist-sized wad of black tar heroin wrapped in aluminum foil. "*Aqui esta* (Here it is)."

"Let me smell it." I unwrapped the foil and brought the dark, sticky wad to my nose. I was familiar with the texture and pungent, acetone odor. It was high quality *chiva*. I wanted to take the heroin with me but the dealer denied my attempt. I rewrapped the heroin and placed it back in the carton.

"It looks good." I said. "I'll go get your money." I began walking towards Yvette and noticed 'Missing Link' following behind. I turned and stopped him by saying, "Wait here or my *ruca* will split."

I scanned the area to determine the location of the other suspects. All were accounted for except one of the men. I was hoping my fellow agents knew his whereabouts.

I walked to the driver's side window. Yvette was sitting anxiously waiting for instructions. Her fake smile and twitching left eye revealed her nervousness. To ease the tension, I jokingly asked her, "Did you bring any bullets with you this time?"

"*Pendejo!*" she said red faced. "You better not have told anyone about that day!"

I was referring to an incident that had occurred the previous week during the execution of a search warrant at a drug dealer's residence. The Group One agents were preparing to raid the house when I noticed Yvette's Glock pistol did not have a magazine inserted into the handle.

Before kicking the front door in, I asked her, "I hope you have a bullet in the chamber."

Embarrassed, Yvette claimed that she inadvertently pressed the magazine release button while loading the raid gear on her Sam Browne tactical belt.

For her safety, I recommended she remain outside and cover the perimeter. The fully-loaded magazine was later found on the floorboard of her OGV. I promised not to tell the other DEA agents because she would never hear the end of it. Her pride was hurt but I found it to be humerous.

I felt someone staring at me over my left shoulder. I turned and saw the missing suspect, identified by agents as 'yellow shirt', walking towards us.

I pulled out my red bandana and wiped my forehead. I then reached under my shirt, pulled out the Glock and kept it next to my right hip with my finger on the trigger.

Yvette grabbed the DEA radio and said, "All units move in!"

The roar of revving car engines from a distance broke the silence. Ideally, agents are focused on converging on the suspects as quickly and safely as possible. Caution for innocent bystanders and themselves must override the excitement. Maneuvering through vehicular and pedestrian traffic is of the utmost importance. No emergency lights or sirens were activated. The element of surprise was critical.

Secondly, positioning the OGV in the most advantageous location to provide cover for agents from incoming gunfire while preventing the suspects from escaping. Agents exited their vehicle with weapons drawn, aiming towards the pavement until their target was in sight. The screams of "Police!" and "Freeze!" startled the violators and alerted bystanders to clear the area.

The synchronized swarm of agents was exciting to watch. Even the suspects were impressed with the swiftness of the convergence leading to their arrest.

Yvette and I remained back until the flotilla of agents covered their targets.

Jake intercepted 'yellow shirt' with his vehicle and forced him to the ground.

Within minutes, four drug dealers and Stinky were laying on the pavement with handcuffs. As a safety measure, the CI was also placed under arrest during buy/bust operations to prevent him from being immediately singled out as the snitch.

Having the CI arrested keeps the defendants guessing as to whom amongst them was the traitor. The uncertainty is a method for the DEA agents to initiate the game of tag during the post-arrest interviews with their captives.

I returned to the old blue pickup and retrieved the heroin. I also produced a Dillie Koppanzi color reagent test capsule to identify the suspected substance. The liquid in the capsule turned a dark purple indicating positive as heroin.

At first, each defendant denied any knowledge of the black tar heroin. During interrogation, an agent tries to keep the defendant from clamming up or asking for an attorney. Persuasion and intimidation can make a suspect forget he requested legal counsel.

The most common method of inducing an incriminating statement was claiming that the other defendants were cooperating. Not wanting to be left out from receiving consideration for their cooperation, the defendant would flip and turn against his associates. This solidified the involvement of those arrested and identified the owners of the illicit drugs for our reports.

The primary drug dealer was adamant of his innocence until he was introduced to the man with the red bandana. His defensive attitude changed and turned to vindication. He claimed the Juarez Cartel had his family hostage. He said cartel members forced him to sell the heroin in El Paso or his wife and kids would be killed. Playing the sympathy card didn't diminish his intent of selling dangerous drugs for profit.

I built my case to conform to a DEA program called Targeted Kingpin Organization (TKO). The project was created by agency heads to have as many suspects arrested in a drug or money laundering operation and claim they were all equally responsible for one person's actions. That meant even the lookouts were just as responsible for the most serious crime committed. This fish net technique was used to enhance the apprehensions to a higher level of credibility within the DEA.

In addition, all four defendants were charged with Intent to Distribute Heroin and Conspiracy to Possess with Intent to Distribute. Applying the conspiracy statute meant everyone received the maximum prison sentence applicable regardless of their minimal participation. Each defendant was punished with five years of incarceration in the federal prison system.

A defendant may drop out of the illicit activity but still be liable for events that occurred before he quit the criminal activity. A mere accusation could implicate someone and they wouldn't know it until after they were arrested.

In the following weeks, Stinky set up two more drug deals. Me and Yvette made a few more arrests while the informant left town with nearly $15,000 of official government funds in his pocket. His motto was, "Crime does pay."

Chapter 7 – Business Before Pleasure

DEA Agent Richard McGee was the epitome of a dedicated agent fighting the drug war. He was a detail-oriented leader who buried himself in his work. He relied on his 6'2" stature, fiery red hair, and 220-pound physique to intimidate those in his way of conducting investigations. And, if he stepped on toes in the performance of his duties, so be it. It could only enhance his reputation.

Some saw his unapproachable attitude and arrogance as overbearing. He didn't care about being popular, only about being effective. He wasn't a back-slapper, or one inclined to unwind by having a beer with fellow agents. McGee didn't have personal hobbies because catching drug dealers was his sport.

McGee thrived on conducting Title III operations, more commonly known as wiretaps, on his targets. Title III refers to the provisions of the Omnibus Crime Control and Safe Streets Act of 1968, relating to interception of wire and oral communications on suspected criminals. He loved spending long hours planning the legal, administrative, and strategic aspects of an anticipated wiretap operation.

Authorization to conduct a wiretap requires convincing a judge that such electronic surveillance is warranted. Specific telephones and cell phones must be identified as instruments used in furtherance of felonious criminal activity.

Judges are willing to extend a wiretap as long as the law enforcement agent shows sufficient proof that an illegal activity is being detected. The U.S. Attorney files the proper motion and requests that the judge grant a motion to continue with the wiretap. McGee never had a problem getting wiretaps approved by a judge because he knew exactly what they wanted to read.

The wiretap operations were complex and time-consuming for everyone involved. The DEA office in El Paso usually requested manpower from local agencies. Taking officers away from their regular assigned duties put a strain on those agencies already understaffed. Administrators complained their limited budgets were drained for the overtime pay required during the extended operations.

The incentives to participate in the DEA wiretaps were the spoils of victory, which was the equitable sharing of property seized such as vehicles, houses, and money. We had first choice of the property seized while the leftovers were distributed to the other agencies. The DEA dangled a financial carrot in front of local police agencies to retain the needed manpower.

According to one of McGee's informants, there was an organization transporting multi-ton quantities of marijuana from El Paso to several northern U.S. cities. Phone records verified the lines of communication between the drug traffickers. Businesses and homes had been identified within the past two weeks. All that was needed was the manpower to follow the suspects and to eavesdrop on their cell phones and landlines.

Once a wiretap is authorized, a listening post is required to house the necessary electronic devices. This location is treated as sacred ground limited to specific monitoring agents. Patience was needed by monitoring agents as they sat in an enclosed area for months at a time. During the eight-hour shifts, the agents recorded only conversations relevant to criminal activity. Privileged, intimate, and sexually-oriented conversations not relevant to the alleged crime should not be recorded. However, the agents would have the option of eavesdropping on the intimacies for their own personal enjoyment.

Calderon liked McGee and provided him with the agents he needed. As usual, the Spanish-speaking agents were assigned to the listening post to interpret and translate the conversations. Working along the Mexican border, most of the conversations were in Spanish. Meanwhile, the non-Spanish speaking agents were assigned to the street surveillance teams.

I was relieved not to be assigned to the listening post or veal treatment for the initial part of the investigation. I preferred street surveillance because of the action. Also, it was an opportunity to bond with local narcotics officers. I had worked with some of them when I was stationed in El Paso with the Texas Highway Patrol. We had played in softball leagues and reveled in many postgame beer binges.

Federal agents and local officers rarely make the time to socialize. Unpredictable work schedules, separate social circles, and different attitudes were the main reasons. One officer put it bluntly, "Dude, it is great to hang out with someone who hasn't let the prestige of being a Fed get to him. You're not anal retentive like most of your co-workers."

The locals invited me to social gatherings because they felt like I was one of them. I came from the same streets they worked in everyday. On one such occasion, a deputy from the El Paso County Sheriff's Office invited me to an outdoor cookout in Canutillo, Texas. I accepted the invitation. Before going to the *pachanga* (party), I asked Paul and Vince to join me for some southwestern-style waterskiing.

I had a flair for adventure and steeled myself against fear by seeking various challenges. I tried hobbies that made me appreciate life more than I would have otherwise. Deer hunting in South Texas, motorcycle riding throughout Central Texas, and snow skiing in Ruidoso, New Mexico. Each provided a satisfactory thrill. I believed risk was part of the process for mental readiness in my line of work.

The most daring challenge came when I jumped out of a perfectly good airplane by skydiving. Before the jump, I told others, "If God wants to take me sooner than later, this will be the best time to do it." Falling to the earth over 100 miles per hour was more than exhilarating.

A videotape was made of my jump. Two songs by 'Tom Petty and The Heartbreakers' accompanied the footage - "Running Down A Dream" (during the terminal velocity) and "Free Falling" (after the chute was pulled and I glided slowly downward). The tempos of the tunes were appropriate for the two stages of the jump.

Just prior to noon, I picked up Paul and Vince in my 1986 Jeep CJ-7. This year model was the last of the original Jeeps. After a series of national safety tests exposed the dangers of the CJ-5 and CJ-7, American Motors sold out to Chrysler. Changes included a wider wheelbase and more aerodynamic design. The originality faded away along with the passing wave usually exchanged by the brotherhood of classic Jeep owners.

I spruced up my toy with oversized Mickey Thompson tires, stainless steel accessories and an awesome Pioneer sound system. Family members and close friends asked if they could borrow my Jeep for a weekend or to participate in street parades. Few were allowed the privilege of riding my pride and joy.

With my sidekicks along, we jammed to "Tres Hombres" by ZZ Top. The rough-looking musical trio made Texas proud with their no frills blues and rock style.

"Man, I haven't been waterskiing in years," said Vince.

"Me too," replied Paul. "We used to go with my uncle to Ascarate Lake every Sunday." The lake is located in the southeast section of El Paso. It measures no more than a mile in length.

"You call that a lake?" Vince yelled. "It's a fucking pond!"

Paul responded, "We're in the middle of a desert. We needed to improvise and make the best of what we had available."

As customary, the men proceeded to chug their first beer. A real man doesn't sip on his beer especially the initial cold one.

Paul wondered why they were headed west on Interstate 10, "Sal, aren't we going to Ascarate Lake?"

I didn't respond. I wanted to leave them in suspense for a while.

"Whose boat are we going to use?" asked Vince.

Again, I didn't answer. I exited at the Texas/New Mexico state line and drove through the town of Anthony, whose motto is 'The Smallest Town in Two States.' I reached the back roads lined with fields of green chili, onions, and cotton.

We were sucking down on our second beer when Paul insisted, "Where the fuck are you taking us?"

"I'm going to show you the poor man's way of waterskiing," I replied. "One needs to adapt to their environment. Enjoy the scenery." I finished my second Bud Light and handed the empty can to Vince. "Bartender, pass me another one of them cold brews." The others chugged their backwash and succumbed to the 'beer pressure'.

The Rio Grande River begins with the snow runoff from the Rocky Mountains in southern Colorado and provides thousands of farmers in New Mexico and Texas with irrigation water. The Elephant Butte Dam and Caballo Lake reservoirs in central New Mexico control the flow of water to those down river.

There are roughly 1,500 large farms and 2,500 small farms in El Paso County that are dependent on the Rio Grande. Water experts believe the City of El Paso's main underground water source, the Hueco bolson, to run dry by the year 2025. The city draws nearly half of its water from the Rio Grande, so obtaining additional water rights outside the county is imperative. Until then, I took advantage of the circumstances by enjoying a unique desert sport.

I turned onto a dirt embankment that paralleled an irrigation canal. I parked the Jeep next to the only tree along the mile-long channel. The canal measured thirty feet wide and was clear of any brush that could hinder the fun.

We stared at the smooth flowing water as I handed the water skis to Vince. "Aids before herpes!"

"I'm not going first!" Vince responded.

"Let me give it a try." said Paul. "How deep is the water?"

I explained, "It's chest high. If you wipe out, the first thing you need to do is grab the skis before the current carries them away." I tied one end of the ski rope to the roll bar of my Jeep and tossed the end with the plastic handle into the canal.

Paul jumped into the canal, grabbed the handle, and stood there for a few seconds.

Vince reached out to Paul with the water skis, but he wouldn't reach for them. "What are you waiting for?"

"The water feels warm. I'm taking a leak." We all laughed.

I continued, "I'm going to pull you upstream for nearly a mile and stop before a small dam. When we get close to the bridge up the road, let go of the handle if you like. I'll turn the Jeep around and we'll come back here. Can you dig it?"

"Let's do it!"

Each of us took turns driving and waterskiing. Our confidence increased with each additional beer consumed. We glided from side to side of the canal while jamming out to the rock-n-roll blaring from the wooden box speakers.

Vince said, "This reminds me of a scene in "Apocalypse Now" when the soldiers were waterskiing in Vietnam. Just like them, we are grunts on the front lines of a war in the armpit of Texas."

I laughed, "Enjoy the aroma of *churos* (deep-fried pastry), my young captain! It smells like victory." It was a play with words from a quote in the movie.

After two hours, we decided it was time to eat something to absorb the alcohol. Not wanting to go empty-handed to the cookout, we made a 'beer run' and resupplied the ice chest. We joined the sheriff's deputies who had beef fajitas and Hatch green chili on the grill.

Upon our arrival, one of the deputies yelled, "Here come the FAFA's!"

"What are they calling us?" asked Vince.

"It means, Fat Ass Federal Agents," Paul answered.

I rubbed my belly and shouted to the deputies, "This is my baby elephant. Want to see the trunk?" I proceeded to unzip my pants but stopped short from taking it too far. There was a burst of laughter.

An intoxicated deputy walked up to Vince and said, "Why is it that we do all the work yet you feds get all the glory? Is that why you guys are considered 'the cream of the crap'?"

Vince asked, "Sal, why are they busting our balls?"

"They're just testing you. Kill 'em with your charming personality and don't lose your temper."

I looked at the deputies and countered, "It's always been the same. The war pigs in D.C. call the shots while you guys are discounted as the soldiers of misfortune. Nothing is going to change so quit your crying and call your Congressman!"

Everyone laughed. Bro hugs (grasp right hand then halfway embracement) were exchanged. The partying continued with the customary tapping of the beer bottles.

As a law enforcement officer, it is easy to view the world with cynical eyes. On a daily basis, they deal with those who don't want to encounter them. They see the worst in people who commit horrific criminal acts on other human beings.

Cops are trained to think and act a certain way in a sub-culture that doesn't tolerate emotional or physical weakness. They put up a barrier and limit their social circle to other cops. They limit their conversations to work-related experiences while other topics of conversation do not interest them.

An 'us versus them' attitude can create a one-dimensional personality. Being a cop is not conducive to healthy marriages and nurturing friendships with anyone outside of law enforcement.

I didn't have many regular friends as a State Trooper. I hung out with other cops because I was in a business that required me to stop people and ruin their day by giving them a traffic citation or arresting them. I gained respect but that didn't help with my social life. I wasn't invited to many parties because people wanted to have fun without a cop being in their presence.

As the deputies began tossing a football, I slipped in a compact disc and cranked up Van Halen's "5150". The innovative and playful guitar riffs of Eddie Van Halen gave everyone an 'eargasm'.

A deputy shouted, "Van Halen isn't the same without David Lee Roth. They sound too commercialized."

I disagreed, "No way! Bringing in the Red Rocker gave them a lot of class. Don't take me wrong, I love the old Van Halen with Diamond Dave, but Van Hagar picked it up a notch in style."

The partygoers kept jamming to the tunes until they were interrupted. An older model Chevrolet Impala, occupied by two teenage boys, pulled up next to me. The front seat passenger asked, "Hey, do y'all wanna buy some weed?"

I adjusted my red bandana, walked to passenger window, and replied, "Yeah. How much you got?"

"Tens and twenties."

"Let me check it out. I want to see if it's fresh."

The boy reached under the passenger seat, retrieved a plastic baggie and proudly displayed his merchandise.

I opened the bag, brought it to my nose and said, "It smells pretty good. We need more than one bag because we just got the party started. Sell me what you've got."

The boy smiled and showed the shoebox filled with clear sandwich bags containing marijuana.

By now, a deputy was standing next to the driver's side window with his badge in hand on top of the car's roof.

I subtly pulled the box away from the boy and looked at the deputies. Two of the deputies had their pistols hidden behind their backs and were approaching the car.

A deputy flashed a police badge in the face of the driver and said, "Police! Get out of the car!" The deputies reached for the teenagers through the open windows to arrest them. I backed away with all the dope.

Instead of cooperating, the driver's 'fight or flight' instinct kicked in and it was flight. The kid punched the accelerator and peeled out.

The deputies quickly stepped away from the vehicle, not risking getting caught in the open windows or being run over. Before the car was out of sight, a deputy memorized the license plate number and called the Canutillo Sheriff's Office sub-station with the description of the vehicle. Although the teenagers were not arrested that day, the car was frequently pulled over by deputies for the next several weeks.

Most of the marijuana was turned over to an on-duty deputy for processing and destruction. Some remained at the party.

The social gathering continued until sundown. However, the festivities would shift to Paul's house to watch a professional football game on television. Paul later regretted offering his humble abode to the motley crew.

After watching "America's Team" get its butt kicked for three quarters, Paul became extremely agitated. He slammed an empty beer can on his ceramic tile floor and stomped on it. He walked briskly to the kitchen counter and grabbed a kitchen knife.

I announced, "I think we need to put Paul on suicide watch."

Paul mumbled something and proceeded to slice into a deer sausage link on a wooden cutting board.

Vince asked, "Why do people show allegiance to any sports team? It's not like a marriage where you have to remain loyal to just one team!"

Paul said, "You just can't jump on the bandwagon of a hot team and root for a different team each football season!"

"Why not? What is your obsession of rooting for a single team regardless of who the players are on that team? There are some thugs on your favorite team who I wouldn't piss on if their guts were on fire!"

I added, "Look, I love sports just like anyone but you don't have to limit yourself to just one team. I watch the games to see the players, not the team. I don't get emotional over the games anymore. It's not worth the agitation."

Paul responded, "I am loyal to 'the Boys'. I've been a fan all my life!"

I added, "The only ones you need to be loyal to is your family!"

Vince said, "In the big picture, how does the outcome of a game affect your life? Paul, you get upset with these overpaid athletes who certainly don't give a rats ass about you."

I said, "That is why I love watching women's beach volleyball. It's a sport where nobody is a loser and everybody is a winner."

Everyone laughed except Paul.

He had enough of the insults, "Shut the fuck up and pass me another beer. Let's take a shot of Tequila, assholes!"

After more beer pressure and tequila shots, high school pride became the topic of discussion. Two of the deputies had attended *La Bowie* High School, Paul graduated from Burges High, and the others had attended schools in the Lower Valley. One challenge led to another and by midnight a three-on-three tackle football game erupted on Paul's moderately-sized freshly cut front lawn.

For the better part of an hour, bodies were flung into rose bushes and manicured shrubs. There were many bumps and bruises exchanged but no pain was felt since all were more than comfortably numb. Except for Paul. He felt his finger was broken. Requesting medical attention would signify defeat for his alma mater. He ignored the agony and continued with the melee.

The next morning, Paul endured the physical punishment inflicted on his body and his wife's verbal tirade over her ruined flowerbed. His uppity neighbors also expressed their displeasure over the scandalous, late night behavior. The only relief he got was from the barbacoa tacos and a Big Red soda for breakfast to ease his hangover.

Partying with the El Paso County deputies and playing tackle football on the grass were times I would never forget. It made me feel young and vibrant. It took my mind off the dangers of my job and rejuvenated my soul. I just wished everyone who shared those times would never forget what we shared. I needed their revitalization in the not too distant future.

Chapter 8 – Back In The Saddle Again

Several men have committed a violent crime. They turn their attention and begin running after me. I am alone. I don't see anyone around! Where was my backup? The men are gaining ground on me. I need to protect myself and resort to deadly force.

I find cover and point my Glock semi-automatic pistol. With a solid grip, I place my forefinger on the trigger with the necessary pressure. I raise the pistol and align the rear fluorescent sights with the front sight. The targets are in the kill zone, and I am ready to double-tap each of the approaching men. I squeeze the trigger but nothing happens. I press it harder, and all I hear is a clicking sound. I pull back on the slide to see if there is a round in the chamber. It is empty!

I push the magazine release button and let the clip fall to the ground. I reach for a loaded magazine and slam it in. I hear it lock and chamber a round. The men are nearly on top of me! I point the pistol in their direction, with no time to align the sights, and pull the trigger. It doesn't fire!

I recognize the frightening scenario. I get a grasp on reality by focusing my efforts on waking up. I shake my head and find clarity. The recurring nightmare has haunted me again. It has been with me since I joined the DEA. What was it supposed to mean? Who were the 'bad guys'? What was the mechanical explanation for the pistol not firing a round? Where was my backup? The nightmare was frustrating in many ways.

I didn't like wasting time analyzing any of my dreams or searching for subliminal meanings. However, this one I have overanalyzed and haven't come up with any discernible answers.

I rose from the bed and fanned the wet pillow. Looked like another early start. I shit, shaved, and showered trying to forget the torment. I got over the hump by listening to REO Speedwagon's live recording of "You Get What You Play For". This album elevated the studio recordings to a higher level of showmanship with an energetic live performance.

Before going to the DEA office, I called Richard McGee. "Good morning."

"What's up, Sal?"

"Just wanted to touch base with you. Do you need me to go on surveillance for your investigation?"

"Not today. It seems the bad guys will be staying in Juarez. There hasn't been much chatter over the wire on this side of the river. I don't anticipate anything happening."

I could hear the disappointment in his voice about the inactivity in the investigation. I tried to console him, "It sucks that we are restricted from playing on both sides of the Rio Grande River while those son-of-a-bitches have no borders."

"No shit! I would love to be on the other side. I can only imagine the many conversations we could intercept if we were there with them."

I closed, "We are in a borderless war yet restricted by an illusionary wall." We would test the wall soon enough.

I entered the DEA office. After getting my first cup of coffee, I walked into the Group One bay and nodded at Vince.

Vince asked, "Do you think Paul will make it to work today?"

"I doubt it. I think his wife still has him doing plenty of honey-do's around the house."

"Shit, we tore up his yard! I don't think we'll be invited to his house anytime soon."

Jose Calderon walked up to us and asked, "What are you guys talking about?"

I changed the subject not wanting Calderon to know about our weekend shenanigans, "We've been debating the possibility of our reincarnation."

Vince played along, "Sal wants to come back as a dolphin. Since he is sexually deprived as a human being, he wants to return as one of the few species that can actually feel sexual intercourse."

I retorted, "Vince wants to come back as a seagull so he can fly around all day and shit on people. Wait a minute, he does that already!"

We all laughed.

"What about you, *jefe* (boss)?"

Calderon joined in, "I have my own dilemma. I am preoccupied with the possibility of spontaneous combustion. Think about it. You're walking down the street, and a chemical reaction occurs. The body explodes, and chunks of flesh are hurled in every direction. Has anybody really seen it happen?"

We got quiet, contemplated the possibilities, and envisioned the gory scene.

Calderon continued, "Onto something completely different. Tell me about your weekend."

I related the eventful cookout with the local cops including the 'pucker factor' experienced by the two stoned teenage boys selling marijuana. I ended the story where the boys drove off.

"And how was your weekend?" I asked.

Calderon described attending an intimate gathering Saturday evening. "It was a peaceful evening with some influential people from the El Paso area. After dinner, we heard a lot of cussing outside. We walked to the front porch and witnessed a knock-down-drag-out party down the street. We were entertained watching grown men reenact their high school glory days on somebody's lawn."

Vince and I looked at each other as our faces turned red. Vince asked, "Did one of those men scream like a little girl?" He was referring to Paul who let out a yell after dislocating his finger.

We all laughed.

Too often, the incessant demand of decision-making leads supervisors to ulcers during their forties, a nervous breakdown in their fifties, or a massive coronary in their sixties. Because of Calderon's deliberate, laid-back demeanor, he had yet to experience any of those afflictions.

He possessed an exceptional talent for evaluating the agents under his command. Not a limelight seeker, Calderon gave credit where credit was due. He had an open door policy and never talked down to his agents. He delegated authority and let them rely on their ingenuity to get the job done.

Lately, he had been riding the crest of a big wave. His youngest agent had made one of the largest cocaine seizures in El Paso DEA history.

Calderon glanced over my shoulder and read a small plaque,

"People with high intelligence, talk about ideas.

People with average intelligence, talk about things.

People with low intelligence, talk about other people."

He smiled, "Wise words. If only we could come up with more ideas in our current situation."

I said, "Law enforcement is an occupation that is primarily reactive. Cops respond to a crime after it has been committed. There are few opportunities for cops to take initiative and prevent a crime from occurring."

Over the office's public address system, I heard the receptionist say, "Spanish-speaking agent needed on Line Two."

I waited a while to see if someone else would answer the phone before realizing I was the only Spanish speaker in the office this early in the morning.

Vince looked at me and said in a poor Spanish accent, "You are the lone *cabron*. Remember, Mexican-Americans don't like to get up early, but they have to, so they do." He was taking a quote from the Cheech and Chong movie "Up In Smoke".

After introducing myself over the phone, I listened as the Spanish-speaking female spoke, "I want to report a lot of cars coming in and out of my neighbor's house. They come all hours of the night. They must be doing something illegal because nobody comes out during the day."

"Have you written down any of the license plate numbers?"

"No, but most of them are the yellow, *Front Chih* license plates." In local slang, she referred to the insignia of the Mexican State of Chihuahua.

"What can you tell me about your neighbors?"

"I don't know them. They recently moved in and never come outside."

"Can you describe any of the vehicles?"

"Not really. The cars are driven into the garage. After about an hour, the car comes out."

"Would you give me the address and description of the house?"

After jotting the information, I made one request, "If it's not too much trouble, could you begin writing down the license plate numbers and a description of the vehicles?"

She said, "I'll see what I can do. You can call me in a couple of weeks and I should have something for you." She provided me with her home telephone number.

I thanked her and hung up the telephone.

Most agents disregard these calls because the vague information generally leads nowhere. It isn't prudent to waste time and manpower on the unknown. Some considerate agents place the notes into their own 'file 13' folder as pending, but not forgotten.

I considered relaying the information to the local cops. The El Paso Police Department and Sheriff's Office appreciated the DEA throwing them a bone. However, I had a feeling about this call and felt obligated to carry out the most fundamental task.

I searched in NADDIS to see if the address had been mentioned in any DEA investigation. The inquiry showed the address as negative in the system.

Later that day, Rudy Montes called me at the office, "I have some good news and some bad news. Can we meet this afternoon?"

I asked, "Can't you just tell me over the phone?"

"No. You know I don't trust your fellow agents. Someone may be listening to our conversation. And another thing, I don't like meeting at busy restaurants."

"Okay. Let's meet at a hole-in-the-wall where we won't be seen."

It was around 5 p.m. when they met at the Circle Inn Bar located in central El Paso. Cold beer and the best buffalo-style wings in town made for a savory power meal. Vince and I were drinking our first beer when Rudy walked in.

Rudy began, "Someone had to answer for the lost loads. Each member close to the lost cocaine loads was interrogated. My brother was grilled for hours. He struggled for answers with questions he didn't want to hear. They threatened to kill him if he did not tell them who snitched on the drivers."

"Where is your brother now?"

"He talked his way out of it. He promised to tie up any loose ends. It would begin with Dan talking to both of his drivers."

Common sense was to avoid any person arrested by the cops. The defendant and his family members were considered hot, or under the watchful eye of law enforcement. Also, they may have cooperated with the arresting authority and implicated other members of the organization.

When a serious problem arises, drug trafficking organizations, similar to the hierarchy of legitimate businesses, meet to discuss damage control. If there were indications that a part of the organization had been compromised, the remedy would be to dismantle and eliminate any further business contracts. That would only be the beginning.

Just like Dan, the boss was unwilling to do anything else for a living. They both had a distorted belief that a life of crime is more rewarding than the responsibility of a legitimate profession. They viewed most people as being content with living in mediocrity and performing routine, meaningless tasks.

Throwing caution to the wind, Dan felt a need to talk to the family members of his drivers. He desperately wanted to prove there was not a leak within his group.

After a few days, the criminal defense attorney for both drivers provided Dan Montes with copies of the arrest reports. The common thread for each event was overly aggressive uniformed officers who made up a reason to detain and search the vehicles.

The ninety-kilogram load in Las Cruces was found by a Border Patrol agent who claimed the driver displayed extreme nervousness, shaky hands, sweaty forehead, and stuttered speech. Dan believed the blame should be directed at an inquisitive agent.

Jason Sanchez's one hundred kilogram load was lost due to a defective taillamp. This was an unforeseen mechanical failure that could have happened to anyone. Who inspects the rear lights of their vehicle?

Defense attorneys usually receive the DEA Reports of Investigation that have been redacted with black marker lines concealing the actual investigative efforts. The rest of the story might be exposed at a trial if the defendant was foolish enough to pursue the extreme option of going against the U.S. government.

In this case, the investigation reports did not disclose the truth or reasons for the traffic stops. Each arresting officer developed reasonable suspicion to detain and search the vehicle. Then probable cause lead to the discovery of the bundles of cocaine. Both cocaine seizures were caused by alert and keen law enforcers. Nothing else.

Dan was relieved that the two events were unrelated and did not suggest a betrayal by his drivers or anyone in his crew. He relayed this naive optimism to his supervisor.

Rudy said, "My brother is hurting for money. He lost his commissions for the two loads of coke that you guys took."

I asked, "What's the good news?"

"Dan's boss said he also lost money and needs to keep the shipments moving. He is willing to test the waters. My brother begged the boss to trust him with another shipment. He wants to redeem himself."

I responded, "Do you think the boss is daring enough to risk sending another shipment of drugs?"

"The boss told Dan to bring a load of money from Chicago to Juarez. I think they need the money or it could be a test. The boss wants to see if the cops are watching them."

"How much money are they wanting to move?" I asked.

"Dan isn't sure. It won't be very much. If the first load makes it safely into Juarez, there will be another money shipment on standby. The second load would be much bigger."

"How is the money supposed to be transported from Chicago?"

"They have a minivan in Juarez that is currently being modified with a false compartment."

"Has your brother brought back money before?"

"We've done it several times. The van will be ready tomorrow, and my brother wants it on the road to Chicago by tomorrow night."

"You've made the money run before?" I was upset with Rudy for not telling me about his prior drug money trips. All would be forgiven if you he could do it again.

"Will you be able to volunteer and drive the van?"

"Yes, I've done it before. I'll ask my bro."

Rudy didn't have any details about the pick up location in Chicago or the travel itinerary. He ended the conversation assuring he would relay any further developments. He left the bar in a hurry. It was obvious he didn't like being out in a public setting, especially with two DEA agents.

Vince and I discussed investigative options. Our fear of surveillance units getting burned was of primary concern. We had to rely on Chicago DEA agents not ruining our plans. After a few more beers, it was time to call it an evening.

As I was leaving the bar, I remembered the call earlier in the day regarding a house with suspicious activity. I decided to drive by and check it out. The house was located in the eastern part of the city that was notorious for stash houses.

I parked down the street, keeping several cars between my location and the suspected stash house. I sat low in my seat, so as to not raise suspicion from neighbors. The OGV had tinted windows, as did most other DEA vehicles in the fleet.

I watched a young couple holding hands, walking on the sidewalk coming in my direction. They were so into each other and oblivious to their surroundings that they were unaware of my presence.

They leaned on the hood of the car parked in front of me. After some passionate kissing, the couple jumped into the back seat of the sedan. Within twenty minutes, the half-naked girl was riding her partner. She occasionally glanced toward the front door of the house, hoping her parents wouldn't come outside looking for her.

I had witnessed some entertaining situations while on surveillance. On one occasion, there were two men smoking a joint in a vehicle parked next to my DEA vehicle. Knowing I wouldn't compromise the operation,

I partially rolled my window down and displayed my DEA badge. One of the men swallowed the half-smoked joint then sped away.

On another occasion, I saw a man hitting a woman in a parking lot of supermarket. I noticed them walking together from the store but wasn't sure about their relationship. I waited a minute, contemplating my involvement, before the man struck the woman again and grabbed her arm tightly.

Not wanting to disclose my identity, I drove my OGV next to the couple and rolled the window halfway down. Without getting out of the vehicle, I said, "Get your hands off her."

The man responded, "Mind your own business!"

I said, "Don't make me get out and kick your ass!"

"Fuck you!"

I pulled up my Glock pistol to the window and showed only the barrel of the gun. I said, "I'm going to pop a cap in your ass, mother fucker!"

The woman escaped from the man's grip and jumped into the passenger seat of their car. The man slowly turned around and took his time getting into the driver's seat. More could have been done but I had other priorities.

It was nearly 8 p.m., when a vehicle arrived at the stash house. The garage door was raised by remote control and the vehicle disappeared. I had enough time to jot the Mexican license plate number and note the vehicle description.

I forwarded the license plate number to the U.S. Customs Service to be placed on a lookout status. That is, anytime the vehicle entered the U.S. through a port of entry, an inspector had two options. The first was to positively identify the occupants and conduct an inspection of the vehicle. If there were no warrants or illicit drugs, they suspects would be released. The information would be relayed to the reporting agent.

The second option, called a silent hit, was a tactic to stall the suspects. The reporting agent, such as myself, would be notified of the detention. I would round up a surveillance team to follow the vehicle once it was released and permitted to enter the U. S. This usually lead to identifying additional suspects, vehicles and locations affiliated with the bad guys.

I waited another hour before calling it a night. It was long after the young lovers had composed themselves and gone their separate ways. It was a school night, and they probably had homework to do.

The following day, I contacted an agent from the Chicago DEA office and discussed the possible scenarios related to the money van. Vince would fly to Chicago and coordinate surveillance efforts to identify the location where the money was to be picked up.

There was only one problem. Chicago DEA supervisors expressed their refusal to let the illicit funds leave their district. They insisted that the van be seized and the stash location be raided. The Chicago supervisors and the desk jockeys at DEA headquarters were unwilling to permit drug money to reach the hands of the traffickers.

Using the utmost tact and diplomacy, Jose Calderon was able to convince the Chicago supervisors to allow the van to proceed as planned. He emphasized the financial benefits of releasing this smaller shipment of money for the anticipated larger shipment.

The transportation group would regain its credibility with the underworld, thus allowing it to transport multi-tons of illicit drugs and large sums of drug money.

Rudy called and said, "My brother was ready to make the trip himself, but I talked him into letting me drive the van. I told him I needed some extra cash."

"Perfect! When do you leave?"

"Tonight."

"Did he tell you where to drive the van?"

"Yes, a motel outside of Chicago. I've been there before. I'm supposed to call a guy when I arrive, leave the keys in the ash tray, and someone will take the van to be loaded with the money."

"Call me when you get the van. I'd like to see it."

"I don't think that will be possible. My brother is real nervous. He will follow me past the Border Patrol checkpoint in Sierra Blanca. He's so paranoid, he may even follow me much farther than that."

It was decided that no DEA agents would follow the van and risk being 'burned' by the Dan.

"Call Agent Sellers when you are near Dallas. He will meet with you to inspect the van before you continue to Chicago."

"What's wrong? Don't you trust me? Do you think I'm taking drugs up north?" I didn't answer.

Vince changed his flight plans to include a stopover in Dallas.

After dark, Rudy picked up the van and headed towards Chicago. As suspected, Dan followed his young brother to the Sierra Blanca Border Patrol checkpoint. Once the van cleared the checkpoint without incident, Dan returned to El Paso.

Upon his arrival in Dallas, Rudy called Vince and the two inspected the Chrysler van. They found a false six-inch high compartment running the entire length of the passenger floorboard. It was empty.

After the inspection, Vince caught a flight to Chicago while Rudy continued his trek northbound.

The following day Rudy called Vince from the motel outside Chicago. DEA surveillance was immediately established on the van.

It was after sundown when an unidentified Hispanic male came out of the shadows. He jumped into the van and drove away.

Unfortunately, Chicago DEA task force surveillance units lost sight of the van when the driver performed evasive maneuvers to elude would-be followers, called heat runs. The van was last seen in a warehouse district in the southside of Chicago.

The Chicago agents were embarrassed and their supervisors were furious.

I wasn't. I was relieved because I didn't trust the Chicago agents from raiding the stash location if had they discovered where it was.

Several hours later, the van returned to the motel. The unidentified driver was not followed by law enforcement after he exited the van into a waiting car. It was unlikely they would return to the stash site.

The van, loaded with money, would remain in the motel parking lot under the watchful eye of law enforcement officers.

The next morning, Rudy left Chicago followed by Vince and other law enforcement agents. After several hours on the highway, it was determined no suspicious vehicles were following the van. The Chicago agents returned to the Windy City leaving Vince and Rudy to head southbound.

I told Rudy to drive the van as far away from Chicago before stopping to inspect the contents in the false compartment. Calderon wanted to wait until the contraband was close to our jurisdiction. It wasn't until Albuquerque, New Mexico, that the van was inspected.

Lifting up the carpet in the rear passenger area, a small, metal sliding trap door was the only way into the compartment. Inside the compartment were bundles of U.S. currency wrapped in masking tape. It took an hour before all fifty bundles were retrieved.

The currency was wrapped in cellophane and masking tape. On the outside of each bundle was a dollar amount written in black marker. According to the markings, the amount of money totaled $300,000. After Vince took photos of the bundles, they were put back into the false compartment.

Chicago supervisors continued to express their anger by complaining to the DEA headquarters decision-makers for allowing the money to leave their jurisdiction. It was not acceptable to allow drug traffickers to receive the profits of their illicit activities.

Completing the trip, Rudy drove to a restaurant in Ciudad Juarez. There was someone waiting for the van. Just as quickly as he entered the parking lot, the van and the money disappeared. Rudy called his brother to give him a ride back to El Paso.

Dan was relieved he completed his contract with the Juarez Cartel. He was determined to redeem the credibility of his transportation cell with additional successful deliveries.

Chapter 9 – Deception And Controlled Deliveries

The next day Rudy called me to say that two large drug transportation contracts were being finalized. Considering the possibility of multi-ton shipments, I decided to accommodate the traffickers with the use of a warehouse, a tractor-trailer, and a truck driver.

I contacted an informant, nicknamed *Chino* because of his Asian decent, to assist us. The informant was the owner of an older model Peterbilt truck-tractor. The well-traveled 18-wheeler would enhance the DEA ruse. All that was needed was for Rudy to persuade his brother that a safe location could be used to transfer the drugs into a rig, slang for truck-tractor and trailer.

I rented a warehouse in an industrial area conveniently located adjacent to Interstate 10 in the eastside of El Paso. Commercial vehicles came and went into the area all hours of the day and night. I believed Dan Montes would feel comfortable blending in with the bustling surroundings.

Two days later, Rudy called me, "Guess what?"

I took my time with the response, "I give up."

"We have been contracted to take a marijuana shipment to the East Coast." Rudy was so excited that he let down his guard and told me over the phone.

"Where?"

"Charlotte, North Carolina."

"How much marijuana?"

"One ton."

I was pleasantly surprised, "Have you ever made a trip to that region before?"

"Never. Is that a problem?"

"No. Actually, I'm happy that Dan and his superiors are willing to expand their list of clients."

"What do I need to do?"

"Persuade your brother to use our warehouse and our rig."

The next day, Dan agreed with Rudy that the tractor-trailer was necessary because of the long haul. Dan wanted to survey the warehouse, meet the truck driver and to inspect the new conveyance. Rudy told Dan that he had a friend who needed work. This friend would help with the labor of transferring the marijuana and stay overnight in the warehouse to protect the precious cargo. Rudy's friend was named Sal.

It is extremely rare that two DEA informants meet or work with each other during an investigation. But in this case, I felt the necessity to introduce Rudy to the truck driver so they could get their stories straight before meeting Dan. We met at the warehouse and the briefing lasted thirty minutes.

Rudy called Dan and directed him to the warehouse.

Upon his arrival, Dan was introduced to *Chino* and I. A handshake was the only thing exchanged at this stage. Dan wasn't interested in getting to know the new subordinates as much as he was in the warehouse. He walked outside and looked over the exterior of the warehouse. He stood by the door and scanned the neighborhood.

He reentered the building and slowly walked along each wall. He closely inspected the aluminum siding panels. He was looking for anything unusual, like a hidden police surveillance camera.

Earlier, Calderon and I debated about installing such a device. After watching Dan's meticulous inspection, I breathed a sigh of relief that we made the right decision not to install any video or audio equipment.

After the thorough inspection, Dan questioned *Chino* regarding the concealment method for the shipment of marijuana. *Chino* replied, "I like using 35-gallon and 55-gallon oil drums to hide the merchandise. I have forty empty drums in my trailer and ten filled with motor oil at my house. I'll place the drugs in the middle of all the drums. Cops don't like to get their uniforms dirty so they avoid moving them to look for drugs. This has worked for me before especially going through the Border Patrol checkpoints."

I leered at *Chino* realizing that the informant had not confessed all his sins. Cops know that most informants have committed criminal violations prior to cooperating with a law enforcement agency. The challenge was to keep them from committing any serious crimes while employed as an informant. It would reflect unfavorably on the controlling agent and the agency.

"I assume that the blue rig parked outside is yours?"

"Yes it is."

"It seems you've used it quite a bit."

"I've been all over the United States."

"How do you feel about taking my product to the East Coast?"

"Not a problem."

Dan turned to Sal, "Where you from?"

I answered, "Ysleta area." I went to high school there and knew the streets.

"My *carnal* (brother) vouches for you. Don't ask any questions and follow my orders. Be ready to pick up the *mota* (slang for marijuana) tomorrow. I'll let you know when and where it is."

I nodded once even though I wasn't clear of my role.

Dan liked what he saw. He told *Chino* to have all his barrels available for the shipment.

The following day, Rudy called me and said, "Dan told me to tell you the van will be in the parking lot of the Pizza Hut restaurant at the corner of Yarbrough and Montana. Look for a gray van containing the marijuana. You are supposed to be there at 2 p.m. The ignition key will be placed in the ashtray. Take the van to the warehouse, and he will be there waiting for you."

Now, I knew my role. I responded, "I'm sure someone will be watching me enter the van."

Rudy ended, "The owners of the weed are big-time players. They are connected to the Mexican Mafia."

I gathered and briefed the El Paso DEA Group One agents. Surveillance was established at the eastside restaurant by noon. The objective was to identify and follow the people who delivered the marijuana.

Paul was assigned to coordinate the street surveillance. Paul positioned the agents for the take aways. It was necessary for each agent to utilize the most recent city street guide for those who were unfamiliar with the area.

The DEA Aviation pilot was available to provide assistance with the eye in the sky. The Cessna 182 had proved to be a most effective surveillance tool in the DEA arsenal. Most drug traffickers might look at their rearview mirror for suspicious vehicles following them but they almost always failed to take one extra precaution by looking up in the sky.

Jake Davis volunteered to be the spotter in the DEA airplane to guide ground units.

I sat with Paul across the street from the restaurant. Paul found a vantage point that gave us full visual access of the parking lot. Paul planned to use his 35mm SLR camera to take surveillance photos through the tinted windows of his OGV of the person dropping off the marijuana-laden van.

At exactly 1:30 p.m., a gray Chevrolet full-size van arrived and was parked in the Pizza Hut parking lot. A man exited and walked briskly to a neighboring convenience store's parking lot. He jumped into the front passenger side of a blue sedan. The car sped away.

There was no time for Paul to take photos of the subject. The transfer took seconds.

Agents fell in behind the sedan after Jake Davis radioed that he had the eye. Paul dropped me off at the restaurant and joined the rest of the surveillance units.

Opening the driver's door, I looked into the van and saw nothing but huge cellophane wrapped marijuana bundles. The rear seats had been removed to accommodate the fresh herb. The windows were covered with cardboard to prevent any passerby from catching a glimpse of a pot smoker's primo dream.

I flipped open the ashtray to retrieve the ignition key. The keychain had a Crime Stoppers logo and the telephone hotline number. I grinned and started the engine. Having only the use of the outside mirrors, I cautiously backed up the van.

I looked around for oncoming traffic and for any counter-surveillance.

I exited the parking lot and turned southbound on Yarbrough Drive.

Although Yvette Gonzalez was unsure if there were any suspects watching me, she followed the van from a distance as a security precaution. We wanted to keep the location of the warehouse our secret. Secondly, to protect me from being carjacked by a third party, as unlikely as it would seem.

Just as unfortunate would be getting pulled over by a local patrol officer. This would leave me having to explain my official capacity to the officer. If the drug traffickers were following the van and saw me being released by a uniformed police officer, they would know that I was a cop.

Like a Sunday morning driver, I cautiously navigated the van to the warehouse without incident.

As for the experienced drug traffickers, they took no chances. They conducted heat runs for nearly an hour in a residential area near the El Paso International Airport. It was an ingenious tactic to prevent aerial surveillance.

The DEA pilot was ordered by the air traffic control tower to stay clear of the airport to avoid entering the restricted air space for incoming and outbound commercial airplanes.

To make matters even worse, Jake Davis became air sick. The pilot was a chain smoker, and even though his window was open, the small plane's cabin quickly filled up with second-hand cigarette smoke.

Jake was using binoculars to follow the blue sedan, but he got dizzy as the airplane circled round and round. He found a barf bag and filled it with the sandwich and chips he had eaten earlier. He lost his lunch and lost the suspects.

Losing the aerial advantage, the burden of the surveillance would on the ground units.

Paul announced over the DEA radio, "All ground surveillance units cease the surveillance! We cannot take a chance of getting burned. Based on the proximity to the airport and evasive tactics, it's obvious these are seasoned veterans."

Rudy and Dan arrived an hour later, followed shortly by the truck driver with fifty empty drums in his trailer.

The four of us transferred the various-sized bundles of marijuana from the van into several barrels. The loaded barrels were sealed with silicon and placed at the front of the trailer.

The remaining empty barrels were then loaded. The final touch was strategically placing the ten oil-filled drums were against the rear trailer doors. This would likely deter a law enforcement officer from trying to move the heavy drums and pursue a more thorough inspection of the contents in the trailer.

Dan was pleased with the concealment method. He was also pleased with his new subordinate named Sal. Dan told his little brother that he liked me because I had the balls to carry a gun. While the men were loading the barrels, Dan noticed my Glock pistol. Although he didn't know it, I would never be part of an undercover operation without a gun under my belt.

After unloading the van, there was some marijuana residue on the floor. Dan picked up a few buds, handed them to me and asked if I wanted to roll a joint. I politely declined, saying I didn't like getting stoned while working. Dan glared at me momentarily.

I needed to clarify my statement, "I used to smoke a lot of bud. Now, I rather puff while I'm chillin' at home with a beer in my hand. I'll take these with me and smoke them later." I placed the marijuana in my rear pant pocket.

Chino showed no modesty by picking up a marijuana bud and rolling a joint. Before sparking it up, he realized nobody else was going to smoke with him. Disappointed, he placed the doobie in his pant pocket.

Dan then took a package of Marlboro cigarettes from his shirt pocket and held it forward. I reached for a protruding cigarette. I didn't smoke cigarettes but knew it was necessary to oblige the offering when working undercover. If I was to be a successful narc and live to tell about it, I needed to do some things I didn't like doing. More importantly, get the bad guy to feel comfortable even when I despise what he does for a living.

Dan ordered me to remain overnight in the warehouse with the tractor trailer. He instructed Rudy to follow him to the Pizza Hut restaurant to return the empty van.

Calderon ordered his Group One agents not to follow the van, as getting burned at this stage of the operation was too risky.

The agents divided shifts to remain on surveillance at the warehouse overnight. This was not only for security reasons, but to warn me in the event Dan decided to check on his shipment.

The truck driver went home for a good night's sleep in preparation for the lengthy trip to the East Coast.

The Charlotte DEA office was alerted of the marijuana shipment headed their way via controlled delivery. With the quantity of drugs flowing through El Paso, it was not at all difficult to arrange drug transactions with one or two-kilogram cocaine dealers. The agents in the El Paso DEA office shifted investigative objectives to conducting controlled deliveries, rather than traditional buy/bust operations.

By undertaking these controlled deliveries, DEA agents desired to seize larger quantities of cocaine and marijuana. The challenge was to get well-connected informants to introduce the agents to mid-level traffickers who had access to hundreds or thousands of pounds of illicit drugs. The informant and agent also had to use persuasion to endorse the reliability of their transportation method to the mid-level traffickers. The ultimate goal was to identify the source of supply in Mexico and the distributors in the U.S., then intercept sizeable quantities of illicit drugs before they hit the streets of America. The theory was simple but the reality was not.

The next morning, *Chino* drove the older model Peterbilt as I rode shotgun. Two DEA agents rode behind in a single OGV providing additional protection.

The caravan departed from El Paso and entered the longest stretch of roadway in the U.S., that is, Interstate 10. The highway runs from Los Angeles, California, to Jacksonville, Florida. The expressway has provided many drug trafficking organizations with safe passage of their product due to the high traffic volume and non-existent checkpoints.

Every three to four hours, the DEA agents took turns sitting next to *Chino*. The topics of conversation between *Chino* and each agent became stale very quickly. Also, the rig was a rough ride and the agents hated the springy passenger seat.

At one point, I desired to acclimate myself to the southeastern region of the U.S. I turned up the volume of the radio to hear some of southern fried Rock's finest - Lynyrd Skynyrd, The Outlaws, and Molly Hatchet. The blend of electric guitars and *macho* vocals provided a feeling of southern comfort.

Before entering the city of Charlotte, *Chino* pulled over to dial a local phone number, as he had been instructed to do by Dan Montes. Next to the telephone number was an alias name. A hotel operator answered and transferred the call.

Dan answered the phone and directed the truck driver to meet him at a truck stop on the outskirts of Charlotte.

After meeting us at the truck stop, Dan jumped into the rig and directed *Chino* to drive about an hour away outside the city limits.

Charlotte DEA agents maintained surveillance as we traveled through the winding roads of the Appalachian Mountains.

Dan guided us to an isolated farmhouse. Dan, *Chino* and I jumped out of the rig cabin where we were met by two 'bubbas' who looked like extras from the movie titled "Deliverance".

The in-breds immediately unloaded the barrels into a corner of the empty barn. One hillbilly exclaimed, "Damn, look at all that wacky weed! I like doing business with you Mesicans!"

The conversations were primarily about the partying that would occur later that evening. The out-of-towners were invited to be their honored guests. One man said, "Moonshine, fresh bud, and hoochie mamas are on tap for tonight!"

Dan told the hillbillies, "As much as we would like to hang out with you guys, we need to get back home and prepare for another delivery. *Adios, amigos* (Farewell, friends)!" After hard-gripped handshakes, the three of us left the local men to prepare for their shindig. We went to a hotel for some sleep before returning to El Paso the following morning.

The Charlotte DEA agents knew their role in the operation. The following day, Charlotte DEA agents had a local deputy sheriff conduct a traffic stop on a car seen leaving the barn. After the deputy discovered fifty pounds of marijuana in the vehicle's trunk, the driver admitted that he acquired the marijuana from the suspected barn.

A search warrant was requested from a local judge with the probable cause based solely on the confession of the driver in the car. The warrant was executed and all the marijuana was seized. The two hillbillies who helped unload the marijuana were arrested and the DEA objectives were accomplished. Arrest reports never mentioned the El Paso connection.

This tactic allowed the drug transportation cell from El Paso to deny any responsibility for the take downs in Charlotte. In other words, it was not Dan Montes' fault that the hillbillies got caught.

There was no rest for the weary. Within a week of returning to El Paso from Charlotte, Rudy called me and said a load of cocaine was to be transported from El Paso to Riverside, California.

Excited about the warehouse, Dan planned to deliver the cocaine personally. He requested the oil drums be used again as the method of concealment. He told Rudy to have me available for this operation.

Group One agents established surveillance on the warehouse and waited for Dan. It was 4 p.m., when a red Nissan Sentra pulled up to the vertical-sliding metal door of the warehouse.

Dan exited the car and knocked on the door. I opened the door and Dan drove the Nissan into the warehouse.

Opening the vehicle's trunk, Dan displayed a glorious sight. He said, "I have exactly one hundred packages of coke."

Dan walked away and pulled a 35-gallon drum close to the car and said, "Let's see how many kilos fit into this drum. Don't lose count!"

Rudy and I helped him extract the bundles from the trunk. In the end, the trio placed one hundred packages into three 35-gallon drums.

Without a word, Dan left in a hurry.

Rudy and I waited patiently for nearly an hour.

Dan returned in a black sports car containing an additional one hundred bundles. The trio filled three more 35-gallon drums with the cocaine.

He instructed, "We're going to conceal each of these 35-gallon drums inside the 55-gallon drums. We'll fill the drums with motor oil. The kind the truck driver uses for his rig." Dan pointed to an oil-filled 55-gallon drum with a pump and hose on top.

"We just need a few things. Sal, let's go to Walmart and buy some silicone to seal the drums." I was hoping the surveillance agents were monitoring the conversation. I was wearing a transmitter disguised as a digital pager. Although it wasn't the most reliable transmitter in the DEA inventory, it was the most appropriate for this undercover operation.

Dan drove while I rode shotgun in the black sports car to the nearest Walmart location. I knew the greatest risk about working undercover in my hometown was getting recognized by someone who knew my true identity. It occurred on several occasions during my seven years as an undercover agent in El Paso. Although the population of *El Chuco* was breaking one million, it was not uncommon to be recognized by someone who was a friend of a cousin of a neighbor.

Entering the store, I surveyed the patrons as Dan and I walked to the hardware department. Dan retrieved a few tools and several tubes of silicone. It looked like the coast was clear. Unfortunately, as we were paying for the items at the checkout counter, out of the corner of my eyesight I saw someone approaching me.

The man yelled, "Hey, Sal! How's it goin'?"

I recognized the man as someone I played softball with in a local law enforcement league. I tried sliding through the checkout line but I was stuck between Dan and the front of the line.

The man continued, "Will you be playing softball next season?"

"No." I responded in a low tone while turning away. I wanted the man to get lost. One word regarding cops on the team and I would be burned. The investigation would cease and people would be killed.

"Do you think we can get Budweiser to sponsor our team again? Man, we got plastered after every game last season!"

I didn't respond.

The man continued, "What was the name of the guy on our team we nicknamed 'The Judge' because he was always sitting on the bench?"

"Hey, dude," I answered, "I'm kind of in a rush because I'm working right now." I emphasized the word 'working' hoping the man would get the hint.

The man didn't get the hint and was insulted when I blew him off, "Take care then."

Dan noticed my rudeness to the overly friendly man.

I shook my head and muttered in feigned disgust, "*Pinchi joto* (Damn faggot)."

Dan smirked. "I don't mind being seen in public with you wearing a Judas Priest T-shirt and the red bandana hanging out of your pant pocket. But do you have to wear that fucking earring? Maybe that's why that guy was hitting on you."

I was wearing a gold cross earring I bought after graduation from the DEA Academy. I deflected the insult by saying, "Hey, it's on my left ear!" Homophobes believed wearing an earring on the right ear meant one was homosexual.

Dan responded, "*Orale*. I just don't understand why men like wearing women's jewelry. You can consider me being old-school."

I wanted to elaborate on the conversation at hand but knew better. I was a subordinate in this relationship. It was safer not to talk and express any opinions. It could only lead to further discussion and raise doubt of my true identity. We returned to the car.

Dan started asking personal questions, "Why are you getting into this business?"

"I need to make a few bucks."

"Do you have the desire to be a millionaire or a drug lord like most of us?"

"I'm not a dreamer. I'm a realist."

"Good answer. Where are your parents from?"

"My parents and grandparents were born in El Paso. Originally, my mother's family was from Chihuahua and my father's family was from Zacatecas."

Dan changed his tone, "Are you expecting trouble?" He was referring to the Glock pistol tucked under my black T-shirt.

"It is better to be safe than sorry."

"Is there one in the chamber?"

"Of course."

"Can I take a look at your gun?"

I pulled it out. Without acting like a cop and ejecting the round in the chamber as a safety precaution, I just handed it over.

Dan inspected it carefully. He was looking for any markings that indicated a government-issued weapon.

He pointed the barrel at my head, "In my business, killing another may be necessary. Especially when someone is a *raton* (rat). Don't you agree?"

I kept my composure, "Fucking A. Anybody trying to take money out of my pocket is dead to me."

Dan held the gun for what seemed like an eternity. Satisfied with the response, he lowered the pistol and returned it to me.

I wanted to return the gesture and pull the trigger. However, a deep sigh was enough for me to alleviate the anxiety.

Upon returning to the warehouse, the cocaine was secured as ordered by Dan. We sealed the smaller drums with silicone and placed them inside the larger ones. Motor oil was pumped into the 55-gallon drums concealing the smaller drums.

After nearly two of hours of completing the task, Dan said, "Have the truck driver ready for tomorrow. This is going to Riverside, California. Deliver it to the Holiday Inn we stayed at last time."

Rudy nodded.

Dan departed the warehouse leaving Rudy and myself to discuss the upcoming trip.

Calderon ordered his agents to rendezvous at a nearby convenience store. He said, "Instead of babysitting the dope, let's secure it in the DEA drug depository. It will be better for all of us to sleep in our own beds tonight instead of the OGV's. We all need to be prepared for a trip to

Califa (slang for California)."

For safekeeping, the two hundred kilograms of cocaine were taken to the DEA drug depository.

I called the Riverside DEA office about the pending controlled delivery. The DEA agent who took the telephone call sounded excited. He said fellow agents and a local task force would be on standby for our delivery.

The following morning, the same agents from Group One that went to Charlotte traveled westbound on Interstate 10. About halfway, entering Phoenix, Arizona, a problem arose with the informant's rig. The transmission was failing and there was no time to wait for any lengthy automotive repairs.

Plan B was improvised. We transferred the barrels filled with cocaine into a rental U-Haul van. The bad guys wouldn't be told of the change of plans until the van was parked at the hotel in Riverside. There was no reason to raise any suspicion for the recipients which would cause the deal to fail.

I wanted *Chino* to continue with the trip just in case Dan wanted to see him. However, the informant did not want to leave his rig behind at the repair shop in Phoenix. We continued westbound without *Chino*.

The El Paso convoy arrived in the parking lot of the designated Holiday Inn hotel. I called the local case agent, or lead agent, to inform him of our presence. The surveillance responsibilities were relinquished to the Riverside DEA agents.

Rudy called Dan, "I'm here. One thing you need to know, *hermano* (brother). The truck driver did not want the *Califa* connection to see his rig. After we arrived, we transferred the barrels into a rented U-Haul."

Dan replied, "Where is the truck driver?"

"He's stubborn. He doesn't want to meet anyone. Do you think this will change things?"

"The Riverside people wanted to meet him but I will tell them it will be after another trip. I don't think it will matter." Dan hung up the phone.

Two hours later, Dan called Rudy, "They're watching the van. At exactly eight o'clock, two guys in a black Ford pickup are going to drive into the parking lot."

Rudy asked, "Are you here?"

"Of course. I want to be here to make sure these guys get their product. We have future shipments planned for these guys."

Rudy remained silent. His guilty conscience kept him from responding.

"Tomorrow morning, get the van and return to El Paso. We have another job next week." Dan hung up.

There were many questions left unanswered. I wondered if the cocaine was fronted, and if the profits would be transferred at a later date. How long had these people been doing business like this? The old-fashioned method of *mano a mano* (hand to hand) was becoming obsolete because it was too risky. That is, it was dangerous having a distributor and buyer conducting a transfer at the same place and time.

Under darkness, a black Ford pickup arrived and backed up to the U-Haul van. Two men exited, opened the rear door of the van and rolled the oil-filled drums onto the bed of the pickup. Within minutes, the transfer was completed.

Riverside DEA agents followed the pickup to a home in a nearby residential area. The drums were off-loaded into a garage. Just like the controlled delivery scenario in Charlotte, the Riverside DEA agents would wait as long as possible to make a traffic stop on a vehicle seen leaving the premises. The responsibility of the cocaine was now in the hands of the Riverside Resident Office.

I instructed Rudy to return to El Paso. Paul, Vince, and I remained in Riverside for some stress relief. We would take advantage of the down time and spend our allotted per diem expense money. After a late dinner, we wandered into a local watering hole. The smell of stale beer and tobacco smoke filled the air. We heard the sound of pool balls clicking at the dark end of the dive. Paul and I grinned while Vince looked disgusted.

Vince said, "Why do I let you guys take me to shit holes like this?"

I responded, "You deserve only the best, my 'brotha from anotha motha'!"

I called over the bartender and quoted George Thorogood, "One bourbon, one scotch and one beer. That's just for me. I don't know what these guys want." The men grunted.

With the first round in hand, we raised the drinks and silently toasted the success of our controlled delivery. Sometimes, words are unnecessary in a close working relationship. One becomes aware of the thoughts of the other.

Vince broke the silence. "Paul, you must have a sponge for a stomach. Didn't you drink two beers before dinner and two more while we were eating?"

Paul retorted. "You got a problem with that?" Then he calmly recited a beer-drinker's anthem, "My head feels heavy and my eyes feel sore. I told myself I wasn't going to drink anymore. A bad hangover I really can't stand yet here I am again with a beer in my hand!" He proceeded to take a big chug of his longneck.

I laughed, "*Chingon* (Badass)."

We talked shop for a time before turning our attention to the surroundings.

Vince complained about the country music blaring. The volume didn't bother me as much as the whiny themes and exaggerated twang of the country bumpkins.

Paul commented on the overweight female patrons, "They need to pass out cow bells at the door. Look at all these heifers."

I added, "Maybe they should place a cattle crossing sign in front of the women's restroom."

The bartender overheard the insults and appeared agitated. His anger was fueled when Paul whistled at him and requested a lighter for his cigar. The bartender ignored Paul.

Paul whistled again, only louder.

The 6'4", 230 pound bartender slowly walked towards Paul and calmly said, "Listen here, Mesican. I don't care for you whistling at me like a dog!"

Deftly, Paul reached over the bar, into the bartender's shirt pocket, pulled out a Bic lighter. Without a response, he lit his Cuban cigar and placed the lighter on the bar.

Fuming, the bartender returned to the opposite end of the bar and told the regulars about Paul. They all glared at us and rose from their stools.

I placed a twenty dollar bill on the bar and calmly said, "Time to blow this joint."

Paul wanted it to turn into a barroom blitz but Vince and I shoved Paul through the front door. I knew if there was anyone I wanted with me in a fight, it was Paul. The problem was that Paul would usually be the one to instigate the fight. Fortunately, this time we made it back to the hotel without incident.

Two days later, the Riverside DEA case agent called to brief me on the investigation. "We saw a Monte Carlo leave the garage, followed it and conducted a traffic stop with a marked unit. The driver had ten kilos in the car. After he sang like a canary, we got a search warrant and found eighty-eight more kilos in the house."

"Only eighty-eight? What happened to the other one hundred and two kilos?"

After a pause, "Are you sure there were two hundred?"

I was insulted, but kept my composure, "Of course. I loaded them myself."

"Well, we seized a total of ninety-eight packages."

"Did other cars go in and out undetected?"

"No. We had the place surrounded."

I thought, "Bullshit! They fucked up on their surveillance and wanted to shift the blame on us claiming we miscounted the number of packages."

El Paso and Riverside DEA supervisors were left to debate the reason for the missing cocaine. Accusations of incompetence and insults were exchanged. It was eventually disclosed that the Riverside agents inadvertently let a few cars slip away through the alley behind the stash house. The vehicles were never identified or followed.

Another tactical error committed by the Riverside DEA agents was not stopping the black Ford pickup that was initially used to transfer the drums after it departed the stash house. The agents claimed since the drums were not visible in the bed of the pickup, it was not followed. Cocaine bundles could have been concealed and transferred to another location.

Poor surveillance tactics allowed a million dollars worth of cocaine to hit the streets of Riverside. If the media got wind of this, they could compare it to the controversial smuggling of drugs by the Central Intelligence Agency into the U.S.

Calderon was more relieved than upset that the issue was resolved. He didn't want the DEA internal affairs section snooping into his agent's activities. The Office of Professional Responsibility (OPR) is the DEA's internal affairs division, fittingly known as the 'rat patrol'.

Other DEA offices had been infested by rats because some agents had the OPR on speed dial. Fortunately for the El Paso office, the scent of cheese had not been detected.

As for the controlled-delivery scenario, the drug traffickers blamed the arrests on the Riverside local dealers. The El Paso connection, lead by Dan Montes, remained legit.

Chapter 10 – Something In The Air

I am being chased by bad guys and nobody is around to provide assistance. I point my Glock at them and pull the trigger. The gun is jammed! I am furious that my weapon isn't working properly!

I seem to recognize this event. This has happened before. I force myself to transcend into another state of mind to get out of the predicament. The fear and frustration wake me up again. Shit, I hate this damn recurring nightmare!

Like most men, I didn't reveal my intimate thoughts and emotions. It was hard to tell anyone about the illogical ending. There is no way the reliability of my pistol or the DEA would fail me when I needed them most. I refused to believe that the dream had anything to do with the abandonment from my fellow agents.

I walked to the restroom and splashed water on my face. I raised my head and stared into the eyes of a man who sensed fear and helplessness. I repressed the doubts and kept them to myself. I got dressed and headed for the office for another early start. I needed to shake off the bad dream. The best way for me was by listening to something in my music collection.

I slipped in a compact disc into the player. "The Spirit of Radio" by Rush stimulated the senses on my drive to the DEA office. I considered Neil Peart, known as The Professor, as the premier percussionist in rock-n-roll history. For me, debating over who was the best drummer, guitarist, or rock band was like asking someone who is their favorite child.

I entered the DEA office and walked to my desk. I saw a stack of messages. For the time being, I ignored them to catch up on current events.

Someone said "reading the daily newspaper was like a dog returning to eat it's own vomit". Newspapers and magazines do not make the space to describe the whole story. The condensed articles are formatted to fit in less than a page leaving out many relevant details.

As much as I despised reading daily publications, I found the Ciudad Juarez newspaper, *El Diario*, to be a sufficient source of information for local events. Unlike U.S. publications, the Ciudad Juarez local newspaper was not completely censored. The stories were descriptive, and the photographs were very graphic.

The murders of countless women in Ciudad Juarez grabbed the headlines. Photos of naked, mutilated bodies left abandoned were published regularly. Most women were abducted on their way to work or school. They were brutally raped, murdered, and dumped in the desert without an ounce of dignity.

Family members were left to comprehend the horrific death of a loved one without any hope of retribution. Mexican law enforcement authorities had no leads to identify those responsible for the slaughter. The carnage lasted for years with no significant arrests being made.

As a law enforcement officer, I wanted do something to apprehend the cold-hearted killers. Unfortunately, there was nothing I could do. Murders of innocent victims were not in my job description.

I put down the newspaper, took a sip of my coffee and turned my attention to the view outside the large office window. The southernmost face of the Franklin Mountains stared back.

I recalled the off-road treks with my high school buddies into the unrestricted mountain ranges. We would sit for hours by a bonfire and admire the panoramic sight of the city lights on the eastern side of the mountain facing Biggs Airfield. Life was uncomplicated back then.

A smile came to my face when I thought of the time when a friend was syphoning gas from his Dodge Charger. The fuel was going to be used to ignite a pile of wood for a bonfire. It was very dark that night and he was unsure how much gasoline had come out through the shortened water hose. Recklessly, he used a Bic lighter to provide illumination.

The fumes were strong enough to cause a minor explosion. As we retreated in shock, we looked at each other and noticed our facial hairs had been singed. More importantly, the hose hanging out from fuel tank was on fire and the flame was working its way up the hose. The car was going to catch fire and explode!

Flight or fight kicked in. My buddies scattered into the darkness including the owner of the car. I didn't run away.

I ran as fast as I could up to the hose and yanked it away from the vehicle.

Very embarrassed, my friend thanked me for saving his car.

Vince walked into the Group One bay and interrupted my reverie, "What are you staring at?"

"The mountain."

"You call that a mountain? It's a fucking rock!"

"Why do you insist on insulting my beautiful city and its gorgeous terrain?"

"Because this place is ugly. Everything is brown. The mountain is brown, the sky is brown from the sand storms, and the people are brown. This is the land of crime, slime, and fat behinds!"

I laughed before gaining my composure, "Yankees and carpetbaggers, like yourself, tend to experience culture shock when they first come here. However, they quickly become acclimated and appreciate the beauty and history. You will, too!"

"I don't think so. There's nothing to do here!"

"Sure there is. There are many old western historical sites to visit around El Paso. You can take scenic drives through southern New Mexico. There is legalized gambling at several casinos, and of course, there is always Juarez."

Vince blurted, "Where two dollars gets you a piece of ass and a shot of tequila!"

I added with a Mexican accent, "Just remember to take your rubber if you're going to be a lover!"

We were laughing aloud when Calderon walked into the Group One bay. In an authoritative tone he said, "Laughing is not permitted here. In fact, I want ten kilos of *soda* (slang for cocaine) or a ton of *mota* (slang for marijuana) on my desk before the end of the day!"

Vince replied, "Okay. Stop any car on the freeway with a Mexican in it, and you've got a fifty-fifty chance!"

"Damn!" I retorted. "Who pissed in your cereal this morning?"

Turning towards our boss, I said, "Jose, I apologize for the ignorance displayed by this WASP (acronym for White Anglo-Saxon Protestant). He is used to demeaning minorities with his butt buddies at the Klan rallies.

He still hasn't realized he is not in Kansas anymore but in a battle zone on the Mexican border."

"Yeah," said Calderon. "And we're fighting this just like Vietnam. The politicians are using one hand to shake the hand of Mexican politicos while the other hand is scratching their nuts. We give millions of dollars to Mexico in foreign aid, but aren't allowed to put any pressure on their law enforcement efforts. It's obvious that the drug war is secondary to politics."

I added, "Our own agency leaders in D.C. have failed to see that we need more personnel and equipment. Out of sight, out of mind. Twenty-two agents and two intelligence analysts aren't enough to put up a fight in this so-called drug war."

The three of us knew that of the El Paso DEA agents, less than half had active drug investigations. Some sat at their desks, waited for their bi-weekly government check, and were content with their support role. These unproductive and unmotivated agents were labeled as slugs. Their motto was "Big cases, big problems. No cases, no problems!"

Calderon did not tolerate idleness in his group. He reassigned the slugs into another group. The Group Two supervisor was a short timer, counting the days until his retirement. He didn't want his agents initiating any cases or causing any problems. As a result, Group Two consisted of slugs working for a slug.

Paul referred to federal agents going their entire twenty-year careers without an arrest or drug seizure as "No Case Fucks." Paul didn't sugarcoat his opinions. Productivity and work initiative are not requirements for federal employment. Federal employees know they won't get fired, so why complicate their life? Many receive exorbitant salaries with automatic yearly increases for doing nothing.

They are afforded privileged, discounted health insurance options and retirement pensions not offered to the general public. Benefits included two-week paid vacations with holidays and weekends off. Sick leave hours can be accumulated and paid as a lump sum if not used. Overtime pay that is included in bi-weekly paychecks even if they didn't work the extra hours. Agents are assigned an OGV that is supposed to be driven for work-related operations but is used for personal errands.

The argument for providing the high salaries and benefits is that there must be an incentive to keep the most qualified people from working in non-governmental jobs. The reality is that many federal employees couldn't make it in the much more competitive private sector.

Calderon said to Vince and I, "Don't make plans for this afternoon. We need two agents from our group to help with a controlled burn. Get with our Evidence Custodian to make arrangements."

With so many illicit drugs seized by the El Paso DEA and the U.S. Border Patrol, the DEA drug depository was usually filled to capacity. The controlled burn was a quarterly ritual necessary to make space in our warehouse.

The DEA Evidence Custodian had arranged a long-term agreement with the American Smelting and Refining Company copper smelter plant, or ASARCO. When the spoils of war were no longer needed for judicial proceedings, the DEA would destroy the marijuana, cocaine, heroin, and weapons seized in the El Paso area.

Disposing of illicit drugs was a collateral duty that did not upset the DEA agents. It only took several hours to complete the task. We were given the option of going home early since our clothes smelled like pot.

Calderon concluded, "One more thing, Sal. You will be accompanied with a camera crew from the British Broadcasting Company (BBC). They are interested in the American efforts to combat the flow of drugs. Show them and the world what is happening here."

Apparently, the Brits were filming a documentary called "The Drug Wars". I was chosen for the cameo by the DEA supervisors because of my knowledge in the El Paso culture. The documentary was later aired on the Arts & Entertainment Network. My claim to fame was diminished as my face was blurred during the broadcast to protect my identity.

Several DEA vehicles were used to transfer the illicit drugs from the warehouse to the smelter plant. Every agent carried extra ammunition and was on high alert as the convoy made its way through downtown El Paso. It was risky to have multi-ton loads of drugs so easily accessible to the public but it was the only way.

The ASARCO plant personnel were instructed to clear the area. The DEA agents did not want an employee familiar with the incineration area to have access to the drugs. It would have been embarrassing if the seized drugs were stolen and redistributed in the streets of El Paso.

Vince and I, wearing protective gear, personally dumped the drugs into a designated incinerator. We witnessed the incineration and confirmed the drugs were properly destroyed.

Because of the proximity of the smelter plant to the UTEP campus, the agents would joke after a controlled burn that the Student Center would be full of students who suddenly developed a severe case of the munchies. A plant official assured the agents that the top of the smoke stacks were high enough for the smoke not to affect the surrounding populace.

The discreet method used by the DEA was very different from the method of destruction used by the Mexican police. I had witnessed one such event in Ciudad Juarez. The Mexican police invited dignitaries and the media to a "dog and pony show". Drugs were piled in an open field and set on fire for everyone to see. The display was supposed to assure the public that the police destroyed the illicit drugs contrary to the rumors that *la policia corrupta* (the corrupt police) kept the confiscated drugs for resale.

However, there was one type of drug missing. I noticed there were no bundles of cocaine in the burning mound. Ciudad Juarez, Mexico, was a major pipeline for cocaine distribution but not a single cocaine shipment was reportedly seized by any regional Mexican law enforcement organization in the past several years.

It was difficult to repudiate an unsubstantiated allegation when the circumstantial facts were in plain view. The Mexican cops were on the take and they had no shame. Who is going to police the police in a third-world country? Let's not be hypocritical. Who is policing the police in our country? Ignorance is bliss and inactivity is cowardice in both undeveloped countries like Mexico and developed countries like the U.S.

Chapter 11 – More Money, More Dope

As I was departing ASARCO, Rudy Montes called, "Two things are happening this week. Big money is coming from Chicago, and another load of coke has been requested by the people in California."

"Whoa! Wait a minute. How much money are we talking about, and how will it be transported?'

"Over a million dollars will be returned in the minivan."

"Are you going to be the one to make the trip in the van?"

"No. Dan wants me to stay in El Paso so I can gather the cocaine. He wants our stepbrother to drive the money back from Chicago."

"Damn, you have another brother? And, he is also involved in the drug business?"

"Yeah. He's made a few money runs."

"What's his name?"

"Kevin Quijano."

"This family affair grows by the day. Why didn't you tell me about him before?"

"Dan rarely uses him. Right now, Dan doesn't trust anyone, and he can't afford any more mistakes! We need to talk. I'm on my way to your office."

So much for me going home early. I was relieved both of our recent controlled deliveries were successful. Now, I became more excited with the possibility of additional deliveries. This time there would be no room for error. None of the dope would hit the streets, and the proceeds wouldn't fill the pockets of the Juarez Cartel.

I thought of the heated discussions between the El Paso and Chicago DEA offices. The debate would be centered on when and where the money would be seized.

Vince was familiar with the Chicago agents and would again travel to the Windy City to participate in the surveillance operation. The same plan of attack would be implemented.

Rudy arrived in the DEA office in fifteen minutes. He was just as excited as I was. I led him to the CI debriefing room.

I began, "Tell me about the cocaine load destined for *Califa*."

"Dan wants me take care of this deal. The people in California liked the way we hid them in the oil barrels. They want our people to do the same thing and send it sometime next week."

Rudy said, "There are two hundred and fifty kilos of coke somewhere on the east side of El Paso. I'm going to meet a guy named *Guero* (light complexioned one) and show him the warehouse. If he likes it, we will go to a stash house and return to the warehouse to put the coke in the oil barrels."

"Have you ever met this guy?"

"I met him once some time ago with my brother. They discussed other drug shipments but they kept me out of the conversation."

"Any idea where the stash house is located?" I asked but I already knew the answer. It's unheard of for any drug trafficking organization to disclose the location of a stash house. It is privileged information and off-limits to underlings.

I was elated at the opportunity to take possession of both the drugs and money. It just seemed a little too perfect. I sensed something was going to quell my excitement.

Right on cue, Calderon walked into the room and sat across from Rudy. "Tell me what your brother has said."

Rudy repeated himself and ended the synopsis with, "The people in Riverside are looking forward to another load of coke going their way."

Calderon said, "I hate to tell you this but we need to take down this load. We won't let it leave El Paso this time."

"Why?" Rudy asked.

"I don't want a recurrence of what happened in Riverside. I won't take that chance. And the money coming from Chicago will be seized, too."

I knew both Rudy and I had to bite the bullet. We had to come to terms that the 'controlled deliveries' eventually had to stop. There were too many risks involved. Arrests had to be made.

"What's going to happen to my brother?"

Calderon answered, "We have to arrest him. He needs to tell us about the people above him giving the orders. If all goes well with the two hundred and fifty keys, we'll have at least one mid-level manager in custody. *Guero* may take our investigation to a higher lever. It appears we're dealing with two different organizations. Your brother is the obvious link. For his safety, arresting him is the best option."

Rudy had his head down. He was shaking it slowly, fearing the worst.

"We will make him understand that he'll be safe in El Paso. However, him going across to Juarez is another story."

The meeting ended.

Calderon would make the call to the Chicago DEA supervisor. He needed his best manners and persuasion to get their cooperation.

The next day, Group One agents established surveillance on Rudy.

Rudy picked up *Guero* at a Circle K convenience store in central El Paso and drove directly to the warehouse.

I greeted them as they arrived. It was obvious to me why the man was nicknamed *Guero*. Most Mexicans nationals have similar physical characteristics - dark complexion, straight black hair, brown eyes, and high Aztecan cheekbones. On the other hand, there are those like *Guero* from European descent with blonde hair, blue eyes, and light colored skin.

When it comes to most Mexican media outlets, from newspaper advertisements to soap operas, the light-complexioned models dominate. The misrepresentation is an example of the discriminatory disregard for the majority of its citizens. The same can be said for the American advertisers. Skinny models eating fattening foods and drinking beer with a third less calories than regular beer. Not realistic.

Guero walked both inside and outside the warehouse, silently inspecting every electrical fixture. He asked Rudy a few questions about the lease agreement. Rudy convinced him that everything was completed under fictitious names.

After thirty minutes, he looked at me and said, "Let's go get the stuff. I'll need you to come with us. We'll use your car." *Guero* couldn't help but notice the brown sedan parked inside the warehouse. He liked the large trunk space afforded by the older model Oldsmobile Cutlass.

I had intentionally parked the undercover vehicle in the warehouse hoping *Guero* would use it. The bait was taken and the payoff was that I would join him on the drug run.

I drove, Rudy sat shotgun, and *Guero* sat in the rear seat area giving directions.

He told me to stay off the main roads and do exactly what he said. For nearly an hour, he instructed me to make heat runs throughout several residential streets in the eastern part of the city. The whole time, *Guero* stared out through the rear window looking for any suspicious vehicles that may be following us.

Like most drug traffickers, *Guero* forgot to look up. The DEA airplane had the vehicle under surveillance, while ground units remained at a safe distance. *Guero* guided me into the driveway of a residence. He said, "Stay here." He exited the vehicle, rang the doorbell, and disappeared into the house.

I couldn't see who opened the door however I memorized the street address. I intended on revisiting the residence at a later date with a search warrant in hand.

Approximately five minutes later, *Guero* came out of the house carrying a cardboard box filled with cocaine bundles.

I exited the car and opened the trunk for *Guero* to load the box. I was actually trying to get a glimpse of the person who answered the front door of the house. No such luck.

Guero said, "Leave the trunk open. I have another package." He went back into the house and returned with another box. After loading the second box, *Guero* closed the trunk and told me to drive away.

Pulling out of the driveway, I recognized a DEA agent parked in a nearby driveway. I knew my fellow agents were remaining close to me for protection and to verify the location of the stash houses.

Guero guided me to a second residence and told me and Rudy to follow him inside. Using my elbow, I nudged my Glock pistol for reassurance and the feeling of security.

This time there was nobody home. *Guero* pulled out a set of keys and opened the front door. The interior was completely void of furniture or appliances. *Guero* walked directly to the hallway and yanked on a cord hanging from a pull-down stairway into the attic. He had been here before.

He climbed up the wooden steps into the unlit attic. After shuffling some obviously heavy items, he began passing small U-Haul cardboard boxes to me. I stacked them on the living room floor close to the front door.

It took ten minutes before *Guero* came down from the attic. The three of us carried the boxes to the undercover vehicle. After some rearranging, the cocaine bundles were secured in the trunk compartment. *Guero* returned to lock the front door. He turned the key and yanked on the door to make sure it was securely fastened. He jumped into the rear seat area of the car and told me to return to the warehouse.

He added, "Drive safely and don't speed. We don't want to grab anyone's attention." *Guero* told me to conduct a few heat runs. Again, he looked obsessively out the rear window until we reached the warehouse. No words were spoken during the trip.

Once inside, *Guero* said, "Let's count the packages. There must be two hundred and fifty."

As an investigator, I wanted to ask *Guero* many questions, such as, "Who owns the coke?" "How was it smuggled into the U.S.?" and "Who owns the stash houses?" However, in the subservient role I was playing, asking questions would be presumptuous and likely fatal.

We counted thirty-five packages retrieved from the first house and two hundred from the second location.

Guero was upset and yelled, "*Pinchi rata* (Damn rat)! There are fifteen packages missing!"

Rudy asked, "Did we leave them behind?"

Guero responded, "No. I know who has them."

I assumed the occupant of the first house was responsible for the shortage. There was no honor amongst thieves.

In most businesses, employee theft is an expected occurrence that is written off and left for the consumers to eventually compensate for the losses. For most drug traffickers, no loss is tolerated. In this case, fifteen may be a small fraction of the total number of packages. But at $10,000 per key, $150,000 was a significant financial shortfall.

Throughout the evening, few words were exchanged. Occasionally, *Guero* asked me about my affiliation with Rudy Montes. Later, he reworded the same question, trying to trip me up.

I kept the answers vague, always leaving myself an opening. I knew not to provide too much information and get cornered by the drug trafficker.

By midnight, the two hundred and thirty-five kilos were secured in the 35-gallon drums then placed into the 55-gallon drums as was done before. *Guero* said he would return the following day with the missing bundles.

After exiting the warehouse, I snapped the dead bolt lock on the sliding door. *Guero* yanked on the lock to confirm it was properly latched. I volunteered to keep a watchful eye on the warehouse throughout the night.

Guero denied my offer. He didn't want any suspicion attracted to the warehouse with someone parked outside. Actually, he didn't trust me being alone with his prized possession.

Guero instructed me not to come back to the warehouse until further notice. He whispered to Rudy that he felt confident the warehouse was a secure location.

After Rudy returned *Guero* to the central part of El Paso, the DEA agents descended on the undercover warehouse. We were not as confident as *Guero*. The cocaine-laden drums would not be left unattended. They were loaded onto a DEA truck and taken to our drug depository for safekeeping.

We wanted to celebrate the acquisition of the cocaine. However, we were exhausted and wanted to go home for a good night's sleep.

Calderon did have something to say. "There are not many DEA agents who have been introduced to a mid-level trafficker, confiscated kilos of cocaine, or actually seen a stash house. Sal, not only have you been to two stash houses but you have gained the trust of this guy. That is simply unheard-of!"

I humbly responded, "I can't believe it either."

The following day Rudy called me. "*Guero* is pissed at the guy who kept the fifteen keys. The guy claimed he needed money for business expenses."

By this time, I knew the identity of the thief. A DEA Analyst had conducted a property check and discovered the registered owner. He resided at the first stash house visited by me and was paying the utilities on the second stash house.

I asked, "Have you ever heard of Alfredo Cisneros?"

Rudy answered, "No. Also, *Guero* wants to wait before moving the cocaine. It might take a couple of days to replace the missing kilos."

"How do you think they are smuggling the cocaine?"

"They hide ten to fifteen keys in the bumpers of vehicles in Juarez. Then they have someone drive across the bridges into El Paso. Smuggling small loads is not as risky large loads getting busted. The cartel can afford losing small loads. It looks like we are headed to the same city but with different customers."

I responded, "Get it into your head! My boss has made it clear that this load isn't leaving El Paso."

Rudy hung up the phone.

I made time to visit with the Assistant U.S. Attorney assigned to this investigation. Investigative reports, witness testimony, and possible scenarios were discussed. He wanted to assure that we had attained the required elements of the crime for a successful prosecution of those involved. The attorney pointed out a couple of loose ends.

The first problem was the lack of proof showing Cisneros was the person who gave the cocaine to *Guero*. None of the DEA agents had actually seen Cisneros open the door for *Guero*. It was merely an assumption he was involved since the house belonged to him.

The second area of concern was determining who was in charge of this transportation organization. In order to grant immunity from prosecution, Dan Montes needed to identify and assist in the prosecution of his superiors. There was no factual evidence to prove that Dan had anyone above him. If there were others to blame, they likely lived in Mexico and out of our reach.

The attorney said the only way Dan could receive immunity was by testifying against the others in a court of law. He reiterated the common practice of reducing or dropping charges against a criminal for his testimony. In this case, even though Dan may have been a more active participant than other defendants, he was in a position to beat them to the punch and provide damaging testimony.

I wanted to implicate Cisneros. I needed to come up with a plan. I asked Paul to cover me during a surprise visit of the Cisneros residence. The objective was to get Cisneros to make any incriminating statement about his affiliation with *Guero* or the thirty-five kilos of cocaine given to *Guero*. It would be a bold yet dangerous ploy.

I wasn't sure how the conversation would go. I would simply improvise based on how Cisneros responded to my approach and inquiries.

Driving the same Olds Cutlass used before and wearing my typical undercover garb, I knocked on Cisneros' front door. I wore a baseball cap with a hidden transmitter so the conversation could be recorded. I was thrilled when Cisneros answered the door.

Cisneros leered at me and didn't say a word. He wondered who this man was wearing a dangling earring, a Styx concert t-shirt, and cheesy baseball cap, at his front door.

I began, "Hey. I was sent by *Guero* to tell you the front lawn at the other house needed to be cut. It looked messy, and he was concerned about it."

"*Guero* sent you here?" Cisneros asked. Thoughts flashed in his mind, "He always called ahead.", "*Guero* wouldn't turn on me, would he?" or "Is this a hitman sent by the cartel because I stole their product?"

I continued, "*Guero* wants to know if you will take care of it as soon as possible."

"I'll take care of it. You need to get out of here!"

"By the way, *Guero* is not happy with you taking those fifteen keys."

"Well, I already talked to him about that. Don't be coming to my house again!" Then he slammed the door.

I turned and walked away. Mission accomplished. The conversation, though brief, was enough to implicate Cisneros. The federal Conspiracy law would be applied, and he would serve a lengthy federal sentence.

We returned to the DEA office and completed a DEA-6 Investigation Report about the interview. I overheard Calderon on the phone using some choice words. After an intense argument between the DEA supervisors, the minivan carrying a large sum of money would be permitted to leave Chicago again. The Chicago DEA agents would raid the money stash house after Kevin Quijano departed in the van. I knew Calderon could play hardball with anyone yet be fair.

When Quijano arrived, the Chicago agents were determined to redeem themselves after being scolded by their supervisors regarding the previous surveillance of the van. This time, they successfully followed the vehicle to a warehouse on the south side of the city.

After several hours, the minivan departed the warehouse and was permitted to leave Chicago. Agents were not sure if the van was being followed by the suspects.

Surreptitiously, Rudy was getting updates on Kevin's whereabouts. Acting like he was concerned about his safety, Rudy periodically called his stepbrother to find out his location on the road.

A search warrant was executed and discovered inside the warehouse were money counters, currency wrappers, and other paraphernalia. Later, additional arrests were made after someone in the Chicago cell became an informant for the DEA.

I wanted to keep the heat off the El Paso connection so a ruse was created. The van would be intercepted far from its final destination. Midland, Texas, seemed far enough from El Paso as to prevent any blame on the Montes brothers.

Jake Davis and I made the four-hour trip to Midland. We contacted the Texas Department of Public Safety office and requested that a marked patrol unit assist with a controlled traffic stop.

I met with the State Trooper. He recognized me from my days as a

State Trooper in El Paso. We discussed the plan to stop the van before turning our discussion to a funny story.

He asked, "Do you remember the two married Troopers who planned a weekend rendezvous with two strippers?"

"Yeah. They told their wives that they were going on a fishing trip by themselves. Well, one of the strippers showed up but the other one was a no-show. The guy with the stripper continued on with the plans of having sex all weekend while the guy who got dumped had nothing else better to do but go back home on that Friday night."

Davis asked, "What's wrong with that?"

I continued, "Well, the wives talked by phone on Saturday and realized one man was home and the other one was supposedly fishing. When the Trooper who was supposedly fishing got home on Sunday afternoon, the wife asked him about his fishing trip."

"He lied and said both of the men had a great time together but no fish were caught."

"She responded with a slap across his face and a never-ending tirade about his infidelity."

Davis asked, "What happened to the Troopers?"

"They didn't talk to each other for a long time. They blamed each other for the misunderstanding." We all laughed and returned to our present game plan.

We parked at a roadside park on Interstate 20 just outside of the city. We had a clear view of all westbound traffic while the State Trooper would be waiting down the road. I instructed the State Trooper to conduct a traffic stop of the minivan and find any probable cause to stop and search it. The officer needed to pretend he didn't know the location of the false compartment. The role-playing was necessary to keep the ruse from being exposed.

About 2 p.m., we spotted the van passing our location. I radioed the State Trooper to pull up behind the minivan.

Anyone who has been followed by a police car knows that it is difficult to concentrate on proper driving techniques, let alone drive within the striped lanes. Kevin got nervous and swerved enough for probable cause.

The van was pulled onto the westbound shoulder. According to script, the State Trooper's actions made it look like a routine traffic stop. This traffic stop was anything than routine.

The State Trooper radioed me, "Agent Martinez, I told him he was pulled over because he was driving erratically. During the interview, he was visibly nervous, so I asked him for consent to search the van. He agreed."

Most police officers take advantage of this natural human reaction while the subject is being detained. 'Nervous' is a catch word used in countless written reports to justify further investigation.

The State Trooper continued, "While looking through the van, I found a trap door under a loose section of carpet."

"Good. Tell him the vehicle must be driven to your office for closer inspection. We'll stay away. I want him to see you find the bundles. Then lock him up in a holding cell so we can help unload the contents."

"10-4. By the way, the license plate is expired."

I laughed and said, "A clear case of HIA."

The State Trooper responded, "Excuse me?"

"HIA means 'head in ass'. You can put that in your report as additional probable cause for the traffic stop."

Davis said, "Can you believe that? Dumbass criminals are caught for making stupid mistakes like this one."

I responded, "Sloth is considered a deadly sin by Catholics. It can also be deadly in the drug business."

Kevin was ordered to follow the State Trooper to the next exit where the Department of Public Safety office was located. He had thoughts of running for the border but he was in the middle of the desert with nowhere to hide. He believed he could outrun the cop, but knew he couldn't outrun the police radio. Kevin felt like a helpless calf being herded to the slaughterhouse.

He was led to an enclosed area where the State Trooper went to work.

The officer slid the trap door open and pulled out a bundle secured in masking tape. A pocketknife was used to cut the bundle and reveal the tightly packed U.S. currency. When questioned about the money, Kevin denied any knowledge. The State Trooper placed Kevin in a holding cell and radioed me.

After nearly two hours, we retrieved one hundred and fifty-eight bundles of cash from the van's false compartment. Each bundle was marked with a dollar amount, the smallest being $10,000.

As the bundles were arranged on the pavement for an evidentiary photograph, we looked at the amazing sight. We glanced at each other with the same thought, "It sure would be nice to take just one bundle as a reward for our hard work."

Integrity is a distinguishing virtue of a DEA agent and a Texas State Trooper. There are many opportunities to cross the line and dishonor the ethics of a law enforcement officer. Self-restraint begins by believing "the thought is as bad as the deed." No words were exchanged.

Kevin was provided with a DEA form known as a Receipt for Items. The receipt indicated 158 bundles of an undetermined amount of cash seized by the DEA. Undetermined amount meant it would take hours to count the piles of currency and tally the exact amount.

He asked, "Why am I being given a receipt by the DEA?"

The State Trooper answered, "A DEA representative was notified of this money seizure. It is a formality for federal forfeiture procedures. If you, or anyone else, want to claim ownership of the money, certain steps need to be followed. In other words, show proof the money was acquired through legitimate means and you can get it back."

It is a legal option rarely pursued by the drug traffickers. It requires someone in the drug trafficking organization to come forward, give personal identification in a court of law, and provide proof for the ownership of the money in question. Unlikely, so they just kiss the money goodbye.

Kevin was released but the van would be seized due to the false compartment. He refused a ride from the State Trooper to a nearby bus station. He needed time to think.

It was the longest walk of his life. Thoughts of suicide crossed his mind.

Dan's boss would be furious for the loss of money. The repercussions could possibly lead to his stepbrother's death.

Kevin wanted to prove it was not his fault. He didn't get a traffic ticket. He wasn't read his Miranda rights. He could explain that it was an overzealous cop that was responsible for the illegal traffic stop.

With a copy of a DEA receipt and $90 in his pocket, he returned to El Paso on the next Greyhound bus.

I was pensive throughout the following day. Rudy had informed me that Kevin was adamant in traveling to Ciudad Juarez to meet with the owner of the seized currency.

Rudy begged his stepbrother not to go alone to meet Dan's boss in Ciudad Juarez. Kevin ignored the request. He felt there was no other way to clear his name and Dan's name. He went alone.

The DEA agents were kept busy throughout the day processing the drug money. After discounting a few counterfeit bills, the total was $1.9 million.

Around midnight, Rudy called me, "Kevin is back home. He talked for hours detailing the trip from Chicago up to the traffic stop. He said the boss threw a fit but settled down after smoking a blunt (slang for marijuana cigarrette) and a few shots of tequila. The boss gave in and said it was just bad luck. Can you believe that shit?"

"I am relieved. What else did Kevin say about their conversation?"

"The boss recommended he remain in Juarez just in case there was heat on him in the U.S. Kevin disagreed and said he wasn't running another load for the rest of his life!"

"What about Dan?"

He said he would stay at his girlfriend's house in Juarez and keep a low profile."

Changing the theme, I said, "Regarding *Guero*, get him to meet you tomorrow."

"Why would we meet?"

"Because the coke will be seized from the warehouse."

"What do you mean? What about the other fifteen keys he was supposed to get."

"We can't wait anymore. Call *Guero* at exactly 9 a.m. Tell him that the warehouse is surrounded by police cars. Insist that you will pick him up and drive by the warehouse. We need to arrest him before he slips out of our hands. Call me after you talk to him."

Rudy ended the conversation, "I hope you guys realize what you are doing."

I was thrilled with the opportunity to arrest and debrief *Guero*. Few transportation managers were ever arrested. Learning the intricacies of this drug cell would be valuable for future Juarez-El Paso area drug investigations.

The next morning, Rudy called, "I'm on my way to get *Guero*. I told him cops have surrounded our warehouse. His first response was to run to Mexico. I told him we needed to drive by the warehouse and see it for ourselves before crossing the border. When are you going to arrest *Guero*?"

"We haven't decided yet." He could not be arrested until Dan was back in El Paso. Arrests needed to be done simultaneously or someone could slip out of the DEA's hands by fleeing to Mexico.

I contacted the El Paso Police Department and informed them of the ruse. A marked unit was parked in front of the warehouse. Yellow crime scene tape was strung around the building. The stage was set.

It was the busiest time of day in the warehouse district. Tractor-trailers scrambled to retrieve their cargos from adjacent warehouses.

Guero ignored the bustling activity as he was fixated on the door that he had specifically latched several nights before. He could visualize the cocaine inside the building that was rightfully his. Rudy drove slowly so *Guero* could get the full effect of the tragic event.

Guero bragged to Rudy that he had never lost a drug load because his precautionary measures were flawless. He was certain this was not caused by anything he had done. Therefore, there was no reason for the cops to suspect him. His ego clouded reality, and he foolishly decided to remain in El Paso to find out why this happened.

Rudy returned *Guero* to his apartment. DEA agents remained on surveillance of *Guero* around the clock.

The following day, an article published in the El Paso Times read, in part, "Anonymous tip leads to seizure of 235 kilograms of cocaine in abandoned warehouse. No arrests were made. The DEA had no leads and no additional information was available." The newspaper article was vague enough to raise doubt in *Guero*'s mind as to the reason for the loss. Although used frequently for bad intentions, deception is sometimes necessary to further the goals of the good.

Chapter 12 – Case Closed

Dan Montes returned to his residence in El Paso after a brief hiatus in Ciudad Juarez.

I explained to Rudy what needed to be done. Dan would be confronted by the DEA agents and provided with limited options. The power of persuasion could only lead Dan to enlightenment and freedom from prosecution.

Dan's first reaction would be shock about his little brother's cooperation with the DEA. The second reaction would be a refusal to cooperate. The responses would be based on emotions rather than intellect.

Rudy pleaded with the agents to let him talk to Dan alone before the introduction.

Vince and I sat in my OGV as the brothers talked outside Dan's house. Although we couldn't hear what was being said, we could see it was a heated discussion. It took nearly thirty minutes before Rudy gave the go ahead sign. He waived us in.

We drove up to the house and exited the OGV. I walked to Dan and extended my hand, "Dan, I'm Sal Martinez. This is my partner, Agent Sellers."

Dan was sweating and visibly shaking. He said nothing. He reached his hand out, and there was no strength in his grip.

"We are here to help you. There are people pointing the finger at you for some drug runs. We know you are not the one responsible. We would like for you to clarify some things. Will you come to our office so we can talk?"

Dan turned to his brother, "I'm going to kick your ass, *carnal* (brother)!"

"Listen to these men, bro!" said Rudy.

Moving in slow motion, Dan reluctantly entered the rear seat of the OGV, "Aren't you going to handcuff me?"

I responded, "You're not under arrest."

"So, if I cooperate with you, are you going to give me a badge?"

The question perplexed us.

Vince turned his upper torso and looked back from the front passenger seat, "Why the fuck would you want a badge?"

"Because I'm going into the DEA office and everyone is going to see me! Especially, the corrupt narc in your office that is providing information to the drug cartels in Juarez."

"Have you ever met or spoke to the corrupt agent?"

"No. But my supervisor says he calls him every time there is a rat squealing about a drug organization in Juarez."

"Don't believe that shit."

"Hell, it could be one of you guys! I just fucked myself by coming with you."

Dan was debriefed for several days. He provided historical intelligence of his nefarious activities that went back five years. There had been tons of cocaine and marijuana that flooded various cities throughout the U.S. by this one drug trafficking cell. Any other person would have been imprisoned for decades but Rudy saved Dan from being sent up the river.

As for the other members under Dan's supervision, it was determined they had limited roles. Of those implicated, we needed to arrest them before they slipped out of our radar.

First on the list was Alfredo Cisneros. A search of his home resulted in the discovery of twelve kilos of cocaine. He skimmed off the top for more than personal use. Cisneros refused to cooperate with us and took his case to a jury trial.

At one stage during the jury trial, his defense attorney argued entrapment by the DEA agent who went to his home. He pointed towards me and raised his voice to the jury, "Look at that man. He looks like a drug dealer! Agent Martinez intimidated my client and persuaded him to say those things that have implicated him in this case. Agent Martinez should be the one to go to jail!"

I sat still on the witness stand as the jury stared at me. I didn't react because I was undecided if the accusation was a compliment or an insult.

The jury believed my account instead of the defense attorney's version. They found Cisneros guilty and sentenced him to seven years incarceration. He vowed to find me after being released from prison.

DEA Agents Rodriguez and Gonzalez arrested *Guero* without incident. The mid-level trafficker denied involvement claiming he had never seen a single kilogram of cocaine in his lifetime. When he was transported to the El Paso DEA interview room, he was introduced to me. His jaw dropped when realizing he had been duped. He was upset with himself because of the way he was set up. Persuaded by a confidant to trust a stranger was simply foolish in the drug world.

I said, "You were caught with your hand in the cookie jar. The only way to help yourself is to tell us about your organization." I patiently explained the options – play hardball with us and it would result in a lengthy prison sentence or cooperate with the DEA to reap the benefits of leniency.

After an hour of contemplation, *Guero* opened up. He described the managerial role he played with the Juarez Cartel. He admitted arranging numerous shipments of cocaine by smuggling the bundles within the front bumpers of modified vehicles. The drugs were stored in rental homes in El Paso before transported to various states primarily California and Illinois.

Guero was also responsible for transferring multi-million dollar cash profits from the sale of illicit drugs in the U.S. He said the accountability of money was much more demanding than counting bundles of cocaine. On one occasion, *Guero* said he was ordered to meet with a man involved in an auto theft ring based in El Paso. After the meeting, several Chevrolet Suburbans were stolen from the El Paso area in a one-week period.

Nine Chevrolet Suburbans were acquired to convoy drug proceeds from Ciudad Juarez to Mexico City. Apparently, the airplane normally used for the monthly transference was being used for something more important. *Guero* guessed the amount of currency was in the hundreds of millions of U.S. dollars.

Guero pled guilty and received ten years in the U.S. federal prison system. He would be deported to Mexico after his prison term.

Jason Sanchez and Kevin Quijano also pled guilty and each received seven years imprisonment. The prison sentences were based on the significant quantity the mules had transported. These were harsh punishments for those at the bottom of the totem pole.

Dan Montes was not charged with any crime since he was the prosecution's star witness. Defense attorney's cried, "Foul!" They argued, "How can the man responsible for their clients committing the alleged crimes not be held culpable and rewarded with no jail time?" The judge and jury ignored the pleas of injustice. They sided with the government's recommendations.

After all the judicial hearings were completed regarding this investigation, an unusual opportunity was brought to my attention by Calderon. Rudy Montes was praised for helping initiate the successful long-term criminal investigation. He should be rewarded for his courage and cooperation with a financial reward that would be taken from the $1.9 million seizure. DEA headquarters approved the request.

Vince and I met Rudy at a local bank to help the former informant open a new savings account. Rudy was provided with a cashier's check for $250,000.

Vince said, "Let me get this straight. You and your brother distributed tons of cocaine and marijuana into the streets of America. Then you find Jesus and help us arrest some of your associates. Now you get rewarded with a quarter of a million dollars?"

Rudy responded, "Don't be a hater."

The bank teller asked, "How does someone earn so much money from the U.S. government?"

Rudy said, "You don't want to know."

Rudy told me he would give half of his reward to his brother since Dan would be unemployed. They planned on opening a legitimate retail business in El Paso.

For their participation in the $1.9 million dollar take down, the Texas Department of Public Safety was awarded $750,000.

The truck driver, *Chino*, was given $15,000 for his assistance. He complained the reward wasn't enough to repair his aging rig.

The remaining amount of the seized drug proceeds disappeared into the federal government coffers.

A good cop doesn't expect any kudos for doing his job. However, accolades can be good for an employee's morale. For our success in the investigation, Vince and I were awarded an Exceptional Service certificate and a U.S. government cashier's check for $500, before taxes.

I responded, "Beer money."

After several years as an effective undercover agent, supervisors acknowledged my accomplishments with a promotion to a Grade Series 12. Being in my early thirties, life was good and on track for further success in the most elite drug enforcement agency in the world.

Several weeks later, Dan Montes called and asked to meet with me. He asked if I could come alone, because he was embarrassed about what he had to say. It was against DEA policy to meet an informant without another agent present, let alone develop an intimate relationship. This was a mortal sin for any DEA agent.

Dan snitched on the Juarez Cartel. The men in the Cartel wanted to get their hands on the man who took their livelihood away. They would be unrelenting in their efforts and I didn't want to be caught in the middle.

I thought of a safe location, "I'll meet you after work. Let's meet at the Dome Bar inside the Camino Real Hotel."

The hotel is located in the heart of downtown El Paso and only a few blocks from the DEA office. With a reputation as the premier lodging for dignitaries and celebrities, the countless ghost stories were just as intriguing to visitors.

El Paso has always been about the past, from its mission trails to the Wild West shootouts. Just across the street, the Plaza Theatre was once the cornerstone of the downtown area. The beautiful, yet eerie, atmosphere surrounded all patrons with a surreal forest while watching the movie screen.

I remembered as a kid spending an entire day in the theatre watching a "Planet of the Apes" movie marathon. My mother permitted my older brother and I to travel across town on a city bus to attend the all day event while she went to work. It used to be safe to allow children to venture out on their own.

Under the Tiffany glass at the bar, I felt the rich history within the walls of the old-fashioned hotel. The Dome Bar was nearly empty. Several middle-aged women celebrated a birthday at one table. At the bar, a very old man sat alone, drinking a beer with a measured pace he probably used for decades. I found Dan sitting alone at a corner table. I would not get caught between being a friend and an acquaintance. I was a good listener and would let Dan do the talking.

We shook hands. "Are you ready for a drink?"

I answered, "Absolutely."

"I have a running tab. I'll get your drinks."

I said, "Hell, I think we paid for a year's supply of your bar tabs."

Dan didn't laugh. He began, "I was in a business that got the best of me. I had all the drugs, women, and cash I needed. It controlled me and made me do things I never would have thought of doing. Don't laugh but my dream was to have a *narco corrido* (drug dealer anthem) written about me."

"Now, I get up in the morning with no place to go. I drive around and notice people performing their daily routines. You don't have to be behind bars to be in prison. Look around and see everyone stuck in daily ruts. I cannot be an Everyday Joe! What am I supposed to do now?"

Without waiting for an answer to his rhetorical question, Dan continued, "Last night, I went back to Juarez to be with my girlfriend. I had loaned her my car and was going to give her some of the money you gave me. My friend drove me to her house where we noticed a man in an unfamiliar car parked down the street."

"I asked a neighborhood kid about the man in the car. The kid said two men walked up to my girlfriend's house, talked to her as she was sweeping the porch, and they never came out."

"I figured the men had seen my car in the driveway and thought I was inside. I knew they were inside waiting for me. I snuck down the alley and jumped over the neighbor's fence. Looking through the kitchen window, I saw the men gang raping my girlfriend. They tied her hands up and had her naked on the couch. I couldn't save her!"

Nor could I save Dan Montes.

Dan asked if he could continue working as an informant for the DEA.

He admitted being low on cash after spending most of the $125,000 he received from his brother.

I knew Dan lost his business contacts with the underworld. Dan was damaged goods after the word spread he cooperated with the DEA. It would be too dangerous for him to try working for any other drug trafficking organization. I denied the request.

I listened to a man who believed there was nothing else to live for. His closest friends weren't actually friends. They were drug dealers just like him. Now, he couldn't associate with them.

After an hour of depressing conversation, I had to stop and remind him that we only had a business relationship. I couldn't help him with his personal problems. I got up from my chair and gave him a bro hug. We would never see each other again.

Chapter 13 - Breaking The Law

In the following weeks, I shifted my efforts to assist fellow agents with other investigations. Richard McGee was still in the midst of coordinating a time-consuming Title III operation. When McGee had initiated this investigation ninety days earlier, he was confident that large quantities of drugs would be seized.

Countless hours of local, state and federal agencies' manpower were expended, and not one ounce of contraband had been confiscated. McGee's pride was hurt, but that never suppressed his drive to continue.

The U.S. Attorney's office warned McGee that a judge would not grant authorization for another thirty day extension unless solid evidence was acquired immediately. Time was running out, and McGee needed something on the table to continue the wiretap.

Few agents are capable of recognizing an opportunity and having the courage to seize it on a moment's notice. I admired McGee's unwavering approach to operations, intelligence gathering and execution of plans. Maybe it was McGee's in-your-face attitude that I revered most. I was on surveillance in the east side of El Paso when McGee asked to meet with him.

McGee said, "I need your help with something. I have a gut feeling there are drugs in a truck being driven by one of my targets. Will you help me take it down?"

"Sure. What can I do?

"I need to get my hands on the pickup without letting the 'bad guys' know we are onto them."

"Why don't you have a marked unit conduct a traffic stop?"

"These guys know better. They will halt all operations and change their method. I can't wait any longer."

"What do you have in mind?"

"Surveillance units will follow the truck and find a suitable place to surround it. We won't identify ourselves as DEA agents. You need to talk to the driver in Spanish and force him out of the truck."

"Carjack?"

"Two reasons I need you. You are Hispanic. Don't take it as an insult."

I smiled, "None taken."

"Second reason. You are the only one I know who would do this. You have no fear! What do you think?"

"Don't flatter me. Let's do it."

On cue, surveillance units radioed that the target was departing his residence in the suspected red Dodge pickup. The vehicle turned southbound onto Lee Trevino Drive.

McGee told me, "Drive my car. Let's get the bastard!"

McGee instructed the surveillance units to surreptitiously circumvent the truck at an intersection prior to entering Interstate 10. They knew if the truck entered the expressway, there would be no way to stop the truck surreptitiously. No flashing lights or sirens could be used. Just a silent wave of enforcers needed to converge on the truck, immediately.

With the truck three blocks ahead of us, I applied my Highway Patrol pursuit driving skills to maneuver through the rush hour traffic. Looking far ahead into the northbound lanes, I noticed little oncoming traffic. Ignoring traffic signals, I moved into the left turn lane of the next intersection and darted between several vehicles.

The most dangerous part was driving through the busy intersections. Peripheral vision is critical when attempting these tactics. I passed two surveillance units caught in the congestion. They saw my gutsy move and squeezed between other vehicles to follow me. Bewildered motorists froze as they watched the outburst of lawlessness.

I relished the adrenalin rush. McGee was in no mood to share in the excitement.

Surveillance units radioed they were reaching the very last opportunity to surround the pickup.

McGee grabbed the DEA portable radio and shouted, "Do not let the truck enter the interstate!"

Someone responded, "Our only chance is the yield lane entering the

I-10 access road! We have the red truck in sight and are ready to block it in."

One surveillance unit was positioned in front of the pickup while the second unit was on the left side to prevent a lane change. The only option for the suspect was to drive onto the sidewalk curb on the right side. It would have been an act of desperation if he was given time to react to what was about to happen.

The light turned green for southbound traffic at the final intersection. The DEA vehicle in front of the red truck came to a complete stop as heavy traffic merged onto the access road.

I forced myself in front of an unwitting motorist who honked angrily. I got behind the red pickup and shifted the gear into park. I jumped out, pulled out my Glock pistol, and ran to the driver's side door.

McGee did not want to be seen. He exited the passenger side door and remained behind his OGV. He was close enough to provide me with backup if the suspect put up a fight.

I yanked on the unlocked driver's side door and pointed my gun 'gangsta' style at the man. I yelled, "*Salte de la troca, pendejo* (Get out of the truck, dumbass)!"

The driver was startled and instinctively raised his arms. He yelled, "*Quien eres tu* (Who are you)?"

I reached over the steering wheel and pulled the automatic shifter into park. I grabbed the man by his collar and yanked him out of the truck.

"*Que esta pasando* (What is happening)?"

I led the man around the rear of the pickup and shoved him to the sidewalk. I positioned the man where he faced towards the west. In Spanish, I yelled, "Stand here and stare at the sunset, mother fucker! Don't turn around or I'll put a bullet in your head. Do you understand?" The harsh language accentuated the violent act. It also bolstered the authenticity that a police officer wouldn't act this way.

The entire episode lasted about a minute. The suspect was stunned and never had an opportunity to defend himself or retain his cherished possessions.

Texas State Trooper
Sal M. Martinez
1985 - 1990

U.S. Customs Service, Air Interdiction Officer, Sal M. Martinez
1990 - 1991

U.S. Border Patrol
Drug Bust
1995

Some of the many Official Awards received by
D.E.A. Special Agent Sal M. Martinez

This is to certify that

SALVADOR MARTINEZ
has completed the
UNDERCOVER SEMINAR

conducted by the
Office of Training
Drug Enforcement Administration
United States Department of Justice

APRIL 8,1993
Date

Administrator, Drug Enforcement Administration

Drug Enforcement Administration

United States
Department of Justice

PRESENTS THIS AWARD FOR

EXCEPTIONAL PERFORMANCE

TO

Salvador M. Martinez

FOR
DEDICATION TO DUTY
AND OUTSTANDING
CONTRIBUTIONS

Administrator
September 1994

Agents take ton of cocaine in bust

A recent drug bust that yielded 2,232 pounds of cocaine was one of the biggest narcotics seizures El Paso has ever seen, said ▇▇▇▇▇▇, a special agent-in-charge for the Drug Enforcement Administration in El Paso.

"One ton is a serious dent to anyone's organization," said ▇▇▇▇▇▇ at a news conference Wednesday. "It's not going to put anyone out of business, but it's not going unnoticed, either."

Two men were arrested Sept. 19 in connection with the case after a joint investigation of the Drug Enforcement Administration and U.S. Customs Service: ▇▇▇▇▇▇ and

Both are charged with possession of cocaine and conspiracy to possess cocaine with intent to distribute.

During a search Sept. 19 search in the ▇▇▇▇▇▇, federal agents discovered an electronically activated door leading to a hidden compartment in the garage. The compartment concealed 1,200 pounds of cocaine that was prepackaged for transportation. Agents also discovered 600 more pounds of cocaine in the garage.

A second investigation in the ▇▇▇▇▇▇ netted about $30,000, a small amount of cocaine and documents linking the occupants to the ▇▇▇▇▇▇.

This latest seizure had ended a long lull in which there was a noticeable absence of cocaine in El Paso, said ▇▇▇▇▇▇, a special agent-in-charge for Customs Service.

"This shows that cocaine is back — big time," he said.

Officials said that evidence at the search site indicated an assembly line was packaging cocaine for long-range distribution. The operation included heat-sealing of assorted kilos sizes of cocaine and the additional packing of cocaine in cardboard boxes used to avoid detection by drug-sniffing do ▇▇▇▇▇▇ said the house was designed to receive and a ▇▇▇▇▇▇ narcotics: "It was made for purpose."

Investigators are still pursing additional leads to identify additional individuals and reside in this narcotics trafficking organization.

An undercover Drug Enforcement Administration agent watches over the 2,232 pounds of cocaine DEA and U.S. Customs Service agents confiscated in a recent case.

D.E.A. Special Agent Sal M. Martinez
standing next to one ton of 'coke'

D.E.A. Special Agent
Sal M. Martinez and
fellow Agent with
confiscated drug
money

A.P.B. issued by El Paso Police
Department on D.E.A. Special Agent
Sal M. Martinez for a Carjacking

Special Agent
Sal M. Martinez in the
El Paso D.E.A. Office

D.E.A. Special Agent Sal M. Martinez conducting firearms training with Mexican Federal Judicial Police

D.E.A. Special Agent Sal M. Martinez in Mazatalan and Guadalajara, Mexico

'Controlled burn' of confiscated drugs by the Mexican Federal Judicial Police in Ciudad Juarez, Mexico

Sal M. Martinez with two groups of Mexican Federales

LA CIUDAD

Localizan a ejecutado

▶ Encuentran cuerpo de hombre atado y con cuatro disparos

MARTÍN ORQUIZ
Diario de Juárez

El cadáver de un hombre, que las autoridades creen fue víctima de una venganza entre mafiosos, fue descubierto ayer en un camino vecinal del ejido Jesús Carranza, horas después de ser ejecutado con tres disparos en la nuca y uno más al corazón.

El individuo, de unos 25 años de edad, se halló atado de pies, manos y cuello, y a su alrededor se localizaron dos casquillos de bala calibre .45.

Al momento de encontrársele vestía una camisa negra, un pantalón marca Pepe's de mezclilla azul, tenis y calcetines de color blanco. Sus bolsillos estaban vacíos, por lo que no se hallaron documentos que permitieran su identificación.

Sus características físicas son: cabello corto negro, moreno claro y de aproximadamente un metro con 75 centímetros de altura.

El cuerpo fue encontrado por trabajadores que realizaban labores en el campo alrededor de las 9:00 horas. Se encontraba debajo de un árbol, boca abajo y —por la rigidez que presentó— peritos del Departamento de Averiguaciones Previas calcularon que el asesinato se cometió el lunes por la noche.

El cadáver —localizado en un camino vecinal, aproximadamente a un kilómetro y medio de la carretera Juárez-Porvenir— tenía las manos atadas a la espalda con un cinto tejido negro, de este partía un cordón con el que le enredaron el cuello con la intención de inmovilizarlo.

Otro cinto, de color café estaba a sus pies. Una de las dos prendas perteneció a la víctima, ya que alrededor de su cintura no se encontró otro cinturón mientras que una de las presillas del pantalón estaba rota.

Los informantes indicaron que no vieran ningún movimiento extraño en el lugar, por lo que no aportaron datos de los ejecutores del homicidio.

Personal de la PJE que estuvo en el lugar de los hechos, dijo que el hombre fue ejecutado en ese mismo lugar ya que no se observaron signos de lucha o de que haya sido arrastrado.

No se apreciaron en el lugar huellas de llantas que pudieran indicar en qué vehículo viajaban los responsables del homicidio. El cadáver fue trasladado hasta el anfiteatro de la Universidad Autónoma de Ciudad Juárez, donde se le practicará la autopsia de ley.

Al momento de recoger el cuerpo

El Diario newspaper article regarding the murder of
Sal M. Martinez's Confidential Informant

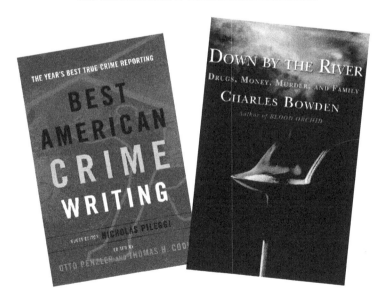

Book by Charles Bowden talks about Sal M. Martinez
after his arrest.

Official request for payment to El Diablo by D.E.A. Special Agent Sal M. Martinez

The U.S. Magistrate Judge in the Southern District of Texas modifies 'defendant' Sal M. Martinez's release to an outrageous $100,000.00 cash bond

164

D.E.A. Special Agent Sal M. Martinez with World Boxing
Champion Julio Cesar Chavez in El Paso, Texas

The only photograph taken of Sal M. Martinez in Federal Prison

Ejecutan a comandante

El Diablo and fellow Mexican Police Officer were assassinated in Matamoros, Mexico in 2001

Arrest in plot stuns DEA agent

Ejecutan a jefe policiaco

DEA agent charged in murder-for-hire plot

DEA agent in murder-for-hire plot pleads guilty

Suspected murder-for-hire plot leads to arrest of anti-drug agent

Cousin: Agent was set up

Ex-DEA official calls murder-for-hire case weak

Bloodshed on the border

Ex-DEA agent apologizes for plot

He gets 7 years for seeking hit man to avenge cousin's death

Newspaper Headlines about Sal M. Martinez

Gear and jewelry given to D.E.A. Special Agent Sal M. Martinez for undercover operations with Mexican Federal Police

American and German Publications with articles about Sal M. Martinez

I ran back to the driver's side of the pickup and jumped in. I shifted the gear into drive and sped away.

McGee jumped into the driver side door of his OGV and got lost in the traffic. The other surveillance units blended into the flow of the heavy traffic.

A product of intuition and guts, the plan worked perfectly. It was one of those moments in life where you've stretched yourself as far as you can, and it worked. There were many looks of disbelief on the faces of those who witnessed the carjacking.

As I was speeding down the access road of I-10, I looked in my rearview mirror and noticed an unfamiliar car following me. The sedan was occupied by an elderly couple. The Good Samaritans had witnessed a violent crime and were taking action. As the male driver accelerated to keep up with the violent thug in the stolen pickup, the female passenger was talking on her cell phone to a 911 operator.

I appreciated the couple's initiative and wished I could have stopped, identify myself, and explain to them why I did what I did. But I had other priorities.

I remained on the access road of the interstate where I came upon a traffic jam waiting at the next intersection. This was no time to stand idle. I drove onto the sidewalk and passed about twenty vehicles idling at the red light. Nobody could follow me after that bit of bravado.

I called McGee from my cell phone. "Where do you want me to take the truck?"

"Take it to the office. We'll tear it apart in the parking area."

Several hours later, ninety pounds of marijuana were discovered in false panels within the passenger area. McGee was elated because he had the evidence to prove he was right all along!

Drug-related conversations on the wiretap increased tenfold. The bad guy called his superior and described the horrific event. The gist of the conversation was debating the reason for the freak occurrence. They concluded the reason for the carjacking was solely for the pickup and not their hidden merchandise. Nobody but them knew what was inside.

They assumed the cops were not brazen enough to do something so outrageous. If the cops were responsible, arrests would have been made for the marijuana. The police are not legally permitted to play this dirty!

In the wire room, DEA agents laughed when they heard the bad guy try to explain to his wife how someone stole his pickup. He claimed a villainous man forced him from the truck at gunpoint and left him standing on the side of the road.

She didn't believe him. He had lied to her many times before. She accused him of selling the truck and its contents for his own personal profit. Deceit had obviously destroyed their marital trust. He had begged her to pick him up after the ordeal.

She responded, "Call your buddies! You're always there for them, now let them be there for you!"

The next day, a Task Force officer handed me a copy of the all points bulletin, or APB, issued by the El Paso Police Department. Based on several 911 calls made by eyewitnesses, the APB accurately described the carjacker as a Hispanic male, dressed like a drug trafficker, brandishing a large caliber pistol.

I wished I could've apologized to the eyewitnesses who experienced such a traumatic event. I would let them know that the victim in this situation was actually the bad guy.

The El Paso Police Department was never told of the operation because it would have created unnecessary friction between the two agencies. There is still an APB for the carjacker.

The U.S. Attorney's office was ready to nail McGee's ass to the wall. Not only were they upset about not requesting legal authorization, they felt charges could be filed on the DEA agents. The head of the El Paso DEA office took the heat, defended his agents, and emphasized there was no time to ask for permission.

McGee and I met the following evening. McGee was grateful and felt like drinking a few beers with me. We drove around central El Paso. After a six-pack each, we drove to the home of the primary target of his Title III investigation.

Inside the palace was a man who had given McGee tremendous grief. Outside in the driveway were several new and expensive automobiles.

I said, "Look at that cocksucker's mansion. Flamboyant asshole!"

McGee said, "He's been moving drugs for years. Nobody has come close to catching him. Other law enforcement agencies have tried but they haven't been successful. I'm determined to arrest him!"

I turned the car around at the end of the street. "According to Sun Tzu, one method to defeat the enemy is to cause chaos among the ranks. Why don't you show this piece of shit what you think about his lap of luxury?"

I drove slowly and lowered the passenger window down.

McGee pulled out his 9mm Glock pistol. He stuck his arm out and shot a round into the front of the two-story dwelling. He screamed, "Fuck you, asshole!" The lights inside the home came on as I sped away.

McGee said, "I'm not sure where the bullet hit!"

I said, "Who cares? It got the point across. This will only create more questions about who is out to get him."

We went home after the alcohol-induced stunt.

The stakes were high, and McGee kept pulling out all the stops. It was time for another radical operation. An informant, who drove car loads of drugs for the organization, claimed two cocaine-laden cars were parked at a house on the east side of El Paso. McGee successfully coordinated a plan to have the several hundred kilograms of cocaine surreptitiously stolen from within the vehicles.

Recently, another drug trafficking group recruited defectors from this organization. This increased the bad blood between the factions putting brother killing brother for the profit of the other. The drug traffickers believed the rival gang stole their product. Who, besides other criminals, could possibly know their modus operandi?

The Cartel leader in Ciudad Juarez wanted someone to pay for the lost cocaine and needed answers. Everyone in the organization who had any knowledge of the lost loads were rounded up. All were blindfolded, interrogated, and brutally beaten, but nobody was killed that night. Retaliation against the rival gang would be sought after a bit of business was completed.

The cocaine destined for demanding clients throughout the U.S.

needed to be replaced immediately to fulfill contractual obligations.

Just before sunrise, it was a typically still weekday morning at the downtown El Paso international bridge. A handful of late night partiers stumbled across from the party zone of downtown Ciudad Juarez. The only sound to be heard on the U.S. side was the breeze shuffling the garbage strewn about the sidewalks of the desolate city streets.

Then a roar of engines broke the morning's silence. It came from the Ciudad Juarez side of the bridge. Eight cars ran bumper to bumper across the Stanton Bridge going the wrong way. The narrow bridge was designed for vehicles crossing from El Paso into Ciudad Juarez.

The first vehicle smashed the wooden tollgate on the American side. The driver was obscured behind dark-tinted windows. The man in the tollbooth on the U.S. side could only watch in bewilderment as the cars sped by him. All eight cars disappeared onto a side street and into the darkness. Each contained a trunk filled with cocaine bundles.

This lawless stunt sparked many other bridge-running ventures for months to come. Drug smugglers realized the Americans did not have a viable response to stop and apprehend the drug runners.

Eventually, U.S. Customs officials strategically placed speed bumps and concrete barriers at each point of entry between El Paso and Ciudad Juarez. It became an inconvenience for all drivers to maneuver through the concrete maze. As for the downtown bridge, one-way metal spikes were installed in the pavement.

After stirring the bee's nest, there were many incriminating statements recorded by the DEA. McGee had sufficient evidence to arrest his targets and decided to shut down the Title III operations. Several homes and businesses would be raided and significant arrests were anticipated.

The best time for law enforcement to conduct a raid is early in the morning. Drug traffickers are usually sleeping at this time after staying up late conducting their nefarious activities. The window of opportunity is considered between a night of partying and waking up to a new day.

I was chosen as lead agent for the raid on the most violent of the drug traffickers. It was 4:30 a.m., and all the lights inside the house were turned off. Surveillance units confirmed the target had arrived two hours earlier. The peaceful, lower-income neighborhood was about to be disturbed.

The preferred DEA eight-man raid technique was used to enter the house. The "snake formation" is considered the safest method for agents to execute a search of a high-risk location. The coordinated effort has each agent performing a specific task and prevents agents from entering rooms randomly that could lead to friendly fire.

Two Task Force officers secured the outer perimeter of the house. The officers stood at opposite ends of the dwelling to prevent anyone from escaping.

After the DEA agents knocked on the door and yelled, "Police! We have a search warrant!", a battering ram was used to gain entry. The snake entered through the smashed front door. The house was dark so we relied on our flashlights while holding our weapons.

A young woman was sleeping on the couch. The coffee table in front of her was covered with empty beer cans, wine bottles, and cocaine paraphernalia. Empty pizza boxes and fast food paper sacks littered the floor. Before the woman rose from a deep sleep, I pulled her by the hair and threw her face down to the carpeted floor. No words were exchanged. Another agent handcuffed and remained with her.

The snake moved down the hallway into the nearest bedroom. Two naked women rose from the queen-sized bed and reached for their undergarments on the floor. Two Task Force officers broke away from the snake and took hold of these temporary hostages by laying them on the floor. An agent stayed with the women as the remaining agents maneuvered methodically throughout the house.

We moved swiftly and methodically from room to room. The primary target was found in the master bedroom struggling to grab his pistol that was laying on the nightstand next to the king-sized bed.

I produced my expandable metal baton and struck the man on the forearm. The man yelled in pain and was yanked down to the floor. We physically punished the man for his failed attempt to shoot us.

Like most assault operations, agents must expect the worst and hope for the best. In this case, we were disappointed that no gunfire was exchanged but relieved we weren't hurt.

Coincidentally, one of the stash locations was related to the anonymous female caller who had provided me with license plate numbers of vehicles.

It was rewarding to know the vague information turned out to be helpful by incriminating the defendants in this case. I had saved the incriminating list of license plate numbers in my File 13 drawer. Again, McGee expressed his gratitude.

The ripples from the aftermath of a DEA operation were usually gruesome. Drug trafficking organizations along the U.S./Mexico border knew that someone must be held accountable. Anyone close to the seized loads were interrogated and sometimes killed. The result was an increase of mutilated bodies found in trash-filled ditches or the remote desert edges of Ciudad Juarez.

Intelligence received by the El Paso DEA office claimed rival gangs fought to take control of the void left in the lucrative drug trafficking trade. For months, the bloodshed escalated, and so did the price of the precious commodity.

El Diario newspaper reporters were busy for months describing the disgusting ways people disrespected other human beings. They displayed graphic crime scene photographs to corroborate the evil exhibited by man. Just like cops, daily readers developed a higher tolerance for violence and death. Our generation would continue to be poisoned with the increased media coverage of the horrors and violence in Mexico and the rest of the world.

Chapter 14 - Snow In The Desert

The El Paso DEA agents continued to flourish with other successful drug-related investigations.

In one case, based on an informant's hunch, Group One agents set up surveillance on a suspected stash house on the east side of El Paso. The informant had proven to be very credible in the past so Calderon ordered his agents to react.

On the first night of surveillance, two unidentified women were seen making a brief stop at the house. Agents could not see if any drugs were carried out.

There was no time to contact a marked unit for a controlled traffic stop. DEA agents followed the duo until they drove across into Ciudad Juarez. The vehicle registration was the only information obtained from this incident.

On the second day, a man was seen exiting the house and departing in a pickup. It was determined he was the homeowner. DEA agents followed him for nearly an hour before conducting a traffic stop.

We tried to persuade the man that it would be in his best interest to admit his illegal activities but he refused to cooperate. He denied us consent to search his home. Without his consent, we knew there was no probable cause to obtain a search warrant.

Now that the man was detained, he now knew the feds were onto him. It would be difficult for us to further our investigation. We had reacted too quickly and hit a brick wall. We just knew there were drugs in the house and were not going to be denied that day.

Americans are tired of criminals having too many rights. Criminals abuse the legal system with technicalities and some get away with murder. To fight the good fight, sometimes rules need to be bent. In this case, the probable cause would be conceived by unorthodox means.

The house keys were taken from the man. He was detained while some agents returned to the suspected stash house.

I knocked on the door. Nobody answered. The door was unlocked. We entered the house and yelled repeatedly, "Police! Is anybody in here?" Cautiously, we conducted a snake throughout the house with our guns drawn.

No one was home. After a thorough search of the rooms, no cocaine or marijuana was found. We struck out! Then something caught my attention.

A wooden panel was separated from a sheetrock wall in the hallway. I walked slowly to the aperture and pulled the panel. I discovered an elaborate walk-in safe. It was expertly crafted to blend with the wood paneling. The careless protectors of the illicit drugs had failed to properly close the door. If it had been shut as originally designed, we would not have discovered the two thousand pounds of cocaine. The cocaine was seized and the homeowner was arrested.

The El Paso DEA agents were ecstatic locating another stash house and taking away some profits from local drug traffickers. While we were giving high-fives to each other, the Juarez Cartel was began conducting their version of damage control.

Anyone with knowledge of the stash house was held responsible for the loss of that cocaine. The first to feel the wrath of the Mexican cartel were the two women seen by surveillance units at the house. Several days later, their mutilated bodies were found in Ciudad Juarez. There were signs of torture as they had been interrogated regarding the loss of a ton of cocaine.

I later learned that the women pleaded with their captors. They claimed to have stopped by the stash house only to purchase a one-half kilogram of cocaine for personal use. The cartel leaders didn't believe them. The women were victims of circumstance.

Weeks later, a *ranchero* bar located on the southeast side of El Paso, called *El Kumbala*, was the scene of a violent act of retaliation. Five men were gunned down as the bar was closing. The intended targets of the hit were two men who were responsible for shipping the cocaine to Albuquerque, New Mexico. Although this type of bold action was not supposed to happen on U.S. soil, the Juarez Cartel left no stone unturned.

In another investigation, an El Paso DEA agent cultivated an informant to set up a seemingly unrealistic ruse. The informant knew someone in Ciudad Juarez who was looking to smuggle large quantities of cocaine across the border. The informant persuaded the drug smugglers that he had a border inspector willing to allow drug-laden vehicles to cross into the U.S. for a price.

Being very persuasive, the informant arranged a practice run for the smugglers. The informant drove a DEA undercover van into Ciudad Juarez, and several cocaine packages were loaded into the van. Under the watchful eye of the smugglers, the informant drove into the designated lane where the inspector was working. The van entered the U.S. without incident.

The cartel members were elated. They had finally attained the ultimate prize possession for any drug smuggling organization – a corrupt U.S. Customs Service inspector on their payroll!

After releasing the cocaine packages to DEA agents, the informant said, "These guys are overstocked with cocaine. They haven't been able to find a trustworthy group to smuggle it across. They are anxious to move it!" The informant returned to Ciudad Juarez with the DEA undercover van. This time it was loaded with hundreds of cocaine bundles.

In a two-day period, the informant made several drug runs. Each time he returned from Juarez, the cocaine was transferred to a DEA agent then directly to our drug depository. We couldn't believe this was actually happening. Approximately six tons of cocaine was hand-delivered to the El Paso DEA.

After waiting a week, the Mexican traffickers became furious when the informant was not returning their phone calls. He couldn't be found. They finally realized they were in a relationship that was too good to be true. They had been swindled.

While there was celebration in the El Paso DEA office, heads literally rolled on the Mexican side. In the days that followed, tortured and mutilated bodies were discovered throughout Juarez due to this major blunder.

I learned that the cocaine had been stored at a warehouse near the Zaragosa International Port of Entry in Ciudad Juarez. Paul Rodriguez and I were willing to conduct surveillance on the warehouse but Calderon didn't want to place his agents in such a dangerous situation without any support from Mexican law enforcement. This information would remain on the back burner.

On another occasion, DEA agents from the Houston area visited the El Paso DEA office to request assistance with an investigation. They were actively watching a stash house in Houston that possibly contained large amounts of cocaine. Instead of raiding the house, they were confident additional loads of cocaine would be coming from El Paso. A coordinated effort was established to determine the location of a related stash house in El Paso.

DEA agents from Houston followed a large Winnebago recreational vehicle (RV) from 'H-Town' to a house on the west side of El Paso. A White male was observed exiting the conveyance and entering a one-story, ordinary dwelling.

Group One agents maintained surveillance on the house for several days. No other persons or vehicles were seen coming or going from this location.

Then, one morning, a new-model Ford Thunderbird, occupied by one Hispanic male, was seen circling the residential neighborhood. The male appeared to be looking for someone or something in the area. Agents believed it was counter-surveillance, as the man was scouting for anyone who may be watching the Winnebago.

After an hour, the man parked the vehicle down the street. Agents saw him make a call on his cell phone. After a brief conversation, the man began reading a newspaper.

Simultaneously, the White male seen before exited the target location and proceeded to transfer cardboard boxes through the side door of the house into the Winnebago. The man made numerous trips between the residence and the vehicle. Afterwards, he locked the door to the house, entered the RV, and drove away.

The man in the Thunderbird remained parked for about another thirty minutes. Agents believed he was making sure nobody followed the RV. The man forgot to do one thing. He never looked up into the sky.

We utilized aerial surveillance to follow the RV as it departed El Paso. We were confused as the vehicle traveled northbound on Interstate 25 into New Mexico. It was headed in the opposite direction of Houston.

Paul called me on the DEA radio, "Where do you think this guy is going?"

"I'm not sure. He may be going to another location."

"He is in no hurry. I would hate to follow this vehicle all the way to

Houston. It could take us all day!"

I responded, "Look on the bright side, he can't outrun you!"

After a brief discussion between the Houston and El Paso DEA agents it was decided there was no reason to wait any longer. Paul and other DEA agents stopped and searched the vehicle. Cardboard boxes were stacked to the roof in the Winnebago's sleeping quarters.

The RV was returned to the El Paso DEA office to unload the many boxes that contained two tons of cocaine.

Paul questioned the cooperative driver, "Where are you going with this cocaine?"

"Houston."

"The most direct route from El Paso to Houston is eastbound on Interstate 10. Why are you going northbound?"

"I travel this direction to avoid the Border Patrol checkpoint in Sierra Blanca. They have canines most of the time and they make me nervous. So, I travel through Albuquerque, take a right on Route 66 to Amarillo, before heading south into Houston. I'd rather take the long way home."

"Why didn't you make an effort to conceal the cocaine packages?"

The haughty driver responded, "I'm a blonde-haired, blue-eyed White male driving a Winnebago. The cops aren't going to stop me! I don't fit the profile of a drug transporter. I've made numerous runs and have never been searched." The former U.S. Navy Seal denied knowing the identities of other members in the drug trafficking organization. He had been trained not to say more than was necessary.

Meanwhile, Jake Davis and I conducted a traffic stop on the man in the Ford Thunderbird. The Hispanic man, identified as Juan Casillas, denied any knowledge or affiliation to the stash house or the RV. He claimed to be house hunting on westside of El Paso.

After an hour of questioning, it was obvious to us there was little evidence to link this man to any criminal act. We knew we would have to release him without any incriminating admissions. With little hope of implicating Casillas, a ray of light emitted.

Paul called me on the cell phone, "We found a shitload of cocaine in the Winnebago!"

I was elated, "Kick ass! Is the driver talking?"

"The jarhead said there isn't anything left from where he got this. However, get someone to search the stash house just to be sure there was nothing left behind. There may be documentary evidence that can lead us to others in the El Paso area. He is denying that anybody else is involved."

I responded, "That's one righteous soldier. As for the guy in the Thunderbird, I'll have to break him." Deception would be my only choice.

I returned to Casillas and asked if I could look through his wallet. With nothing to hide, he confidently consented. I found a picture of a young girl. "Is this your daughter?"

"*Si.*"

"It's a shame you are not going to see her grow up."

"What do you mean?"

"Our agents found a lot of cocaine in the Winnebago that you were watching. The driver confessed that you were responsible for the shipment."

"That's a lie!"

"Tell it to the judge. You won't have your day in court for months. In the meantime, I feel really sorry for your daughter. Federal prosecutors love to send people like you to prison for a very long time." I rubbed the photo with my fingers keeping it out of arms reach from Casillas.

I continued, "Take a breath of this fresh morning air because it is the last time you will smell freedom. I'm placing you under arrest."

"Wait! What did the *guero* say?"

I continued with the deception, "He's blaming you. He said you are responsible for the cocaine and that he is merely a driver working under your direction."

"He said that? I don't believe it."

"Mr. Casillas, you have wasted our time out here long enough! There are two options for you. Tell us what you know, and we will help you. Or, play hardball, and we will make sure you go to prison for a very long time."

It was considered a victorious day for the DEA by seizing the large quantity of cocaine and arresting a driver. However, it would be extraordinary to arrest the person who actually owned the illicit drugs. Casillas was folding and I was confident that I could make it happen.

Casillas asked, "What can I do?"

"Tell me who is the owner of the cocaine?"

After a few minutes of deep contemplation, Casillas said, "He's from Juarez."

"I need a name."

"I can't. If I give you his name, he will kill me!"

I continued, "Nobody is going to lay a hand on you. I know this is very difficult for you but you need to think about your family. You're not the one we want. We know you're not the main guy of this organization. Don't take the blame for this large load of cocaine."

"He knows everything about me. He is going to find my family and kill them!"

"We need to get our hands on your boss. We need you to get him to come across the river into El Paso."

"There's no way he'll come here. He's afraid of being arrested by you guys!"

"What's his name?"

Casillas shook his head and nervously paced in a small circle. He whispered, "I can't do it."

"They won't come into the U.S. to retaliate. It never happens."

Fear of death was outweighing his fear of incarceration. Casillas reverted back to a defensive attitude claiming there was no legal proof to connect him to the cocaine in the Winnebago. I got impatient, "If you want to act like an attorney, then I'm done with you!"

"I'm just saying you can't threaten me with prison!"

I interrupted by yelling, "I'm not threatening you. I'm promising you. We need his name, now!"

Reluctantly, he whispered, "Fernando Amaya."

I calmly asked, "Who else do you know close to Amaya?"

"I've seen other men with him, but I was never introduced to them. They all work for Amado Carrillo-Fuentes."

I gave Casillas a chance to think. "Here's the deal. I'm sure the U.S. Attorney will consider dropping or reducing the criminal charges against you. The only way it can be done is if we get our hands on Amaya."

"And if I don't do it."

"You don't want to consider the other option." I tossed the photo of the little girl on the dash of the OGV. I handcuffed Casillas with his hands behind his back and shoved him into the front seat of my OGV. I wanted him to feel the tightness of the cold steel on his wrists during the drive to the El Paso DEA Office.

In the DEA debriefing room, I connected the recorder to the undercover telephone. It was the power of persuasion and confidence that the set up was going to happen. I said, "This is your last chance to see your daughter." I laid the photo on the table next to the telephone.

After a moment of contemplation, Casillas began dialing Amaya's cell phone number.

Amaya answered, "*Bueno* (Hello)."

"*Buenos dias, señor. Tienes un momento* (Do you have a minute)?"

"*Si. Que pasa* (What's happening)?"

The conversation continued in Spanish, "I don't want to talk over the phone. Can we meet?"

"Sure. Let's meet at *La Cueva* (The Cave)." It was an underground piano bar with a cavernous motif located in the downtown nightclub strip of Ciudad Juarez. Complete with artificial stalagtites and stalagmites, it was the perfect hideaway for an intimate rendezvous.

"No. I don't have time to go across, because I'm making sure our shipment departs. Can you come to this side for a minute?"

"You know I don't go across anymore!" shouted Amaya.

"I know, but I have great news for you."

After a pause, "I guess. Meet me on the other side of the downtown bridge. Do you remember where we met a few months ago?"

"*Si, señor.*"

"Be there in thirty minutes." Amaya hung up.

Casillas was sweating profusely. "We're meeting on Second Street near the Santa Fe Bridge."

I asked, "What happened when you last met him at this location?"

"He never got out of his car. We talked for a few minutes before he returned to Juarez."

There was no time to lose. I gathered several DEA agents in the office and briefed them. Surveillance units set up in adjacent streets waiting on Amaya to arrive.

Jose Calderon said, "This could be icing on the cake. Arresting the owner of multi-ton quantities of coke is unprecedented. I am going to be there when this happens!"

Casillas insisted that he drive alone to the meeting. "Mr. Amaya will drive away if he sees someone else in my car."

I said, "There is no way I am going to let you drive alone." I grabbed a portable DEA radio to monitor the activity of my fellow agents. I would improvise with the unique situation.

Vince asked, "How do you want to do this?"

"I placed a mini-cassette recorder in Casillas' shirt pocket. He needs to incriminate Amaya with any bit of conversation about the cocaine load we just seized. As for me, I will hide in the back seat of the Thunderbird. I don't want Casillas having a change of heart and escaping into Juarez."

Vince responded, "You are one crazy dude."

Casillas drove his vehicle to Second Street and parked on the roadway facing the Santa Fe International Bridge.

I lay on the rear passenger floorboard and covered myself with the newspaper Casillas was reading earlier. I said, "When you see him, get out of your car and walk to his driver's side window. I don't want him to get out of his car and find me here. Don't try anything foolish, or I will shoot you. Do you understand me?"

"There's no turning back now." Casillas answered. "There he is!"

"What's he doing?" I couldn't see anything from my position.

"He's parked in front of me and is motioning for me to come to his Cherokee."

"Go ahead. Just don't get into his vehicle!"

Casillas exited his car and walked over to a new Jeep Cherokee. He opened the passenger door and sat in the front seat.

I heard Calderon yell over the radio, "Everyone move in now! Do not let them escape!"

Before Amaya could shift the gear of his Cherokee into drive, three DEA vehicles surrounded him. There was no time to react. With guns pointed at his face, Amaya instinctively raised his hands.

Amaya and Casillas were ordered out of the Cherokee with their hands up. They were thrown to the ground and handcuffed.

I remained out of sight, so as not to burn Casillas as a cooperating individual.

Calderon placed Amaya in his OGV and transported him to the DEA office. Yvette placed Casillas in the passenger seat of her car. The scene was vacated by all as quickly as we had arrived.

Vince walked up to the Thunderbird and knocked on the window. "Hey, *pinchi* homeless, it's over. You can come out now."

Peeking through the newspapers, I smiled at Vince. I tossed the papers aside and climbed out from the floorboard.

Amaya's vehicle was driven to the DEA parking garage where it was thoroughly searched. A pamphlet from a Mexican herbal company was found in the glove compartment. It was bagged and tagged as evidence with other seemingly insignificant items.

One incriminating statement was recorded in the brief period Casillas and Amaya sat together in Jeep Cherokee. Amaya asked, "Are the courts open?" It was their code regarding the safe departure of the cocaine shipment.

Casillas responded, "*Si, Jefe* (Yes, boss)."

Amaya refused to cooperate with the DEA. He hired the best criminal attorney in Texas but lost in a high profile jury trial. Amaya was recorded on the mini-cassette recorder admitting knowledge of the two tons of cocaine that were in the Winnebago. Along with circumstantial evidence, it was enough to send Amaya to federal prison for thirty years.

DEA agents raided the Houston suburban house and discovered three tons of cocaine. The Houston and El Paso DEA agents determined there was a common factor amongst the recent cocaine seized. The label on the majority of the cocaine bundles was the marketing symbol of a Mexican herbal company.

It was common to see cocaine kilogram bundles labeled to identify the source of supply, the drug trafficking organization, or the quality of the product. The emblems emulated company logos, such as Nike's swoosh or McDonald's arches. Some markings mock famous names, such as Clinton or Bush.

I received congratulatory calls from DEA headquarters. One International Operations head said, "You apprehended a major player from the Juarez cartel. It will impact their operations drastically. We cannot express our gratitude for your efforts. Also, we are impressed by the way you got him to cross over into El Paso."

In the midst of these successes came a rare visit from the DEA Administrator. He was not there to congratulate his agents but to discuss budgetary issues and his bureaucratic efforts in Washington.

After his uninspiring speech, the Administrator asked for questions. Nobody had any, except me.

"Are there any plans to increase manpower in the Southwest border offices?"

"I plan to send the next academy graduates to New York, Miami, and Los Angeles. Those cities need more agents to help with the enormous case loads."

Not happy with the response, I prodded the bureaucrat.

"Is it possible to reinstate the Spanish Language Bonus Program?" I was referring to an incentive program that rewarded agents who had foreign language abilities. This was a morale booster for those agents involved in undercover roles, wiretaps, and other Spanish speaking activities.

"I feel that Spanish speaking agents were hired for their ability to speak a foreign language. I don't believe they should be given extra money for that reason."

Somehow, it was the response I expected.

When in the presence of a man like this, there was no need to ask questions any more than necessary. The man did not want to hear anything outside of his personal agenda. Like most political appointments within the U.S. government, he wasn't in touch with the real needs of his personnel.

A close friend of the FBI Administrator, he ran the DEA just like the feebs. There was an increase in micro-management, procedural bickering, and internal back-stabbings. The general mood of the DEA personnel declined during this man's tenure. The DEA would never recover from the transition and the deterioration of morale.

PART TWO
FOREIGN OPERATIONS

Chapter 15 - Keep Your Enemies Closer

Jose Calderon summoned Paul and I into his office. There was seriousness in his tone.

I refilled my cup of coffee and walked into the room, "*Que pasa?*"

Paul dragged himself into the room with a cup of coffee in hand. He appeared agitated as usual. There were no salutations or acknowledgements. It was a defense mechanism to avoid conversation, because he was always one word away from an argument.

I regarded him with a mixture of admiration and amusement.

Paul and I had developed a bond because we were both from the *barrio* and had made it to the big leagues. We had similar off-duty interests - primarily drinking beer and playing golf. When on-duty, a level of toughness with us had to be imbued, especially with what was in store for us. We balanced work and play for most of our careers.

Calderon rose from his high-back leather chair, but there was no usual handshake or greeting. The facial expression was indicative of a supervisor having to deal with unwanted bureaucratic stress.

He took a deep breath, "I have been on the phone all morning with Headquarters. As we know, all the drugs seized in the El Paso area are coming from across the river. Just because there is an imaginary international line and a river dividing our cities, this shouldn't prevent us from working over there."

Paul asked, "What do you mean?"

"There are U.S. agencies, such as the CIA, FBI, and Department of Defense, who may be involved gathering drug trafficking intelligence. But we are the lead agency in the war on drugs. Our agency has finally realized that we have ignored Juarez for too long."

Paul reacted, "I knew it. I transferred out of Mexico to leave the bullshit behind and now I am supposed to get back into it. I came home so I could work domestic cases."

Calderon paused, "We have to address an unspoken issue. You two are the only male Hispanics in this office. You both need to get familiar with the city of Juarez. You are about to enter unchartered territory. Decision-makers in Washington and Mexico City have ordered us to set up shop in Juarez."

Paul burst out, "Wait a minute! That's not our responsibility. It's up to the Mexico City DEA Country Office to assign their agents."

The Mexican government had permitted thirty-nine DEA agents to reside in seven cities as advisors. The unwritten arrangement gave the agents semi-diplomatic privileges. In reality, Mexican officials did not want any DEA agents in their country, but they owed the U.S. at least that much in return for the multi-million dollar financial aid donations given to "their" war on drugs.

The DEA agents were assigned to Mexico City, Guadalajara, Mazatlan, Merida, Monterrey, and Hermosillo. No agents were assigned to the most strategic location for the drug cartels – Ciudad Juarez.

There had been occasional joint investigative efforts by the DEA and the Mexican federal police in the border city. Administrators had failed to recognize the importance of the region and the drug traffickers took advantage of the free reign.

Calderon said, "We need to establish a working relationship with the other side. If things work out, you guys will be fixtures in Juarez. A permanent presence is necessary if we are going to be effective."

I said, "I've been down that road once with a previous supervisor. Before you got here, we tried a joint effort with the *federales* (Mexican federal agents). The plan was to establish rapport and have them pursue investigative leads. They had a different agenda than we did!"

Calderon laughed, "I heard about that fiasco."

Paul asked, "What happened?"

"We went to Juarez to meet an elite team of *federales*. My former supervisor had worked with the Comandante while stationed in Mexico. After a pleasant brunch, the rest of the day was spent partying like college kids. Nothing was ever accomplished except creating large tabs at sleazy strip joints."

Paul added, "I've worked with some decent *federales* while I was stationed in Guadalajara. The key for success is to stay on top of them so they don't stray from helping us to join the cartels."

Calderon said, "Where there's smoke, there's fire. We're the closest to the fire. We will meet with a team of *federales* handpicked by the *Procuraduria General de la Republica* (PGR) and vetted by our people. Clear your agenda and transfer all your domestic investigations to other agents."

I said, "I have an informant ready to set up a few drug deals next week here in El Paso!"

"Sorry about that. Give your informant to another agent and let that agent run with the investigations."

"Shit!" I would miss out on doing a few of my favorite things - buy/bust operations. I would miss out on a lot of other desires as my job description changed completely.

Calderon added, "We will exchange information with the *federales* on active drug investigations on both sides of the river. They will be reporting directly to their headquarters in Mexico City. It goes without saying that we need to be selective about the information we provide them. Both of you and this special unit have been dubbed by someone in our headquarters as the Bilateral Task Force or BTF."

I thought, "Great, another acronym to remember."

Calderon concluded, "Just like you, I have many questions but nobody to answer them. We will take this a day at a time, and it begins tomorrow morning. We will meet our counterparts for breakfast."

Paul and I were never provided with any official rules of engagement. We would need to improvise with logistics, investigative techniques, and the punitive measures against the Juarez Cartel.

The next morning, the three of us traveled in one OGV to Ciudad Juarez.

We discussed the rampant corruption evident in every aspect of law enforcement in Mexico. We agreed the primary factor was that officers were paid low wages making them easy prey for bribes from drug traffickers. Most policemen had begun their careers with honest intentions but succumbed to the temptation of money or coercion from threats.

Protection of the Mexican cartels had reached the upper levels of the Mexican government. Politicians, military brass, and police heads had been accused and arrested for affiliating with drug trafficking organizations.

Many Mexican officials believed that the militarization of enforcement efforts would eliminate the deep-rooted corruption. But in 1997, they received a big slap in the face by the arrest of General Jesus Gutierrez-Rebollo, then head of Mexico's anti-drug agency. While being praised by both U.S. and Mexican authorities for his integrity, Gutierrez-Rebollo was found guilty of being on the payroll of numerous drug trafficking organizations. In addition, U.S. investigative strategies and the identities of confidential informants operating in Mexico were compromised.

It will take generations to overhaul Mexico's terribly ineffective, graft-ridden police agencies. Raising salaries and cutting the bloated bureaucracy may help, but the culture that accepts corruption is hard to change.

A popular saying is, "If you are being mugged on the streets, don't scream or you may attract the police." The Mexican people are accustomed to *mordidas* (payoffs) to avoid being harassed or arrested by their own police. Sometimes, extortion accompanies the bribery.

As we entered the *Las Palmas* (The Palms) restaurant, a young Mexican male wearing a shiny green shirt, blue jeans, and snakeskin boots greeted us. He extended his hand to my supervisor, "*Señor Calderon?*"

"*Si.*"

"My name is Francisco Morales-Telles, *Segundo Comandante* (Second-in-Command) with the *Procuraduria General de la Republica*. Would you please join us at our table?"

Most Mexicans identify themselves with more than one last name. The first is the father's last name followed by the mother's last name. Many Americans haven't figured out which of the two is paternal or maternal.

There were few patrons in the restaurant. Mexicans have breakfast around the same time Americans eat brunch.

Five young Mexican men were seated at a large rectangular table. Each was wearing multi-colored silk shirts, blue jeans and cowboy boots. They all rose as the DEA representatives approached.

A slender, light complexioned man at the head of the table was the first to introduce himself. "My name is Hector Mendoza-Brusuelas, *comandante de la PGR.*"

Everyone shook each other's hands and said their names very matter of factly. None of the men spoke English. After the introductions, they all sat down.

Calderon and Mendoza did most of the talking while the rest of us listened attentively to our supervisors. The two leaders discussed administrative and investigative objectives. There was an urgency to get the BTF established immediately. Not only did each supervisor want to understand the other, but he also wanted to express his respective agency's agenda for the undertaking.

After an hour of conversation and several drink refills, Calderon and Mendoza agreed to order breakfast. A few more details were resolved over *huevos rancheros* and *huevos con chorizo* plates.

Comandante Mendoza said, "We are all from the Mexico City area. We were ordered to say goodbye to our families and board the PGR plane. We did not have time to take care of personal affairs before departing. All we have are the shirts on our backs. Nobody in my agency provided me with money to establish ourselves here in Juarez."

This did not come as a surprise to Calderon. He was familiar with the lack of financial assistance by Mexican bureaucrats for their frontline agents. The obedient grunts were left to fend for themselves.

Calderon produced a manila envelope containing $8,000 of U.S. official government funds. He handed it to the Comandante saying, "Additional funds will be provided monthly."

The Comandante placed his hand on the package and humbly responded, "*Muchas gracias.*"

Calderon said for all to hear, "There is a lot of work for us in this area, and both of our agency heads want us to be up and running as soon as possible. We will provide you with the necessary equipment to establish a base of operations. Sal and Paul will meet with you on a daily basis to help with your efforts and to exchange relevant information."

Wiretaps on suspected drug traffickers would be a priority for the covert operations. Audio recorders, audiotapes, and any electronic devices would be purchased in El Paso, from a Radio Shack. It was easier for us to buy the necessary equipment from a public vendor than documenting the withdrawal from the DEA inventory. Also, we didn't want any U.S. government markings on the equipment just in case it fell into the wrong hands.

A house in a residential area would be rented as the operational base. The inconspicuous listening post would be restricted from anyone outside the BTF. One Mexican agent would always remain at the base for security and to record relevant telephone conversations.

Nobody, especially the Mexican media, could know that the *gringos* were conducting wiretaps on their soil. The disclosure of the unauthorized U.S. law enforcement presence in Mexico would cause a political uproar regarding violations of sovereignty.

The *federales* desired to make *Las Palmas* Motel as their temporary sleeping quarters. It would be easier than renting another house that required furniture, appliances, and other costly amenities. The motel was conveniently located several blocks from the listening post.

Calderon concluded, "We will provide each of you with a passport so you can personally see our operations in El Paso. You will work with us on the American side just as we will work here with you."

This brought smiles to the faces of the *federales*. The idea of Mexican cops working on American soil was unprecedented. Apparently, the brass in DEA headquarters viewed this program with the utmost of optimism.

This was the first time Paul and I heard about this. We looked at each other wondering, "How the hell are we allowing Mexican cops to be roaming El Paso streets?"

The introductory meeting between the *federales* and the DEA representatives ended with everyone exchanging bro hugs.

On the drive back to El Paso, I said, "I don't want to rain on this parade but Mexican cops on U.S. soil? Can you imagine the fury of the American people if they caught wind of this? Shit, we thought the 'Remember the Alamo' battle cry was profound!"

Paul looked at me, "We live in the 'Land of *Mañana* (Tomorrow)'!

It is a culture that delays responsibilities with a 'come back tomorrow' mentality. It would be naïve for us to believe we will receive any immediate investigative efforts from these guys."

I added, "More importantly, any exchange of information with the Mexicans must be viewed with a great deal of skepticism. We can't trust them with our sensitive information."

There was no response from Calderon.

In the coming weeks, I was responsible for purchasing the necessary equipment to make the BTF operational. I made several trips to an El Paso Radio Shack store for wiretap apparatus, cassette players, cassette tapes, etc. Also, since the *federales* were not provided with ammunition for their weapons, a visit to a local gun shop would be on the itinerary.

Although DEA agents are required to submit receipts for expenditures, I was instructed not to leave any paper trails. There must be no red flags raised along the audit channels within the Department of Justice. Any questions or scrutiny by pencil pushing accountants would disrupt the clandestine affair.

Vince constantly reminded me, "CYA (cover your ass) by documenting your purchases and expenditures. If you don't save receipts, at least log everything in your Pocket Day-Timer booklet. You don't want the 'rat patrol' coming after you with nothing but your dick in your hand!"

I followed my partners advice and used catch-all phrases, like investigative expenses or emergency purchase to justify the clandestine purchases on the DEA vouchers. Receipts were stored in my desk drawer next to the File 13 accordion folder just in case the rat patrol came after me.

While in college, I had taken the Myers-Briggs Personality Type evaluation. I was characterized as outgoing, loyal, and curious by nature. A great sense of humor on one end of the spectrum and a suck it up mentality at the other end. I liked order and never failed to answer unexpected calls for help.

When it came to funding the BTF operations, I did not want any accountants scrutinizing or asking questions about any expenditures. Unafraid of any consequences, my mindset was "it was better to ask for forgiveness rather than ask for permission".

I believed the DEA Headquarters was counting on me. I knew my supervisors and the agency would not let one of its most dutiful agents hang out to dry. A trusting belief shattered in the end.

Chapter 16 – Crossing The Line

After weeks of collective planning, the BTF would get its first test. Paul said, "I have a snitch who met a guy with forty ounces of black tar heroin. The problem is the dealer refuses to make the transaction in El Paso. He insists the negotiations and the heroin delivery take place in Juarez."

DEA agents are strictly prohibited from engaging in undercover work on foreign soil. They are directed to act only as advisors and gather intelligence. The restriction was to prevent any physical harm from direct contact with drug traffickers. Politically, it would insult the credibility of the host law enforcement agency by allowing *gringos* to do their job.

Comandante Mendoza and Supervisor Calderon agreed to conduct the undercover meeting to justify the existence of the BTF. There would be no written documentation by either agency.

Since assigned to the BTF, I habitually carried my service pistol into Ciudad Juarez. Although there was not an official agreement between the DEA and the Mexican Government regarding possession of weapons, I refused to be caught unarmed in the event of a gun battle. My motto being, "It was better to be tried by twelve than to be carried by six."

Located near downtown Ciudad Juarez was a partially open air market known as *El Mercado* (The Market). This long standing tourist attraction allowed shoppers and vendors to negotiate prices of handmade boots, leather goods, *serapes*, and various *curios*. Like every other tourist trap, it was swarming with strolling vendors selling Chiclets gum, pirated CD's, or useless trinkets.

Within *El Mercado* were three adjacent restaurants offering local cuisine. *Mariachis* walked from table to table cajoling tourists for a musical request. The musicians relied on the festive setting and alcohol-related occasions to charge five dollars per song.

It was 11:45 a.m., on an unusually hot, spring day. Paul and his informant, nicknamed *Gato* (Cat), sat at an outdoor table sipping on Tecate *cervezas* (beers). The heroin dealer had agreed to meet the buyer around noon.

I sat with a *federale* at a nearby table sipping on Fanta sodas. I would remain close to Paul in case of an emergency.

The rest of the BTF agents waited in their vehicles. It had been decided that if something needed to be relayed to the surveillance team, a meeting would surreptitiously be held in the men's restroom.

Just after noon, a thin, Hispanic male about forty-five years old walked up to Paul and the CI. After introductions, the drug dealer sat at the table and ordered a round of Tecate *cervezas*.

They talked for nearly an hour before Paul excused himself and walked to the men's restroom. Comandante Mendoza met Paul in the restroom. Paul said in Spanish, "The guy is playing hardball. He insists we give him $20,000 cash upfront and then he will produce twenty ounces of heroin."

The Comandante responded, "Does the DEA have that kind of cash available?"

"We are not going to hand over any cash to this guy!"

Mendoza offered, "Let me get my hands on him. I'll find out if he is legit."

Paul ended the conversation, "Hold on. Let me try to get a sample of the heroin. He may lead us to the rest of the drugs." Frustrated, he returned to the table with slim expectations.

Drug negotiations of this type usually involve demands from each side. The seller wants to see the money before displaying the product. The buyer wants to see the drugs before revealing the currency. Patience is necessary to reach a compromise acceptable to both parties. But that didn't work this time.

To my surprise, Mendoza ordered his men to move on the table. The *federales*, pointing AK-47 automatic rifles, surrounded Paul, the informant, and the dealer. The three men raised their hands and fell face down on the hot cement. The look of shock on their faces rivaled that of nearby tourists.

The *federales* grabbed the dealer by his shirt and forced him into the back seat of a Ford Crown Victoria. People watched in horror as the man was seemingly kidnapped and the car sped away.

I walked up to the informant and Paul as they rose from the ground.

I asked, "Why did Mendoza pick him up so quickly?"

"Fuck if I know," retorted Paul. "That was messed up! I'm getting out of here and taking *Gato* back to El Paso."

I said, "I'll stay here. Let me see what the Comandante has planned."

I called the Comandante and asked where they were taking their captive. He asked to meet him at an isolated motel on the Pan American Highway leading to the Ciudad Juarez International Airport. The *federales* would be in a room furthest away from the highway. I accepted the invitation.

Mexican cops almost never allowed a U.S. agent to observe their methods of interrogation. Not only was I wondering about the Comandante's decision to abruptly end the undercover meeting at the restaurant, I had a morbid curiosity of the misfortunes the heroin dealer was about to experience.

As I entered the parking lot of the Corona Motel, there were no people or vehicles visible. Window curtains were drawn, and the tenants remained in their secluded suites. Each room had an adjacent two-vehicle garage whereby guests concealed their vehicles. The hourly rate and parking arrangement made the motel a popular place for those desiring extramarital trysts.

I drove to the rearmost section of the motel. I entered through the partially open door and walked into the room. I would not give any indication that I was a U.S. agent. I would blend in as one of the *federales*.

Mendoza, sitting on the only recliner in the room, looked at me and said, "This could be a long afternoon. Before we begin to interview our friend, why don't you make a beer run and bring us something to eat?"

Without questioning the Comandante, I acted as a subordinate and nodded. Mendoza ordered one of his men, named *Oso* (Bear), to accompany me.

The *federales* often confided in me, and I listened attentively. I took this opportunity to learn more of the Mexican culture, the mentality of its citizens, and motives of the law enforcers I was working with.

Oso came from a poor family outside of Mexico City. He had hopes of becoming a law enforcement officer to provide a decent living for his wife and newborn child. He couldn't afford attending college so he went to the PGR training academy.

Like the rest of his fellow agents, he had no prior law enforcement experience. They were grunts in a system that provided a low salary with little opportunity for advancement. They understood the inadequacies of their profession and the inevitable proposition of *plata o plomo* (silver or lead)?" In other words, accept the bribes demanded by the drug cartels or take a bullet to the head.

Oso relied on the guidance and expertise of their commander. With four years in the Mexican military, Comandante Mendoza was the only person in the team with any significant training. He emanated a brashness and confidence that let everyone know he was in charge of his crew.

Oso said, "I hope we can get some drugs from this guy. It will help justify our joint efforts."

I responded, "Absolutely. However, this guy is just a small-time dealer. We should be focusing on gathering intelligence and identifying members of the Juarez Cartel. Do you think we can accomplish that?" I was trying to get a feel for the *federale*. I was hoping for a response that would indicate a bona fide desire to arrest Mexican drug traffickers.

"We are still getting to know people in this city. We can't trust anyone. It would be very dangerous for us to ask the wrong person about the Cartel."

I could see there was a legitimate fear in this man's eyes. There was no reason to continue with the subtle interrogation. After nearly an hour, we returned to the motel room.

The Mexican agents were sitting on a king size bed, staring attentively at the American made porno flick on the 19-inch television. Hamburgers and *cervezas frias* (cold beers) were passed around.

Having no appetite, the heroin dealer refused a hamburger offered to him. He sat quietly as the *federales* ate, drank, and joked about the lesbian sex scene.

The Comandante said, "*Pinchi gringas* need to do this because their *gringo* husbands don't know how to satisfy them."

Morales added his *machismo* opinion, "It's because their husbands are out grabbing ass with their buddies on a golf course."

The Comandante added, "The *gringos* are preoccupied with making money instead of taking care of their women. Let me tell you something. You will never find a Mexican lesbian because we Latin lovers know what women like. Isn't that right, *paisas* (countrymen)?"

All the men started hollering.

After the *federales* finished their power lunch, the Comandante stood and instructed the hostage to stand. Handcuffed with his hands behind his back, the drug dealer trembled with fear.

Mendoza asked, "Where's the heroin?"

"I don't have any."

"Why did you say you had forty ounces?"

"I didn't."

"Are you saying I am a liar?"

"No."

"What about the twenty ounces you said you would bring to us if we gave you $20,000 in cash?"

"I was just making it up."

"Why are you lying to me? I don't have time for lies!" The Comandante punched the man in the stomach.

Doubled over, the man looked up at his assailant and seemed to be more surprised at the cheap shot than in physical pain.

I began to feel sick to my stomach. The hamburger I just ate wanted to come back up. It wasn't right for a handcuffed man to be hit like that. This was not fair, and this was not the DEA way. But I couldn't say anything because it wasn't my show.

Comandante Mendoza calmly removed the man's eyeglasses and asked one of his agents for a bag.

The *federale* produced a clear plastic bag from his rear pant pocket. Mendoza slowly placed the bag over the dealer's head and wrapped his hands around the neck to seal the bag.

The second punch to the stomach took the prisoner's precious air out of his lungs. The bag collapsed around the contours of the man's face as he gasped for air that was not there. His skin began to turn a sickly blue color and the stare of utter fear possessed the prisoner.

The thoughts that raced through his head were apparent, "How am I going to get out of this? How much punishment can I take? Maybe he'll hit me only once or twice more."

Mexican police are known for their brutal interrogation methods. They beat people so severely that their captives eventually confess to crimes they never committed. Human rights violations have been a major grievance from many citizens of Mexico, but there has never been any political pressure to correct the injustices or punish the abusers.

Mendoza stated, "Only complications can come from lies. The truth is very simple. Now tell me where you have the heroin!"

The captive did not say a word. He only shook his head. His resolve would only cause him more pain.

Showing no expression, Mendoza tightened his grip on the man's neck.

The victim's legs started shaking uncontrollably before buckling.

Mendoza removed the bag as the man fell to the floor gasping. He was given five seconds to gather his senses before Mendoza pulled him up like a rag doll.

The man just shook his head and said, "I don't have any heroin. Please believe me!" Then he began sobbing.

Comandante Mendoza walked the man to the bathroom. He kicked his prisoner behind the knees and simultaneously pushed his shoulders down toward the toilet.

After submerging the man's head in the toilet, he flushed it twice.

The man tried to raise his head as the water ran into his nose and cut off his air.

Mendoza forcibly held the man's head steady for what must have felt like an eternity.

This method of interrogation is commonly referred as *el ahogadito*, translated as the little drowning.

The Comandante finally gave the man an opportunity to catch his breath.

The man began to throw up the Tecate beer he drank earlier. He screamed, "Please believe me. I made it up!"

Mendoza gave the man a towel to dry himself and wipe the puke from his dress shirt. He grabbed another towel to dry his own arm from the toilet water.

The prisoner was ordered to sit on the toilet seat. The Comandante lectured him, "I know you will eventually tell me the truth. I have never failed. You need to tell me something now or I am going to use other methods to find out what I need to know."

Gasping for air, the prisoner contemplated his demise.

The Comandante turned to me, "Let's step outside."

The Comandante pulled out a Texas driver's license and showed it to me. "Here's the guy's address in El Paso. He has dual citizenship. I need Paul's informant to tell me more about this guy. Will you let me talk to the informant?"

The DEA prides itself on not disclosing the identity of its informants. It is rare for the DEA to permit another law enforcement agency to meet their informant especially a Mexican cop. In this unusual situation, the *federales* had seen Paul's informant. I did not want to hurt any feelings so I said, "I'll get back to you."

The Comandante concluded, "It's going to take some time to break this guy."

I tried to defend the victim, "If he didn't tell you the truth after that, I doubt if he has anything to say."

Mendoza opened up about his background, "I was a Special Forces officer in the Mexican military. I learned the best interrogation method to elicit information from our captives was to inject heroin into the wrist. Heroin can be used as a truth serum. The burn of the dragon in their veins makes them feel like I am their greatest friend. They tell you everything you need to know."

I just listened.

Mendoza continued, "Some would become addicted to the drug and become dependent on us. They would do whatever we wanted them to do."

"You turn them into junkies?"

"That is the consequence of not cooperating from the beginning. Now, I am going back inside and taking this interrogation to a higher level. Do you want to stick around?"

I had heard and seen enough. "I need to take care of some other business back in the office. Let me know if this man says anything."

The Comandante shook my hand and said, "Get me more information about this guy, and we'll show our leaders that our task force can be effective." The Comandante hurried back to the motel room.

I climbed into my GMC pickup and drove to the exit.

Before merging into traffic, I looked in my rearview mirror and watched a *federale* retrieve a cattle prod from a vehicle. The prisoner had another thing coming. It appeared the captors were going to practice various interrogation techniques with a live subject.

I drove off wondering if I should say something to my superiors. What good would it do? How would I describe the post-arrest interview in a legitimate DEA report? It would read the standard introductory, "The defendant declined to make any statements and requested legal counsel." Realistically, "The defendant failed to cooperate with his captors therefore traditional Mexican interrogation techniques were implemented."

"No, this interview would not be documented". While on the road, I answered my cell phone.

It was Paul, "Are you still in the Land of *Mañana*?"

"Yeah. I'm heading back to the office."

"Did the dealer have anything to say?"

"He said the *federales* violated his constitutional rights because they failed to Mirandize him."

Paul laughed, "I can only imagine what else will be violated."

"The guy was adamant that he didn't have any heroin. Mendoza felt otherwise and proceeded to use interrogation techniques not taught at the DEA Academy."

"I could tell the guy was bullshitting me. He was stalling during the negotiations and didn't talk like a dealer. As for getting any drugs from him, I think we're SOL, shit outa luck!"

"The Comandante requested additional background information on the wanna-be dealer."

"All we know is that he lives on the east side of El Paso. He has a wife and two daughters, attending UTEP. No prior drug arrests or criminal history. He has a regular job with decent pay. I'm not sure why this guy claimed to have heroin. He fucked up and wanted to play in the big leagues."

I said, "I'll tell the Comandante we don't have much. By the way, Mendoza wants to talk to your informant, *Gato*."

"Hell no!"

"I figured you would say that."

"Unless the man can come up with some drugs, this case is over!"

I agreed and ended the conversation, "As for the bad guy, he is out of our hands. I just hope they don't kill him."

Driving in Ciudad Juarez irritated me. Being a former state trooper was a curse as I observed traffic violations that most motorists never noticed. There were inconsiderate drivers not yielding for those who had the right of way, cutting off others by changing lanes constantly, or running red lights.

The Mexican drivers' mantra is, "He who does not cheat does not advance!"

I resisted the urge to pull out my pistol and shoot the assholes because I didn't have enough bullets! I found myself in one of several half-mile long traffic lines waiting to cross the Bridge of the Americas International port of entry, known as the free bridge.

Unlike the other major entries between Ciudad Juarez and El Paso, no user tolls were imposed at this bridge. The toll fees collected were intended for local projects, but true to form, the money never remained at the border. The funds were sent to Mexico City and never returned to those who needed it the most.

Waiting patiently, I ignored the traffic violators and snubbed the annoying street vendors. Avoiding eye contact, I looked in the distance to see a larger than usual dust devil whirling towards them. It snuck up on the pedestrians and vendors, raising skirts, blowing off hats, and knocking over displays.

I reached into the center console and extracted the Rolling Stones from my collection. The wicked lyrics of "Sympathy for the Devil" added to my contemplation. I thought to myself, are people inherently evil, or is it learned behavior? Is it easier to be cruel than it is to be kind? How does one derive gratification from inflicting physical harm on another human being?

I reached for the fan switch on the truck's air conditioner to increase its speed only to discover it was already on high. "Damn the heat!"

Chapter 17 – Black Bag Jobs

Calderon began taxing the patience of his agents by insisting on productivity. He was being pressured from DEA Headquarters to ensure his agents were productive in Ciudad Juarez. Daily communications via teletype and investigative reports regarding BTF developments were needed to justify the funding for the bilateral operations.

Calderon said, "You guys need to be in Juarez everyday. Get those assholes to start kicking down some doors. Headquarters believes we should be making drug seizures and arrests with all the money we're giving them."

Paul said, "Tell Headquarters to shove it up their ass! They can't expect inexperienced Mexican cops from another area of the country to be hell bent for leather. It's going to take some time to put any drugs on the table."

Paul and I respected our supervisor but we despised taking orders from those above him with little or no street experience. There is no real gain from micro-management as it only breeds resentment. Mindful of our subordinate positions, we tried to appease the suits only to keep the heat off of Calderon.

After several months of inactivity, Paul and I insisted on a face to face with the Comandante. A meeting was arranged at *El Matador* (The Matador) restaurant located just outside of downtown Ciudad Juarez.

We rode together in my OGV. As I was turning the dial on the radio, I found a station playing Mexican ballads with a western cowboy tone known as *rancheras*. I considered the tunes to be similar to the bouncy beat of polka music.

When the song finished, a commercial for a local supermarket came on the air. Mexican radio stations increase the volume for commercials, and commonly use an echoing voice. I remembered hearing the same type of commercials as a kid when my father would take me to Ciudad Juarez.

In those days, one could get a hair cut for fifty cents, a car trunk full of groceries for thirty dollars, and a full gas tank for less than ten dollars. Many El Paso families made the weekend excursions into Ciudad Juarez to take advantage of the peso devaluation. However, the increased violence in the border city changed all that.

In the mid-1990's, the city's reputation was tarnished with the hundreds of women being raped, tortured, and killed. In addition, the escalation of drug-related violence began claiming the lives of innocent bystanders not related to the illicit activities. Being at the wrong place at the wrong time was reason enough for American visitors to avoid the lawlessness.

I thought to myself, "This city used to be a tourist destination for anyone who visited El Paso. It was a must for shopping, attending the bullfights and greyhound races, or night clubbing in the downtown strip. Juarez would showcase their tourism by entertaining college football teams participating in the annual Sun Bowl. Now, it has become one of the most dangerous cities in the world. It is heartbreaking."

Paul and I waited almost forty minutes parked outside the restaurant. We did not like waiting in a car on the streets of Ciudad Juarez. We felt like sitting ducks. Although we had our sidearms at the ready, we felt uneasy in this part of the city.

Trying to calm his irritability, Paul opened the center console thumbing through the music collection. "Metallica, Queensryche, AC/DC!" he blurted. "Why do you listen to this devil music?"

I explained, "Heavy metal music is an aggressive, energetic form of expression. These musicians have more musical talent than any of those commercialized pop groups you listen to. Most music companies use the media to promote the no-talent, bubble gum groups instead of this top quality music."

"I can't understand what they say. It's a bunch of noise with lyrics about evil shit!"

"Although I love classic rock, I need to hear something new. That's why I listen to hard rock, too. It provides an adrenaline surge when I am working out or when I need motivation."

Paul pulled out Aerosmith's, "Toys in the Attic", saying, "Okay, I can handle this." He then sarcastically added, "Sal, I think you're running with the devil."

I laughed, "You can be witty for a *cabezon* (hard-headed person)."

At that moment, a green bullet-riddled Mercury Marquis sped around the street corner headed towards us.

I shifted my truck into drive. I revved the engine and was ready to press the accelerator. It took a second glance to realize that it was Comandante Mendoza.

The Marquis was parked and positioned at an angle in front of my truck. Comandante Mendoza and his right-hand man, Francisco Morales, exited the car wearing shorts and tank tops. Sweating and with messy hair, they nervously looked around. It was obvious that someone or something had flustered them.

The Comandante yelled, "*Pinche locos*! Someone was shooting at us as we were leaving the gymnasium!"

I replied, "Why did you come here and jeopardize our butts?"

"Don't worry. I've been clearing our trail for the last half hour. Nobody is following us. Let's go inside and eat."

I inspected the bullet holes in the hood. The pattern and size indicated a large caliber weapon, such as an AK-47. It is the weapon of choice for both drug traffickers and Mexican law enforcement agencies. I had many questions for the Comandante but knew they would never be answered truthfully.

Mendoza reached into the rear seat area of his vehicle and retrieved his own AK-47. He passed it to Morales who slung it over his shoulder.

We entered the restaurant and walked briskly to the rearmost table adjacent to the rear exit door. It looked like a game of musical chairs as each man wrestled to get the chair against the wall. As a cop, an escape plan was always aforethought. One could never be too cautious especially under these circumstances.

El Matador restaurant was considered the primary hangout following a Sunday afternoon at the bullfights. The interior had a bullfighter's motif with an extensive collection of autographed pictures of local and national *matadors* lining the walls.

The waiter brought the customary bowl of *tostadas*, *guacamole* and *pico de gallo*. He noticed the automatic weapon hanging on the customer's shoulder but did not say anything.

The Comandante requested a bucket of Dos Equis *cervezas* and a round of Jimador tequila shots. Quality alcohol has a way of calming the nerves while cheap alcohol causes a hangover. He also ordered the waiter to make a special *habanero* sauce for his guests.

Mendoza claimed, "Tourists eat salsa while real men eat *chile* (spicy condiment)." *Chile* can put hair on your chest and it has a medicinal value. How many Mexicans do you know with ulcers?" The Comandante was trying to divert us from the real issue at hand, an assassination attempt on his life.

Paul and I forced a smile.

I played along, "The test of a good *chile* is when one develops a sweaty forehead and a runny nose."

Morales joined in on the detraction, "What kind of gun do you have in that bag?" He was referring to the leather pouches lying on the table, in front of the DEA agents.

Some American police officers carried their cell phone, wallet, badge and, most importantly, handgun in a fanny pack. It was a convenient apparatus to keep essential items organized.

I usually wore my fanny pack around my waste. On this occasion, I placed the black leather pouch on the table. The gun needed to be easily accessible. It would be better to shoot from above the table than to shoot from the hip.

"Glock 9mm," I answered.

Morales shot back, "Those guns are made of plastic. You can't hit anyone on the head without breaking the handle! Let me show you the type of weapon the DEA needs to issue to its agents." He reached back and caressed the AK-47, known as a *cuerno de chivo* (horn of a goat) because of the curved-shaped magazine.

"Look at the solid wooden butt. It is guaranteed to send a clear message to its target."

I defended my agency, "The advantage of carrying a government-issued pistol is uniformity. It could be a matter of life or death during the chaos of a gun battle. Any agent can pick up a fellow agents pistol and use it without worry. Because of their reliability, our agents favor them."

It was a practical defense in comparison to the *federale*'s opinion. I knew the government-issued Glock 17 pistol and the Colt 9mm submachine gun would not fair well against the firepower of an AK-47 assault rifle.

The waiter returned with an ice bucket containing eight beer bottles. He uncapped four and passed them out.

Raising our beverages, in unison we said, "*Salud!*" After a couple of large gulps and tequila shots, the tension subsided.

I asked, "Do you have any idea who would have shot at you?"

"No. Someone is aware of our presence on their turf. This was their way of welcoming us. You don't need to worry about this incident. We will find out who was responsible and resolve this issue."

The Mexicans excused themselves to the restroom to freshen up.

I knew there was more to the story than Mendoza was telling. I asked Paul, "What do you think?"

"They haven't been here long enough to make any enemies. According to them, they have not made any arrests or drug seizures to piss off the cartel."

I responded, "I hate to think they crossed the line with the local cops. It could complicate things."

Mendoza and Morales returned to the table. They sat down and raised their second beer bottle. "Here's to cheating death!"

I shifted the conversation to the reason for calling the meeting. There were two objectives that needed immediate attention by the BTF.

I had read many investigative reports about the Amado Carrillo-Fuentes drug cartel. Though there were many active DEA investigations, few significant arrests had been made. Members of the drug organization were out of reach from U.S. authorities as Mexico was their safe haven.

Not wanting to insult the Comandante's intelligence, I began, "As you know, Carrillo-Fuentes heads a business that earns a profit of $10 billion annually. He is known as *El Señor de los Cielos*, The Lord of the Skies, because he moves multi-ton loads of cocaine from Colombia into Mexico in 727 airplanes."

Mendoza responded, "Everyone knows the capabilities of Amado."

I continued, "When he loses a load of drugs to law enforcement, everyone associated with the cargo is beaten or killed just to make sure he punishes the snitch."

Mendoza added, "Amado sends a message to those suspected of informing on his organization. Sometimes, a finger is cut off and put into the mouth of the victim. Or, a body will be found with its throat slashed and the tongue pulled through the opening that is known as the Columbian necktie."

I said, "We know he barricades himself behind family members and only a few confidants. U.S. law enforcement agencies have found it difficult to get close to him. Bottom line, since we are in the midst of Amado's territory, he will be our priority. We need to identify his people working in Juarez."

The Comandante responded, "You are asking me to be a dragon slayer. You want the head of the beast with only seven men on my team!"

"We will provide additional manpower when necessary. Just like we plan to next week."

"What is happening next week?"

"There's an upcoming wedding for a relative of Carrillo-Fuentes here in Juarez. Amado is expected to attend."

"How do you know Amado will be at the wedding?"

"We have an informant who will be here in a couple of days. He is one of the special guests invited to the private ceremony to be held at the church in *El Campestre*." The majority of the city's populace lives in slum-like housing settlements with unpaved dirt streets. *El Campestre* consists of large, well-landscaped homes with cobblestone streets. The exclusive residential section of town has a private golf course and a Catholic Church reserved for the elite.

Looking at the disbelief on Mendoza's face, I confided, "Just like you, I question Amado being seen in a public place. I am one who doesn't believe anything I hear, and only believe half of what I see." After a pause, I offered, "We have to begin somewhere."

Mendoza asked, "Was there anything else you want me to do?"

"We received orders from Washington to set up surveillance on a medical office not far from here. There is a hot telephone number in Colombia that is calling someone at this location. We need to tap the telephone line and set up a pole camera to see who is coming and going." I described a gray imitation transformer usually found at the top of utility poles. The signal from the concealed video camera would be transmitted to a portable receiver with recording capabilities.

The Comandante nodded and said, "I will have your pole camera set up, and the telephone lines tapped tomorrow. My men will watch the business tonight to see if anyone is there at night."

"Can we take it one step further and install hidden microphones inside the business?"

The Comandante said, "I will need your people to do that."

I knew Vince was itching to do a 'black bag job'. Vince would pick the lock and place microphones inside. If there were going to be any conversations in this place, the BTF was going to know about them. I handed the Comandante a slip of paper with the business' address and telephone number.

Sarcastically, Mendoza asked, "Anything else?"

Paul and I grinned.

After consuming the fourteen ounce ribeye steaks, numerous *cervezas*, and a cognac for dessert, the agents prepared to go their own ways. Everyone rose from the table to exchange bro hugs.

Mendoza walked to the restroom. The others headed for the exit.

I couldn't hold back the beer and didn't want to wait until I reached El Paso. I turned and walked towards the restroom. I walked in on Mendoza who was scooping out a bump (small amount) of cocaine from a small, plastic 35mm film canister.

Mendoza continued to snort the white substance and reached for another mound with his long pinky nail. "Here, try some."

I cordially declined. "I can't do that. The DEA gives us random piss tests."

"Don't worry. It doesn't stay in your blood system very long."

"Maybe another time."

He didn't let it go to waste. Mendoza snorted the second bump into his other nostril.

Both of us would overlook the incident, for now. I had more important things to focus on. The BTF was being called on by DEA Headquarters and needed to prove its validity.

On the drive back, Paul and I were wondering if our efforts to encourage the *federales* was worth putting our lives on the line crossing into Juarez. I said, "Every time I cross into Juarez, I feel the tension here. There is a sense of uneasiness and insecurity. When I return to American soil, I feel a sense of relief every time I cross the bridge. I mean, I actually let out a sigh and feel like I can breathe easier."

Paul said, "Yeah, I feel safer, too. It's as if we have more control of our surroundings."

The next evening, Vince and I drove in a DEA surveillance van containing audio and visual recording equipment. The Comandante met us at the Mexican port of entry on the free bridge. It was a precautionary measure in the event an overzealous Mexican customs inspector discovered the electronic surveillance equipment with DEA serial numbers.

We traveled to the medical office. Waiting was a technician from the Mexican telephone company named *Telefonos de Mexico*, or Tel-Mex. The Comandante bribed him for his unofficial services. The technician opened a switchboard box down the street and crossed a few wires. Hardline conversations from the medical office would be monitored at the BTF listening post.

Vince asked me to translate, "Comandante, do you need any form of judicial authorization for the wiretaps? In the U.S., we need a judge's approval for any electronic surveillance."

Defiantly, Mendoza responded, "I've never needed permission, so why start now."

Vince looked at me and said, "It was about time you let me play in your reindeer games. Just because I don't speak Spanish doesn't mean I can't work with you."

"Don't take it personally. In fact, you and several other DEA agents will be needed for the upcoming wedding at *El Campestre.*"

Vince added, "I need to work on my Spanish. The only words I've learned are the bad words you've taught me. Last week you called me 'cool arrow' realizing you were surreptitiously calling me an asshole. I'll catch on *cabron*!"

I said, "The only way to learn a second language is to practice as much as possible. Not just by listening but actually speaking it."

Vince said, "Let's see if you can understand me. *Yo no hablo español, mojado* (I don't speak Spanish, wetback)!"

I laughed, "*Perfecto.*"

I continued, "Seriously, if the shit hits the fan during this operation, your main objective is to get back to El Paso, ASAP! While you're running for the border, use the star on the mountain as your guide." I was referring to the large El Paso Star illuminated nightly by the local electric company on the southern face of the Franklin Mountains. It can be seen up miles away and is clearly visible from any section in Ciudad Juarez.

I noticed Vince's Glock protruding from under his belt and asked, sarcastically, "Are you planning to conceal your gun?"

Vince shot back, "No. I'm going to walk down these streets of Juarez carrying it where the 'bad guys' can see it so they can shoot me full of holes. Of course I'm going to conceal it, *culero!*"

At 10 p.m., the eight-room business complex was empty. The Tel-Mex utility truck raised the pole camera and the technician completed the task within an hour. Simultaneously, Vince had surreptitiously entered the targeted office. Microphones were installed in the foam ceiling tiles.

Earlier in the day, Mendoza had one of his men act as a businessman and rented a vacant office space at the end of the complex. The rented suite would contain the BTF voice-activated recording equipment. The audiocassettes would be retrieved in the middle of the night by the *federales.* To avoid detection, nobody in the BTF was to enter it during daylight hours.

By midnight, the mission was accomplished.

For the next several days, me, Vince, and a *federale* spent most of our time inside the DEA surveillance van. We listened to insignificant conversations and videotaped people that did not look like they were seeking medical attention. I knew the office was a front for something yet unknown.

Then a telephone call came from someone in Cali, Colombia. There were no formalities between the two men. Only an 18-letter cryptic message was exchanged. The alpha code resembled a cryptoquip game found next to crossword puzzles in many newspapers. The caller recited each letter clearly and distinctly, giving the receiver time to write it down correctly.

The next morning, I forwarded the cryptic code to the DEA Headquarters Intelligence Analysts. I never got a response. I later found out the message was passed on to the CIA. Their analysts couldn't figure it out either. Nobody was able to decipher the message. Only the two men on each end of the telephone line understood what it meant.

I learned while working in a world of deception that there were aspirations leading nowhere. Even the obvious was not as it seemed. I tried to adapt to my limited role but it got very frustrating. I discovered not refraining from the inherent deceitfulness would have devastating consequences in my future.

Chapter 18 – Massacre Of The DEA Agents

There was a nervousness in the El Paso DEA office. The extraordinary opportunity of getting our hands on the "Lord of the Skies" was just too good to be true. Fueling the tension was wondering what kind of resistance we would encounter in the chapel.

The designed military-style operation required superior firepower and additional manpower. Comandante Mendoza and the BTF would have their wish granted.

Three days prior to the scheduled wedding, a PGR Lear Jet landed at the El Paso International Airport. The airplane was instructed to land in El Paso so as to avoid detection by informants working for the drug cartels at the Ciudad Juarez airport.

A DEA Supervisor and five Special Agents were there to welcome the visitors. A very irate U.S. Customs Service inspector was also there.

The Associate Director of the PGR, a Comandante, and fifteen handpicked agents exited the plane. The U.S. Customs inspector examined each of their newly-printed passports.

The unannounced arrival was nothing compared to the unauthorized importation of AK-47 assault rifles and .45 caliber automatic pistols. The inspector frantically called his supervisor and said the Mexican airplane yielded enough weapons and ammunition to start a small war.

The shit rolled uphill as one U.S. Customs supervisor called another superior until it reached their headquarters. Then they called DEA supervisors to complain about the failure of notification and inconsideration. It took three hours before the U.S. Customs Service permitted the PGR personnel and the weapons to enter American soil. The weapons would be secured in the DEA office until the day of the operation in Ciudad Juarez.

From the inception of this Top Secret operation, the PGR took precautions to prevent any leak of information that could compromise the plans. Without prior notification, the selected *federales* were ordered to board the PGR Lear Jet outside a Mexico City airstrip and wait to be briefed about their mission while in the air.

Their personal cell phones were taken away and told not to make any telephone calls during this mission. In that regard, the PGR and the DEA weren't looking so much for elite agents as much as they wanted loyal ones.

The *federales* were driven in two transport vans and housed in isolated barracks at the Biggs Airfield military base in El Paso.

Vince and I were instructed to take the *federales* to dinner and allow them to purchase hygiene products. The gestures of appreciation were for their cooperation, as well as a way to keep an eye on them. I was authorized to spend two thousand dollars of DEA funds. Any additional expenses would be covered with a government credit card.

Once they found their designated bunks, I asked the agents where they wanted to go. In chorus, they responded Walmart. They wanted to buy American products. Each *federale* was provided with fifty dollars, compliments of *Tio Sam* (Uncle Sam).

The *federales* were excited to be in the U.S. They begged to be driven around to see more of the American city. They didn't want to spend their first night confined in the dismal military barracks. I was empathetic to their desires. So, the two-vehicle caravan changed course to the safer side of El Paso, that is, the Westside.

After dinner at a Golden Coral restaurant, we ventured to a bar called Papa's Night Club. A place frequented by many of El Paso's finest young women. Vince and I were familiar with the layout of the establishment. It was an open venue where we could keep an eye on all the *federales*.

Since we had a late start, we shut the place down. I footed the eight hundred dollar drink tab with the allotted U.S. tax dollars. No receipt was required for the expenditure. I liked it that way.

Within the PGR group was one very attractive female *federale* whose company Vince enjoyed. Although the pair spoke little of each other's language, the language of lust was universal that evening.

I noticed that the couple danced casually, but at one point disappeared for almost an hour. After returning, I leered at Vince and asked, "Smile if you got any."

Flustered, Vince responded, "I don't kiss and tell."

I retorted. "She's not your type because she is too old for you. You like girls in their teens…tenteen, eleventeen, twelveteen."

Vince laughed, "You're sick!"

It was Saturday afternoon. The wedding ceremony was scheduled for 7 p.m. Calderon and the PGR Associate Director did not want to leave any gaps in the tactical design. This was anything but a straightforward, plain vanilla operation. Their priority was ensuring the safety of their agents with the anticipated firefight.

The plan assumed the DEA and PGR agents would raid the church and arrest Amado Carrillo-Fuentes. We expected resistance and chaos. Each DEA agent and *federale* was given a bright, yellow piece of cloth to wrap around his left bicep. This would help with recognition to prevent friendly fire during the gun battle.

Instructions were clear. If anyone in the church showed anything resembling a weapon, they would be shot without hesitation! We knew to expect the worst but hope for the best.

Verbal communication was of the essence between the U.S. agents and the *federales*. Vince Sellers, Jake Davis, and Yvette Gonzalez would join the operation. Although Davis did not speak Spanish, he was a team player and had no qualms participating.

It was a tough decision for Calderon to include Yvette in this dangerous engagement. Although she was the only other Spanish speaker in the office, Calderon hadn't included her working with any previous BTF operations. Most assumed he paid deference to her role as a new mother. Others knew it was because she was a woman.

Six DEA cars and four PGR cars were scattered throughout *El Campestre* area. Each vehicle was occupied by one DEA agent and at least two *federales*. Calderon drove the PGR Associate Director and a Comandante who came with his unit from Mexico City. Most of the surveillance units set up in the *Soriana* Supermarket parking lot located near the main entrance to *El Campestre*. The weekend shoppers would provide plenty of pedestrian and vehicular traffic to conceal the police presence.

The wedding party and their guests began arriving. Paul Rodriguez' informant was in attendance. He was instructed to walk outside, call Paul on his cell phone, and specify the seating location of Carrillo-Fuentes. The anticipation grew by the minute expecting the arrest of the most notorious drug trafficker in Mexico.

The DEA and the PGR agents tried remaining calm by engaging in small talk. The conversations were brief, and the usual joking around was obsolete. There was more silence than conversation.

Then, a loud "Wham!" broke the silence. There was a slamming sound on the windshield of my OGV. Instinctively, I reached for my Colt submachine gun. Looking out the driver's side window, I found myself looking into the muzzle of an AK-47.

A Mexican teenage boy with a twitchy finger on the trigger screamed for me to get out of the car.

The PGR agent seated next to me said, "Don't do it. He has the drop on all of us."

I released the grip on my submachine gun and slowly raised both hands. Thoughts raced in my head. Is this a carjacking? A robbery? Or, was this an orchestrated setup for a mass killing of DEA agents? Anti-American sympathizers and Carrillo-Fuentes' supporters would brag about this day forever!

I looked to where Calderon and the PGR Associate Director were parked. Gun-toting men had surrounded their vehicle, as were the other DEA vehicles in this covert operation. All the DEA agents had their hands in the air, staring down the barrel of automatic rifles.

There was chaos throughout the supermarket parking lot. Shoppers were running wildly, dropping their grocery bags, grabbing their children, and looking for cover.

My PGR comrades looked at each other as to contemplate who was in the best position to reach for their weapon. The heroic effort would mean some would get shot while the others had a slim chance of surviving the incoming fully-automatic gunfire.

The kid screamed, "Get out, now!"

I yelled at the kid, "*Calmate* (Calm down)!"

The PGR agent sitting next to me whispered, "Get out of the car. Distract him and I'll shoot him from here."

I realized getting out of the vehicle would be the only chance of survival for at least one of us. It seemed like an eternity. I stalled wondering what the other DEA agents were planning to do to get out of this dilemma. In the meantime, my right hand had slid between the driver's seat and the center console. I had a firm grip on my Colt Submachine gun with the finger on the trigger. Instinctively, I was determined not to die without a fight.

Before any foolish act could take place, a pickup screeched to a stop in front of my OGV. The driver yelled at the young gunman to get into the truck. The boy lowered the automatic rifle and jumped into the bed of the pickup. The truck sped away.

I turned to Calderon's location and saw two Chevrolet Suburbans converge on his vehicle. I grabbed the DEA radio and said, "El Paso 106 to 101!" The radio call numbers were assigned to each agent based on their group assignment and seniority in the El Paso DEA. Group One had the 100 series with Calderon being the number one man in the group at 101.

There was no response from Calderon. I shifted my OGV into drive and sped towards his location. He responded on the DEA radio, "All units, do not engage! Each agent, let me know you are okay, in numerical sequence!"

Paul began, "102 is okay." Then Gonzalez said, "103 is fine." All the DEA agents used their radio call number and said they were okay.

Calderon said, "These are Plaza Agents. They were tipped off about our presence. It looks like this operation has been compromised."

The local federal police in Ciudad Juarez, referred to as Plaza Agents, knew exactly where each DEA agent was positioned. Someone tipped off the Plaza Comandante that the *gringos* were in his city and planning on being wedding crashers.

I could see a furious PGR Associate Director standing outside of Calderon's vehicle. He had his finger in the face of the Plaza Comandante and was scolding him. After thirty minutes, the PGR Associate Director ordered the Plaza Comandante and all his agents to report to the local PGR office immediately. Each *federale* had some critical questions to answer.

The DEA entourage was invited to the roundup after Calderon said he was very interested to know how the operation was exposed. We anticipated witnessing what few Americans have ever seen.

The PGR office was located in a residential area in the southern part of Ciudad Juarez. The one story, six-bedroom compound had been seized in the 1980's from a local drug trafficker and converted into the local federal police base of operations. The Mexican cops, like us, took advantage of the fruits of a crime.

The DEA agents were reluctant to take their vehicles inside the facility. There was a sense of vulnerability when enclosed in an unfamiliar setting. We parked our OGV's on the street outside the front entrance.

Calderon, Paul, and I decided to join the Associate Director and his agents inside the dwelling. Each Plaza agent was interviewed based on rank, from senior to junior. Initially, questions were directed to the divulgence of today's operation. The inquiry then switched to a systematic form of interrogation regarding their affiliation with the Juarez Cartel.

The Associate Director was certain the Plaza agents were on Carrillo-Fuentes' payroll. And if it required cleaning house, then it would begin tonight with him taking the first steps. Sterilizing the dark corners of the entire PGR agency would require a thorough reformation of personnel. A good place to start would be with the *federales* stationed in Ciudad Juarez.

Standing high and mighty next to the interrogation chair, Comandante Mendoza played with a pair of handcuffs. He twirled them around his forefinger and kept swiveling the ends. He knew the sound of the metal teeth grinding intimidated anyone being held against their will.

The Associate Director's men and Mendoza had no intention of employing the 'good cop, bad cop' interview tactic with their captives. It wouldn't work. So they resorted to the 'bad cop, bad cop' interrogation technique. They got in their face and proceeded to beat them to a pulp.

The Plaza agents claimed they had been tipped off by anonymous callers as to suspicious vehicles in *El Campestre* area and responded as any legitimate cop would. The problem with their story was that this type of call would normally be handled by the municipal police.

I studied the faces of the assembled PGR agents to see if there was any remorse or regret. I saw none. Each agent knew if he spoke of Carrillo-Fuentes, he would be killed along with his family. Their denials only brought them more physical affliction.

I remained inside the building to witness a few of the interrogations.

After an hour, I witnessed enough of the cruelty and decided to join Yvette, Vince, and Davis. They waited outside patiently by their OGV's.

Throughout the night, many dark-colored Chevrolet Suburbans sped into the enclosed compound. None were seen leaving. As they arrived, the occupants displayed apprehensive, frightened faces. They probaby knew what was in store for them.

Occupants in one particular vehicle caught my attention. It was a minivan driven by a woman with curlers in her hair. A man, likely her husband, was observed in the passenger seat hurriedly tucking in his button-up shirt and combing his hair. I imagined the couple spending a quiet night at their home before being disturbed and ordered to report to the office.

The minivan did not enter the compound. The woman stopped by the front entrance. The man hurriedly kissed his wife on the cheek and ran towards the front door of the building. The woman sped away as she burst into tears.

It had been a long day for us but it would be a longer night for those on the hot seat. The beatings continued well into the early morning.

Hunger and thirst set in for the DEA agents waiting outside. A young Mexican boy brought a bucket filled with glass bottles of Fanta sodas submerged in ice water. Each agent grabbed a bottle and chugged it. The carbonation quenched the cotton mouths caused by the harrowing day.

Knowing he was going to sell another batch of sodas shortly, the boy watched intently at what looked like a chugging contest. He not only sold all his sodas, he talked the agents into buying *gorditas* that his mother had prepared in the family kitchen.

The agents were skeptical of eating the unknown. But the boy, wiser than his years, dared them, "Aren't you *gringos* tougher than these *federales*? They always eat my food and never get sick!"

Accepting the challenge, the hungry DEA agents ate the proffered *gorditas*. It would take several hours for the agents to feel the consequences, commonly known as Montezuma's revenge.

Aware of their surroundings, the agents engaged in discussion related to Mexican socio-economic factors. They were in a section of the city that most Americans never see. Local tourism officials showcase fountains, statues, and flowers along main streets. It was not to beautify the city, but to appease foreign visitors. It was a façade that hid the truth about the plight of the majority.

The monumental economic gap between the rich and poor is growing wider. The rich get richer and say, "Fuck the Poor!" The poor are beset by high unemployment rates, low wages, no retirement benefits, and forced child labor.

The young boy selling sodas was a prime example of a difficult life that forced a child to mature before his time. Poverty is one thing, but inequality is another.

Narcodemocracy is a term used to describe democratic nations whose economic, political, and social situations have been influenced by the money and power of drug trafficking organizations. Ciudad Juarez was a microcosm of the national crisis.

Most citizens are destitute and out of work. They believe they have little or nothing to lose by engaging in criminal activity. While that may be no excuse to work afoul of the law, it does explain their complete sense of hopelessness.

Jake Davis asked an insightful question, "Why can't the PGR take initiative and arrest Mexican cartel members without our assistance?"

I responded, "It depends how badly they want to risk their lives and fear the repercussions. They don't want to piss of the cartels so they need someone else to take the blame. If they really wanted to arrest cartel members, they call us for assistance and say it was the *gringos* who were responsible for the arrests."

"You mean to tell me that they don't want to arrest cartel members in their country because of the fear of retaliation?"

"Yup. The PGR leaders know they would be the first on the cartel hit list. For the DEA, our effectiveness in Mexico depends on the PGR weighing the repercussions of a significant arrest versus the purpose of their existence as a law enforcement agency."

Conversation among the DEA agents shifted to the issue of immigration. Constant migration from Mexico to the U.S. results in some of the more resourceful citizens forsaking their homeland for better opportunities. Unfortunately, these are the same people who, if they stayed home, could spearhead much of the needed reform within Mexico.

Vince said, "Mexicans need to stop crossing into the U.S. and stay here. They need to fix their own country instead of running away!"

I responded, "If you were in their shoes you would be doing the same thing. Desperation would lead you to risk going anywhere for an opportunity to put food in your mouth."

"We can't feed and house all these people. We need to stop letting them into our country."

"Europeans, Chinese, Africans and other people are also being smuggled into the U.S. Not just brown people! The politicians and media are obsessed with the southern border.

"We already have too many people in our country that aren't welcome. At least deport the ugly ones back to their homeland."

Yvette got upset and said, "Just because they aren't kissing cousins and banging their sisters like your relatives doesn't mean they are inferior. Ya'll White people look the same to me, *cabron*!"

We all laughed. Then I ended the conversation, "Well then you'd better learn how to pick your own fruit and vegetables, learn to cook at your favorite restaurants, clean your own home, and landscape your neighborhood."

It was nearly 3 a.m., when Calderon walked outside and said to his agents, "The Associate Director just fired the local PGR Comandante and every agent assigned to this Plaza. Come Monday, this office will be under new command. None of them admitted to being on Carrillo-Fuentes' payroll because they knew it would mean their death sentence."

Paul said, "Shit, some were almost killed tonight! The Associate Director's men put on a hell of a show for us."

Calderon said, "Let's get back to El Paso. Half of the elite PGR team will return with us while the rest will remain in Ciudad Juarez to coordinate the transition of power." Calderon led the BTF caravan to the Bridge of the Americas port of entry.

At this hour, there was no vehicular traffic on the international bridge. A look of bewilderment could be seen on the face of the U.S. Customs inspector as he saw six vehicles in tandem approaching him.

Calderon said, "I am a DEA supervisor from the El Paso Office. We are returning home after conducting an operation in Juarez. The cars behind me are occupied with my agents and Mexican police officers that assisted in the operation."

The inspector asked more questions about the Mexican agents and their official business in the U.S.

Calderon respectfully provided a not too detailed synopsis of the operation. The joint operation was Top Secret and on a 'need-to-know' basis.

The befuddled inspector did not want to hear that. It was his inspection line and was insulted by the secrecy. He directed the entire convoy to a secondary inspection area.

A U.S. Customs supervisor was summoned. He approached the lead vehicle. Calderon briefed the man, but that wasn't enough. The supervisor refused to let anyone enter the U.S. until each DEA and PGR agent was fully identified. The supervisor insisted the weapons, including those belonging to the DEA, be seized and criminal charges considered.

Calderon was furious that a fellow law enforcement agency would make such threats. He told us to remain in our vehicles. Calderon went inside the supervisor's office to explain his actions on the telephone to someone higher in the U.S. Customs chain of command.

U.S. Customs officials were upset that they were left out of the loop again. This was the second time that the DEA insulted them by failing to advise them of an international operation in their area of responsibility.

Calderon insisted there was no devious intent by the DEA. He explained that both faux pas were a result of unexpected turn of events.

This situation was an example of the failure of intra-agency communication. Federal, state, and local agencies are guilty of not encouraging joint investigations and not sharing gathered intelligence with each other. Much of the problem can be blamed on bureaucratic jealousy, turf wars, and animosities.

The inspector ordered Calderon to open the trunk of his OGV. He reluctantly obliged.

However, Calderon lost his temper when the border inspector asked him to remove the spare tire so that a thorough inspection could be conducted. Calderon yelled, "I opened the trunk for you. If you want to see what's under the spare tire, you take the fucking thing out yourself!"

The inspector replied, "You don't need to use that language with me. I could seize your car if you don't cooperate."

"You want the car? Here are the fucking keys!" He held them out to the inspector. "I'll take a cab!"

Watching their boss lose his cool, the DEA agents wanted to laugh, but held back so as not to agitate the already tense situation.

It took two hours before cooler heads prevailed. The caravan of DEA and Mexican agents was finally released and permitted to enter American soil.

Several days later, I learned that the PGR elite team took over the Ciudad Juarez Plaza office. It would be a difficult yet cyclical process of assigning trustworthy *federales* to maintain the hottest spot on the border.

As for the recently replaced Plaza Agents, no criminal charges were filed against them. In the Mexican legal system, it was easier to terminate cops from their position than to pursue criminal charges.

One last event occurred regarding this Top Secret operation. All activity by suspects at the medical office ceased. Nobody ever showed up again after the mysterious 18-letter cryptic message was relayed. We decided to terminate the surveillance.

Based on the timing of our operation, I could only assume that the cryptic message was a warning to Carrillo-Fuentes about our plans to arrest him. The Colombian and Mexican cartels utilized a highly sophisticated system of electronic eavesdropping equipment that kept them one step ahead of American law enforcement.

Chapter 19 – Death Is A Part Of Life

I tried to balance my role as a domestic and international agent. Administrative reports were overdue and my domestic informants were feeling neglected. Few, if any, DEA agents had ever been put in my position. Yet, nobody heard any crying or complaining coming from me. I rose to the challenge and did more than what I was told to do.

I continued pursuing the ambitious and difficult task of recruiting Mexican informants who actually collaborated with upper-level members of the Juarez Cartel. Two informants, named Roberto and Jaime, were in a position to identify some key members. The men were instructed to aggressively gather fresh intelligence on the inner workings of the Carrillo-Fuentes organization. For months, the informants tried penetrating the inner circle of the cartel.

Tragically, they got too close to the fire and were burned.

Roberto was a childhood friend of Carrillo-Fuentes. He provided me with historical information about the drug trafficker's family members. He worked for me about a year before his body was found in an abandoned vehicle on a desolate highway outside of Ciudad Juarez. He was stabbed five times in the chest after enduring extensive torture. Mexican law enforcement authorities had no leads as to his killers.

Jaime was a young, energetic informant who desired to be involved in the espionage of the drug world. He claimed to have a sister dating a Lieutenant in the Juarez Cartel. For six months, he could only provide me with vague information. I pushed him to corroborate his story. We decided to record the Lieutenant utilizing a mini-cassette recorder. The device was small enough to hide in Jaime's shirt pocket.

The following morning, *El Diario* newspaper showed a graphic photo of Jaime lying in a pool of blood in an empty dirt lot. His hands were tied behind his back and he had been shot in the back of the head. I noticed the clothing. It was the same clothes Jaime was wearing the day before when we met in the DEA office.

I wondered, "Did the lieutenant discover the recorder? Did the informant ask too many questions? Was the ill-fated meeting a tactical error based on our desperation?" I felt responsible.

Relationships between a DEA agent and their informants must be limited to business only. Sometimes personal issues were discussed, and one couldn't help being empathetic. On a few occasions, I became acquainted with the immediate family members of my contracted employees. When something tragic happened to my informants, I felt the sorrow of their relatives. Several of my informants were killed because of their noble efforts. I couldn't help but feel guilty and accountable.

As a State Trooper, I had seen countless traffic fatalities. I asked myself questions of morality, such as, "What kind of person was he? Who loved him? How many children did he leave behind?"

To dismiss these thoughts, I would focus on my investigative duties of securing the scene of the accident and reconstructing the events that lead to the fatal accident. This was the only way of dealing with the death of a stranger. Seeing the mutilated bodies increased my tolerance for death. Unfortunately, I would remember each dead body I saw for the rest of my life.

Especially the fourteen year-old boy struck by a car. One evening, the boy was home watching television with his parents. They were interrupted by a knock on the front door. Three neighborhood boys invited him to get an ice cream from a local convenience store. His parents encouraged their son to spend more time with his friends.

Reluctantly, the kid put on his sneakers and joined his older buddies.

All the boys made it across the unlit country road safely except for the youngest of the bunch. The kid must have not tied his shoes properly and tripped on his laces.

The driver of the car never saw him enter his path. At forty miles per hour, the front of the sedan slammed into the young, frail body.

Everyone in the neighborhood heard the screaming. They came out of their homes to see the horrific scene. They cried aloud and helplessly watched one of their own children suffering on the asphalt as paramedics frantically tried to keep him alive.

I arrived at the scene of the accident in time to feel the child's last breath. It broke my heart to see this little boy die in front of me.

As part of my follow-up investigation, I needed to confirm the cause of death. I traveled to the El Paso morgue to see the lifeless body embalmed on the metal table. The image still haunts me today.

Death was a part of my profession as a State Trooper and it was certainly a part of the violent illicit drug trade I was in as a DEA agent. I tried to be philosophical when I witnessed death. It was a matter-of-fact aspect and I refused to concede to sadness. "I'm a cop!" I thought. "I must invalidate the mortality and move on!"

It was not a requirement for the DEA to provide restitution to the next of kin of a Confidential Informant. However, I believed it was the least I could do. Roberto's wife was given a consolation check of $30,000. Graciously accepting the gift, she said the money would be used for their three children's education.

Jaime's death came when operational funds in the El Paso office were low. DEA headquarters made no effort to help with the cause. I squeezed out $7,000 from a depleted informant fund. I was embarrassed of the paltry sum. Jaime's sister humbly accepted the check. We conceded there was no amount of money to compensate for the death of a loved one.

Relentless, I continued to pursue any investigative leads into the Carrillo-Fuentes drug trafficking organization. I believed someone or something would knock this cold-hearted bastard off his throne. One such opportunity fell into our hands.

An informant told DEA agents in El Paso, that a Colombian named Eduardo Flores, head of the northern transportation cell of the Carrillo-Fuentes organization, was due to arrive in Ciudad Juarez. Flores desired to renew his passport so he could enter the U.S. whenever he felt like it. Flores would need to take care of this by walking into the Immigration and Naturalization Service (INS) office in downtown El Paso.

The informant, also Colombian, claimed Flores kept many buffers between himself and the drug shipments. Flores was confident that U.S. authorities could not arrest him without any probable cause. The DEA and FBI felt otherwise.

As the word spread through the DEA channels of Flores' impending visit, countless inquiries from Headquarters and Intelligence Analysts were directed at the El Paso DEA office. All wanted to know the operational plan to detain Flores.

The DEA wanted to make Flores an offer he couldn't refuse – immunity from prosecution and a hefty payday for his cooperation. He would be a wealth of information regarding the Colombian and Mexican drug trafficking connections.

Unassumingly, Flores walked over the Santa Fe Bridge international bridge into El Paso. Under pressure from various agency heads, INS agents detained him.

Somehow, the FBI got their hands on him first. The tactless feebs were out of touch with reality and threatened Flores with prison. It ruined any opportunity to obtain his cooperation. By the time the DEA agents were permitted to interview him, Flores refused to talk to the *gringos*.

Flores remained in custody for several days as U.S. law enforcement agencies scrambled to produce relevant documentation to indict him. Numerous intelligence reports with circumstantial evidence implicated Flores in some nefarious activities. However, a federal judge felt otherwise and ordered his release from U.S. custody due to lack of sufficient evidence.

The FBI and DEA were viewed as impotent as the high-level drug trafficker slipped out of their grasp and would be permitted to return to his nefarious lifestyle.

I heard several federal agents express their outrage. One agent said, "If I had a sniper rifle, I'd shoot the son of a bitch as soon as he crossed the border." Another asked me, "Can't your *federale* friends do something about this? They would know how to take care of him."

I did not respond.

Only a few people knew when Flores was going to be released from U.S. custody. Escorted by U.S. officials, Flores and his Mexican attorney were led across the Paso Del Norte International Bridge. Flores and his attorney crossed into Ciudad Juarez and were never seen again.

I sat pensively at my desk, losing myself in the ghoulish lyrics of Jim Morrison. The eerie sounds of "The Doors" paralleled my psyche. Although I was disappointed with the weak U.S. judicial system, I was delighted with "The End".

Eyewitness accounts claimed the two men were met by PGR agents as they entered Ciudad Juarez. They were forced into a dark Suburban and driven away. They vanished.

Flores' wife initiated a public campaign in Ciudad Juarez to pursue and identify the ones responsible for her husband's disappearance. Allegations of police corruption and a need for political change were raised during organized protests. All eyes were on the most obvious target, the local police.

In the drug trafficking world, anyone from a Colombian or Mexican cartel who was detained for any significant amount of time by American cops, and then released, did not live long. The punishment was administered for being reckless and the likelihood of snitching to their captors. Death outweighed faith and loyalty.

No one was ever held culpable for the kidnappings of Flores and his attorney. I later learned that the men had been thrown into barrels of acid so their bodies could never be found.

The following Friday, I arranged a meeting with Comandante Mendoza. DEA Headquarters ordered me to place two telephone numbers on the priority list of wiretaps in Ciudad Juarez. I crossed into Ciudad Juarez around 6 p.m. Upon my arrival at the trendy Chihuahua Charlie's Restaurant, I walked into the VIP section. Each of the well-dressed *federales* was paired with a young, attractive woman. The Comandante gave me a firm embrace and insisted I join the party.

As I greeted the *federales*, I was surprised to see Paul's informant, *Gato*, sitting in their midst. Paul had been wondering why he had not heard from his informant. Paul would be livid to learn his informant was moonlighting with the *federales*.

I sat down next to Mendoza and provided him with the telephone numbers. After finishing the first beer, I made eye contact with the informant. I raised my eyebrows and looked to the right as to signal *Gato* to meet me outside.

I apologized to the *federales* for not staying longer and enjoying the pending orgy. I said I needed to return to El Paso for other business and excused myself from the table.

The informant waited a minute before leaving the table and finding me outside, away from direct view of the *federales*.

"What the hell are you doing with these guys?" I asked angrily.

"Don't worry. It's okay. I'm working with them on a case that involves some Colombians. They're going to pay me a lot of money."

"Why haven't you told Rodriguez about this?"

"I just found out. I'll get with him on Monday."

"No you won't! Get the fuck away from these guys and drive your ass to El Paso now. You can't trust them."

"Calm down. I'll go inside for a couple of drinks, and then I'll call Paul when I'm on my way to El Paso."

I wanted to forcibly take the man with me, but the informant wasn't a child. That was the last time *Gato* was seen alive.

The following Monday morning, *El Diario* newspaper ran a story of a man found dead in a rental car parked near Chihuahua Charlie's Restaurant. The story said that a thirty-five year old man had died in the vehicle of natural causes. There were no visible signs of foul play. The man in the photo was wearing the same clothes I had seen *Gato* wearing on Friday evening.

Paul Rodriguez and Jose Calderon went to the Ciudad Juarez coroner's office to read the autopsy report on *Gato*. No bruises or indications of torture were apparent, only a tiny puncture wound on the inside portion of his right wrist. The coroner concluded that the victim had been injected with a fatal dose of heroin.

Gato was not a heroin user. Paul knew Mendoza murdered the informant. It was the same modus operandi once bragged about by the former Mexican military investigator.

When confronted by Paul, Mendoza claimed the informant was acting strange as they partied late into the night at the Mexican restaurant. *Gato* disappeared during the fiesta. His agents were not concerned with the informant as they were preoccupied with their female companions.

Paul and I envisioned the downward spiral of the BTF under the leadership of the roguish Comandante. We hated being hypocritical with someone who didn't care about our interests. We felt like pawns in a game that we couldn't win.

Chapter 20 – Everyone Has Their Price

Paul and I knew the DEA hierarchy didn't want to hear our complaints. We kept our opinions to ourselves. Paul said, "Daily communications have ceased and no follow up information has come in weeks. We're giving them info and getting nothing in return."

I added, "The business meetings meant to exchange information have lost their significance. Have you noticed that Comandante Mendoza insists we meet with him in the late afternoons?"

"No shit. The meetings turn into drinking affairs. I've never drunk so much Chivas Regal Scotch with mineral water."

"He's been very generous lately. He flaunts a large wad of U.S. bills and now foots the bar tab. Also, his men are better dressed than before, with name brand clothing."

Paul said, "That doesn't bother me as much as the large entourage of *madrinas* he's recruited." *Madrinas* are underlings who do anything to appease someone in Mendoza's position. These wanna-be cops do the dirty work for law enforcement agencies including drug dealing, extortion, and murder. Mexican citizens fear the *madrinas* more than they fear the corrupt cops.

During one meeting, there was one face that caught my attention. It was the man that Mendoza had tortured in the motel room. He was now part of their crew! How could this be? When asked about the man, Mendoza claimed the man was willing to set up other drug dealers for the *federales*.

I wasn't buying it. The man looked strung out on heroin. Mendoza likely injected the man with drugs and made him one of his 'go-fers', or errand boy.

Paul refused to follow orders from DEA headquarters regarding traveling to Ciudad Juarez on a daily basis. I understood his frustration and told him I would handle the tasks at hand. I didn't want our resentment with the BTF to reflect on Calderon.

The DEA's rule is that agents must travel in pairs when meeting informants or performing investigative operations especially when working on foreign soil. Never go it alone! None of the other agents wanted to deal with the untrustworthy *federales*. I didn't complain.

Several days later, a DEA International Operations supervisor from Headquarters traveled to El Paso. Steve Ray was responsible for authorizing funds for the BTF operations and wanted to see where the money was being spent.

I met the honored guest at the El Paso International Airport and drove him directly to the listening post in Ciudad Juarez. During the drive, he admitted never working outside the U.S. in nearly ten years with the DEA.

Upon arrival, Ray walked through the front door of the covert listening post and walked directly to the Triggerfish. The expensive piece of DEA equipment was a prized-possession for any legal or covert wiretap operation. The mobile, suitcase-sized device could intercept cellular telephone conversations within a mile radius.

Ray said, "I'm glad you are utilizing the Triggerfish. I am getting a lot of flack from my cohorts for allowing it to be on foreign soil. Other DEA offices are putting pressure on me to release it to them so they can conduct domestic wiretaps."

I responded, "We should have priority. We are at the primary point of entry for the distribution of drugs into the U.S. This piece of equipment is needed to begin a concerted effort to penetrate the Juarez Cartel. Steve, things are moving too slow for us in this area. I need something to generate productivity."

"I heard the *federales* are not as motivated as we would like them to be. I understand you can only do so much."

Ray turned his attention to a small, white box, known as the AT&T Telephone Security Device (TSD) 3600. The device is used for encrypted conversations by U.S. national security advisors, business executives, and unfortunately, drug cartels.

The adjoining table housed ten Marantz audio recorders. The voice-activated devices were connected to pirated telephone lines from nearby homes and businesses. On another table were a police scanner, stacks of audiotapes, and a paper document shredder.

Ray was impressed with the electronics I purchased for the clandestine operation. He was pleased that his funding was being put to good use.

Mendoza arrived and took about an hour to express his pride and optimism for the BTF operations. The presentation would be enhanced with some wining and dining. The Comandante invited his American guest to a local watering hole for a few drinks.

La Rueda, The Wheel, featured a circular bar surrounded with high bar stools. Within the circle was an elevated floor where a dozen scantily clad young women tended to each male patron. A clear view of the variety of cleavages complemented the flirtatious interactions.

Mendoza ordered a bottle of Chivas Regal Scotch for the threesome. A *botana*, or complimentary appetizers, was available for customers who wanted to eat something to absorb the alcohol.

Shortly, Segundo Comandante Francisco Morales arrived with two *madrinas*. They sat at a separate table by the side entrance. They made no effort to conceal their AK-47 assault rifles. It was difficult for anyone in the bar to ignore the brassy display.

Mendoza said, "You can never be too safe, especially in this part of town." He insisted the DEA agents not pay attention to the armed men.

I felt responsible for Ray's protection. I drank in moderation knowing I had to safely return the DEA dignitary to the American side. Even when Ray went to the restroom, I stayed behind to keep an eye on the man's nearly full drink. It was a safety precaution learned from past experiences.

I learned from my days in the Texas Highway Patrol not to leave my beverage unattended. Playfully, my senior partners would pour salt in my iced tea when I excused myself to the restroom. Now, I always finished any beverage, regardless of who was with me, before excusing myself from the table.

Another tactic used was pulling the top right corner of the label on the beer bottle to mark my beverage. That way my bottle wasn't mistaken with another. My friends thought me paranoid, but I considered it safeguarding my property and health. Jokingly I would respond, "I don't want to be swapping spit with any of you!"

It was 2 a.m., when Mendoza invited us to Las Palmas Hotel. I was feeling edgy after seeing Morales and his *madrinas* snorting lines of cocaine on the table.

Ray was oblivious to his surroundings and was feeling no pain. He accepted the Comandante's invitation to continue the party. I reluctantly agreed after insistence from Ray.

Mendoza led the entourage to the hotel. Ray and I sat with Mendoza at the bar for a so-called nightcap.

Morales walked up to the table and said to Mendoza, "They are here." Several women from *La Rueda* were invited to the motel to keep the party going. Mendoza said, "*Señores*, pick the one you want and enjoy yourselves."

Believing that Ray would be insulted, I said, "We appreciate the offer *jefe* (boss) but it is getting late."

Defiantly, Ray said, "We can't insult the Comandante and run away like scared children!" Ray selected one of the young ladies and walked hand-in-hand to a motel room. He turned back to me, "I just hope my get up and go hasn't got up and went."

It was something about going into Mexico that would make people feel like they were on a vacation. I entertained many visiting coworkers while I was with the DEA. The business trip would turn into a pleasure trip. They would feel comfortable, let their hair down, and rely on me for their entertainment.

Mendoza and I conversed with the women for a time over a full bottle of Buchanan's Scotch and Topo Chico mineral waters. Mendoza admitted bragging to others about working with the *gringos*. It elevated his stature amongst the other local Mexican law enforcement agencies.

I had slim hopes that the Comandante's power trip would pay off with some kind of virtuous investigative efforts for the BTF. Mendoza was only concerned with his personal gain in the underworld. After nearly killing off the bottle of scotch, I was ready to go home. I went looking for Ray but walked into the wrong motel room.

When I opened the door, I saw Morales with two nude women doing lines of cocaine on the nightstand.

"Is something wrong?" yelled Morales.

"Sorry. I'm just looking for the *gringo*."

Hearing the commotion, Ray opened the door in the adjoining room. Wearing only his underwear, he asked, "Are we ready to go?"

"Yeah."

He shut the door to put his clothes on. When Ray exited his room, I could see a look of distraught on his face.

I tried to make light of the awkward situation, "He's coming out of the phone booth, displaying a big 'S' on his chest!"

Feeling guilty, Ray shook his head and forced a fake smile. He had a moral blackout. He got drunk and should have not let his behavior go as far as it did.

I drove the man to his hotel room in El Paso. Few words were spoken. He would return back to Washington, D.C. the following day.

After Ray's brief affair, we never spoke of that night. For months, our long-distance telephone conversations were limited to business only. I was never denied any requested funding for the BTF program.

The next day, I received information from an El Paso DEA Intelligence Analyst. The analyst claimed various sources identified a warehouse in Ciudad Juarez as a hub for multi-ton quantities of cocaine before smuggled into the U.S. It was the same site identified in the six-ton cocaine seizure months before. There was no doubt that this location was a Juarez Cartel asset.

I traveled alone to the warehouse near the Zaragosa International Bridge. I was anxious to see it for myself. The dismal-looking gray, cinder block warehouse was located in a desolate area. It was nearly impossible to establish surveillance because there was nothing to conceal my presence. I took photos of the compound from a distance.

There was nothing that could be done without relying on proactive Mexican law enforcement. I humored myself when I thought of the oxymoron – proactive, Mexican law enforcement.

I met with Mendoza and insisted that the compound be raided and searched by any means. "Comandante, the DEA has sufficient evidence to prove this location is a transportation hub for large cocaine shipments."

Mendoza responded, "I will have some of my men watch the place. It could take several days to get permission from a local judge to search the warehouse."

I was blunt, "What do you mean a search warrant? Since when do you need legal authorization for something like this?" I knew Mendoza had searched other homes and businesses without asking for permission and with lesser probable cause.

Mendoza said, "There are specific elements needed to obtain a search warrant for certain operations. I will advise our legal section in Mexico City. Let's be honest. The probable cause to search the warehouse is going to be difficult to apply since the evidence is in the U.S."

I was upset that Mendoza was talking like an attorney. It was obvious he was stonewalling. I volunteered to accompany the *federales* with surveillance, but Mendoza denied the request. Mendoza demanded that no one go near the warehouse so as not to alarm the inhabitants.

After the second day of waiting, I went to the warehouse without telling Mendoza. From a distance, I recognized a PGR vehicle parked near the rear entrance of the complex. There was activity in and around the compound. There was nothing I could do but watch.

The following day, Vince and I visited with Mendoza. The Comandante claimed he finally received legal authorization to conduct a search. His agents had conducted a thorough search of the warehouse and found no indication of any illegal activity.

Furious, I insisted that we be accompanied by the *federales* on a personal inspection of the facility. I wanted to see the compound from the inside. The Comandante reluctantly agreed.

I walked up to the front door. I pushed the elegant wooden door because the handles were removed. Nobody was home. Not a single piece of furniture or décor were present.

The entire compound had been meticulously stripped and cleaned. Window frames, electrical outlets, and all fixtures had been removed. I was amazed with the efforts of the Cartel members to remove any and all physical evidence.

Vince asked, "Why did they go to such extremes?"

I said, "The traffickers did not want to leave anything behind that might have their fingerprints on it. They knew we were coming."

We walked to an opening that led to a spacious outdoor patio. On the right was an outdoor entertainment stage next to a party room. I could picture the flamboyant *fiestas* held for the honored guests. Someone special, like Amado Carrillo-Fuentes, stood on this very spot.

Behind the stage was an inconspicuous gray, steel gate that concealed a loading dock. The platform was obviously designed to load large shipments of cargo onto tractor-trailers.

Noticing a piece of paper under the stage, I picked it up and put it in my pant pocket. I recognized it as a label from the same herbal company found on the cocaine packages of the multi-ton loads recently seized in El Paso and Houston.

I felt both elation and anger. I knew I was on the heels of Carrillo-Fuentes. On the other hand, I concluded Mendoza was on Amado's payroll.

As weeks went by, Mendoza became involved in a power struggle with local Mexican cops. The dispute was over who would be selected as the enforcers for the Carrillo-Fuentes organization. It would be a prestigious and extremely lucrative distinction within the Juarez Cartel.

Public executions and armed confrontations escalated in the streets of Ciudad Juarez. The media captured public displays of chaos and their bloody aftermath. The violence damaged the city's image even more.

A Mexican photographer captured one such violent skirmish. A large photograph of Mendoza appeared on the front page of an issue of *El Diario* newspaper. The Comandante was caught walking down the middle of a city street, wearing a torn t-shirt, carrying an AK-47 assault rifle, and looking very angry.

Paul looked at the photo and said, "So much for keeping the BTF agents under the radar. I'm done with those assholes."

The turf battle did not exempt me from getting caught in it. On one occasion, it was late on a Saturday night. I traveled alone to the listening post. I was met by the *federale* nicknamed *Oso*.

I said, "The Comandante told me to meet him here. He said it was important. What's going on?"

"He told me to take you to another location."

"*Chingado*! I don't like surprises and I don't like coming to Juarez this late."

"I don't know what to tell you. I was ordered to drive you to meet some local dignitaries."

"I thought he had information for me."

"Please come with me."

"No. I will follow you in my own vehicle." I did not want to be at the mercy of someone else. Being a passenger and not in the driver's seat was a personal control issue that is still with me today.

Oso lead me to another section of the city into an unfamiliar residential area. The streets were dark and all the homes seemed to look the same. There were no visible street signs. The *federale* lead me into a driveway of a house.

We walked into the home and there was a party in progress. In attendance were local politicians, businessmen and many beauty pageant contestants. Most of the young women were still in competition mode as they were modeling their swimwear ensembles. Some of the women ignored the regulations of the pageantry as they walked around in their 'birthday suits'.

Mendoza made his way through the crowd and walked briskly to me, "*Bienvenidos mi estimado* (Welcome my esteemed guest)! Join us on this special occasion."

I was not amused with the Comandante's awkward reception and I did not care to ask about the reason for the celebration. I was introduced to some of the dignitaries. Handshakes were exchanged and aliases were declared.

I asked Mendoza to step outside. We exited through a kitchen door into a poorly lit backyard patio. As my eyes adjusted to the darkness, I saw several *federales* standing in a corner of the barren enclosure next to an open fire pit. I acknowledged them with the wave of a hand. I also noticed several large dirt mounds against the high, gray cinderblock walls.

Mendoza interrupted my visual inspection, "*Amigo*, let's party!"

I turned to him, "I thought you had something important to tell me!"

"I wanted you to share my affiliation with these beautiful people. Here, have a bump of this pure coke." Mendoza produced a small clear container called a bullet. He turned the tiny knob that produced a portion of the white powdery substance, known as a bump.

"Maybe later."

I could see the Comandante was under the influence of many Chivas Regal and *agua mineral* mixed drinks. That didn't bother me as much as the edginess displayed from the excessive number of bumps Mendoza had already done.

Mendoza said, "I've been wanting to tell you that I am impressed with you. You have no fear by continuing to come into Juarez, especially alone, and work with my men on our operations. My men respect you and appreciate everything you have done for them. I would like to give you something as a token of our appreciation."

Mendoza handed me a Mexican police raid vest that displayed a large PGR insignia clearly visible to anyone in my kill zone. In other words, someone in gunshot range during an actual police raid.

"*Gracias.*" I liked the gesture but wasn't sure when I would actually wear the specialized article of clothing.

The Comandante continued, "Aside from this, I have something else for you."

I had a feeling the vest was a proffer for something bigger.

Mendoza began asking questions regarding my motivation for being a DEA agent. After dancing around the issue, the million-dollar question was asked. "How much would it take for you to provide information to the other side?"

There was a long, uncomfortable pause. We stared into each other's eyes. Mendoza added, "Let's say someone approached you and made you an offer. Would you consider it?"

I responded, "The last thing I would do is jeopardize my career for dirty money. I am very happy with my job, my salary and have no desire to do something so foolish."

Mendoza did not say anything. There was a look of disappointment on his face.

It is believed that people under the influence of alcohol say things that they will later regret. On the other hand, it is said people speak their mind and say what they really feel.

I could see Mendoza thinking out loud. The Comandante wondered how he would report the failed attempt to the Juarez Cartel. Also, how would they respond to the agent's denial.

Mendoza said, "Let us pretend this conversation never happened. I want you to take Miss Juarez upstairs. She will show you why she was selected as Miss Congeniality by her peers."

I was ready to leave but I realized I didn't know how to get out of the area. Also, none of the *federales* were anxious to leave the party. A believer of business before pleasure, the task-at-hand was concluded. There was time for some self-indulgence with Miss Juarez.

Two hours later, *Oso* volunteered to escort me out of the subdivision. He led me to a major roadway. The *federale* turned around and returned to the *fiesta*.

I knew exactly where I was. So did six men in two Ford Crown Victoria sedans. I was forced off the main thoroughfare onto an adjacent street. I couldn't maneuver out of the well-rehearsed rolling roadblock.

My first thought was, "Damn! The Juarez Cartel was going to make me pay for not accepting their bribe!"

On the other hand, something about the traffic stop and the situation did not raise my level of fear. After surviving several deadly confrontations in Mexico I had a sense of invincibility. Maybe working in Juarez alongside the *federales* provided me with an increased tolerance.

Two men flashing police badges approached the driver's side of my OGV. The men asked me step out of the vehicle.

Before exiting, I questioned the men about the reason for the stop. They claimed someone reported a maroon truck leaving the scene of a traffic accident. I knew it was a lie. It was a ruse to identify me by the Ciudad Juarez municipal police or the State of Chihuahua police. I had nothing to hide and would cooperate with the rogue cops.

They asked, "Where are you coming from?"

I responded, "I was visiting a friend."

"I don't believe you. You need to tell me who was at the party you are coming from!" These men were Mendoza's rivals. They wanted to know who attended the party.

"I don't know what you're talking about."

The dialogue changed as the men insisted they search the passenger area of the pickup. I refused because I did not want them to see my Colt submachine gun on the floorboard. An American in possession of a weapon in Mexico would create an international incident.

Two other men produced AK-47 assault rifles and pointed them at me. I was within arm's reach from gun toting men eager to empty their 'banana clips' into me.

I responded, "You need to know who you are fucking with before you go any further! Who is in charge here?"

One officer said, "You're not in a position to ask any questions. I suggest you get out of the way and let us search your vehicle."

With my cell phone in hand, I dialed Comandante Mendoza. Surprisingly, the intoxicated man answered on the first ring.

"*Que pasa, amigo* (What's happening, friend)?"

Speaking loud enough for everyone to hear, I said, "Comandante, I have some men here pointing their *cuerno de chivas* in my face. Should I tell them who I am?"

"Let me talk to the man in charge!"

I passed the cell phone to the man closest to me.

The man lowered the assault rifle and reached for the cell phone. He passed it to his superior. I heard him say, "You know anyone you associate with is fair game. Why should I let him (me) go?"

I don't know what Mendoza said but I assumed it was my being an American law enforcement officer. Hurting me would complicate their personal feud with a much larger adversary - the U.S. government.

Within a minute, the man returned the cell phone to me. He said, "Don't let me catch you here again." The six men got into their sedans and left without another word.

I got back on the well-lit main road and returned to El Paso.

DEA supervisors overlooked my encounters as long as I did not complain. I felt there was no reason to make it an issue.

Vince and I were pressured by DEA Headquarters to utilize the Triggerfish cellular telephone intercept equipment or it would be taken away from us. Use it or lose it.

When the violence escalated in Ciudad Juarez, I was not going to put us in harm's way. I decided to remove it from the listening post and transfer it to the DEA surveillance van. We would make it mobile and utilize the device on American soil. Although it was against U.S. law, it was a tactic that kept us out of harm's way.

We parked along the banks of the Rio Grande River whereby conversations were intercepted from both sides of the river. Few names, addresses, or telephone numbers were submitted into the DEA archives. We did not want to explain our source of information.

As for intercepts regarding criminal activity, the details were given to the El Paso Police Department and El Paso County Sheriff's Office. The small-time drug dealers and criminals arrested never knew how the police discovered their illicit activities.

Time was running out for the most notorious drug kingpin in Mexico. After a botched assassination attempt on his life, Carrillo-Fuentes knew he was a marked man. While he and his family were dining in a Mexico City restaurant, gunmen entered and raked the place with automatic weapon fire.

Carrillo-Fuentes and his family miraculously escaped. Many suspected that someone in his own organization was responsible for the attack. Others believed it was an orchestrated effort by one of the rival Sinaloa or Gulf Cartels.

Oddly, the end of Carillo-Fuentes' reign did not come from any police action or a bloody gun battle. It came at the hands of plastic surgeons. While attempting to change his physical appearance, Amado's heart could not take the trauma of the extensive body reconstruction. He died on an operating table.

Amado's brother, Vicente Carrillo-Fuentes, ensured those responsible paid for the mistake with their lives. The surgeons were found dead in 55-gallon barrels soon after their medical snafu.

Many law enforcement investigators, including myself, were disappointed that Amado would never see life from behind U.S. prison walls. The extensive incriminating evidence and countless DEA case reports would now be left to collect dust. With Amado gone, the Juarez Cartel now belonged to Vicente.

Comandante Mendoza and his team were transferred out of Ciudad Juarez. Either Vicente Carrillo-Fuentes made the change for other enforcers or the PGR administrators wanted to replace their rogue representatives.

In the following months, I was ordered by DEA headquarters to work with another group of vetted *federales*. Initially, the young agents were eager to participate with the DEA in the BTF operations. Within months, their initiative dissipated. There was inactivity in the listening post, misleading information regarding requested intelligence reports, and blatant refusal to pursue any active leads on the Juarez Cartel.

The corruption and payoffs were apparent at all levels in the Mexican federal police.

On one occasion, a Lear jet arrived at the Ciudad Juarez International Airport from Mexico City. In the plane was the Assistant Attorney General for Mexico who was to supposed meet the newly-vetted group assigned to Ciudad Juarez.

The following day, the diplomat departed with an undisclosed amount of cash claimed to be in the millions. Intelligence reports claimed the money was a payoff from the vetted group to the Juarez Cartel to remain as the enforcers in the area.

As time passed, it was the same old story. The joint efforts with the *federales* were leading nowhere. Being the pawns for the DEA heads with imaginary programs was very time-consuming and unproductive for me. More frustrating was listening to Confidential Informants say the Juarez Cartel members were boasting that they did not fear the DEA. They would continue their illegal operations with impunity in the Ciudad Juarez area.

We did not take the insult lightly. A verbal consensus was reached. An unorthodox method of punishment would be implemented. We would make the cartel members, who believed were immune from prosecution in the U.S., contend with another form of justice. We decided to let corruption tangle with evil.

Names and addresses of confirmed drug traffickers were provided to the *federales*. Extortion, kidnappings, and murders were optional. The demise of the *narcos* (drug traffickers) would never be questioned or discussed by the El Paso DEA agents and the *federales*. We didn't care what happened to them.

In the midst of the purge, local newspapers reported that many dead bodies were discovered in the backyard of a home in Ciudad Juarez. The gruesome footage was broadcast for weeks in the El Paso and Ciudad Juarez area. To me, the enclosed backyard with dirt mounds and high cinderblock walls looked very familiar. It looked like the place Mendoza had offered to change my ways.

PART THREE
THE NIGHTMARE

Chapter 21 – Roll With The Changes

The Group One Special Agents developed a renewed interest in overhauling their careers. They took advantage of the notoriety achieved by the El Paso DEA office with its recent successes of the multi-ton drug seizures and rode the wave for personal advancement.

After a lengthy career in the U.S. military followed by a decade with the DEA, Calderon felt the need to be closer to his family. He was promoted and transferred closer to his family in Puerto Rico.

With a transfer to the multi-agency information gathering facility known as El Paso Intelligence Center (EPIC), Yvette Gonzalez remained in *El Chuco*. In this safe position, she sat behind a desk for the rest of her career.

 Vince Sellers spoke his mind, and it got in the way of promotion. He never cared about that because he had other interests that fulfilled him. A lesson everyone should follow.

Richard McGee, recognized for his outstanding tactical decision-making abilities, was promoted to a supervisory position. This was a well-deserved honor for someone I considered the most innovative agent I ever worked with.

The DEA managers never viewed Paul Rodriguez as supervisory material. His rough personality and not playing well with others kept him from any consideration for advancement. He expressed his disappointment, "After all the shit I've done for this agency, and the bastards won't even let me sit behind a desk to shuffle papers. Fuck those pencil dicks!"

I recommended, "I know something you would be good at. Why don't you start thinking about retiring and opening a bar?"

Paul responded, "Are you crazy! I won't make any money because you and I will drink all the profits."

Cops tend not to think outside the box when it comes to career changes. Upon retirement, many pursue private or government-contract security occupations that make them feel as if they were still in law enforcement.

Paul said, "You can never retire from being a cop. It's the one profession that will never let you go."

As for me, I believed anyone who lacked ambition was being untrue to himself. It is a sin to be content with mediocrity. I enjoyed working in my hometown but had to make the most of my abilities.

For those aspiring to become a supervisor in the DEA, a transfer to another office or Headquarters was obligatory. Both my supervisors and peers urged me to pursue a foreign assignment. I was selected for a position in Monterrey, Mexico.

My mindset and guts were essential qualities for working in a place like Mexico. I was confident I could balance the political arena in another country and the cruelty of the international drug trade.

Of all the going away parties in recent months, mine was the best. The owner of the Circle Inn Bar shut down the place for the private party. Family members and co-workers from the El Paso DEA office filled the joint. The gifts of appreciation were piled on a corner table next to my favorite dessert, carrot cake with cream cheese icing.

Co-workers made speeches about shared exploits and adventures during the past seven years. They described my wholehearted efforts to help fellow agents with their investigations especially with undercover operations.

One agent announced, "I have never known anybody who could talk someone into doing something they hadn't thought about. Sal persuaded lots of bad guys to produce drugs and walk away as if they made a new friend. Only after they were arrested and saw Sal with a DEA badge hanging from his neck did they realize they were fooled."

Veteran agents gave me advice based on their experiences abroad. However, the best advice came from my father, "Son, remember where you came from. It wasn't easy but you were determined to succeed. Now, you are entering into a dangerous situation in Mexico. Don't trust anyone!"

I assured my father, "I've been working with the Mexican cops for awhile. I've come to understand the best and worst of them. I'll be fine."

With beers in hand, fellow agents and administrative staff members used this occasion to broadcast how much they cherished our friendship.

They presented me with a Texas-shaped wooden plaque with the words engraved, "You will be greatly missed." Nobody anticipated the sentiments would be retracted very soon.

It took several months for the DEA and State Department bureaucratic process to be completed. The move from my hometown to the city known as the Pittsburgh of Mexico was a test of patience and a forewarning of things to come.

It was not easy to adjust from the comforts of a modernized country into the conditions of a third-world country. The frustration began after settling into the government-leased quarters that lacked water pressure, natural gas pressure, and chronic power outages.

Secondly, there was a limited selection of desired grocery items and household products. The quality of Mexican consumer goods was substandard at best. The depravity was compounded with the limited retail merchants and their disinterested sales personnel.

The U.S. Consulate was located in the downtown area of Monterey, Mexico. The exterior of the building was viewed as dull in an eye-catching landscape. I was assigned to an 8' by 14' office space. I looked through the narrow window to see a gray wall from another building. The paltry office and dismal view made me feel caged in. The conditions were indicative of the limited role I would have as a cop in a foreign land.

I tried to spruce up the room with personal décor. The cement walls made it difficult to hang DEA certificates and awards to create my "I Love Me Wall". I was forced to store them in a desk drawer to collect dust.

The only picture frame that held up was a photograph of me with Mexico's most admired boxer, Julio Cesar Chavez. It was the first thing Mexicans saw when they entered my office. The conversation piece elicited excitement and the question, "How did you meet *El Campeon* (The Champion)?"

I had fun making up the story that I trained with Chavez and accidently knocked down the World Champion during a sparring session. This evoked many animated responses of disbelief. The truth was I met him at a restaurant in El Paso. It goes without saying, "Don't believe anything you hear and believe only half of what you see."

The DEA Monterrey Resident Office consisted of four agents and a

RAC, Resident Agent in Charge. Our area of responsibility consisted of five eastern Mexican states. We relied heavily on each other for business and personal matters.

Orientation required traveling to various Mexican cities to meet government and law enforcement officials. At times, it felt like political pandering. I hated the hypocritical conversations and empty handshakes. Working as an emissary took me away from doing what I wanted to do - arrest bad guys!

Considered an expert, I was instructed to establish and coordinate several BTF's with vetted *federales* just as I had done in Ciudad Juarez. It took a few months to set up the wiretap operations with listening posts in several Mexican border cities including Reynosa and Matamoros. The onus of obtaining technical equipment and providing operational funds fell on the DEA, again.

I learned firsthand that the multi-million dollar financial aid packages provided by the U.S. to Mexico never made it to the people who needed it the most. The money remained in the upper levels of the government, likely pocketed by administrators.

American officials did not want to insult Mexican bureaucrats by questioning the distribution of the specifically earmarked funds. The soft stance for requesting any auditing procedures was contemptible and made the U.S. look spineless.

One Comandante confided, "I can't rely on my supervisors with any financial support. I am left to trust only the handful of agents under my command. We feel abandoned and discarded living only by rationing our meals and necessities."

I spent tens of thousands of dollars on basic equipment and supplies for countless *federales* - the same Mexican cops who would likely be bribed by drug cartels within months. Just as I experienced in Ciudad Juarez, the problem of institutionalized corruption existed in the heart of Mexico.

Mexican officials insisted they were making great strides by terminating and replacing incorrigibles in their ranks. To disaffiliate the old from the new, the transition was coupled with a change of agency name and acronym. Theoretically, the house cleaning was a good idea, but corruption will remain chronic for generations.

One fruitless effort made by the DEA was an all-expense paid training session for thirty *federales*. The vetted agents were flown to Baltimore, Maryland, where they spent over a month learning U.S. enforcement and investigative techniques.

On weekends, the *federales* were entertained by attending a Baltimore Orioles baseball game, bar-hopping in Georgetown, and taking shuttles to Philadelphia and New York City. I was ordered to provide the necessary funds to keep their interest and, literally, buy their friendship.

Upon completion of the training, the *federales* returned to their assigned locations with the intent of working with the DEA. It didn't take long for apathy or a better offer to override their commitment to us.

This was made clear to me during a fugitive operation in the Mexican state of Michoacan. I was assisting in the search of the accused killer of a DEA agent from Arizona. The lengthy investigation required many DEA agents to follow leads in locating the killer in the mountains near the city of Morelia.

One opinionated Mexican Comandante told me, "You *gringos* spend a lot of our time and manpower to look for one person. Just because one American cop was killed, you have to engage in such an exhaustive project. We have Mexican police officers getting killed everyday, yet we don't see your agency making an effort to help us!"

I responded, "Your people never ask for help. You know better than I do that there isn't a sense of pride or unity among your agencies."

"You *gringos* have an Imperialistic attitude in law enforcement just like all your other political agendas. You feel like you must be known as the primary police force of the world. Politically, you force your will on foreign countries for financial reasons. The idea of helping others, even when they don't desire change, is arrogant."

I wanted to tell him, "Get your shit together and we wouldn't have to come here and do your job!" Instead, I just ended the conversation knowing politics was a topic I avoided.

I knew my limitations. I couldn't make a dent in the Mexican pysche or institutional agendas. All I could do was perform my responsibilities hoping not to get caught in the crossfire of their corruption and the cartels' lawlessness.

While in Morelia, several DEA agents met for dinner and drinks at a Señor Frogs restaurant. After flirting and dancing with some of the local college girls, we called it a night. We lodged in different hotels to prevent any attention by the locals of too many *gringos* in one location. So we thought.

I was staying at a hotel across the city of Morelia. I jumped into a plain, compact rental car. I pushed play to hear the sultry sounds of Santana. For decades, the untiring, versatile Carlos Santana represented his *raza* (race) proudly. I rolled the windows down to feel the breeze of the crisp night air.

There wasn't much traffic around midnight. I approached a poorly lit, outlying four-way stop traffic intersection. The isolation and darkness were perfect conditions to hide the four dark-colored Chevrolet Suburbans waiting for me.

The swift blockade prevented any second-guessing. Two AK-47 assault rifle barrels were pointed at me - one from the driver's side window and the other through the passenger side window. I slowly raised both hands.

Although the six beers and two mixed drinks dulled my alertness, my instincts remained sober. I looked for an escape. I kept the car running and in gear preparing to ram through the much larger vehicles.

I saw several men surround me wearing black military fatigues with no insignias. I wasn't sure if they were police officers, military personnel, or drug traffickers.

I was ordered out of the car, but I refused. One man forced open the passenger door and reached for my fanny pack lying on the front passenger seat. The leather pouch contained my credentials, wallet, and Glock 17 pistol. I slapped his hand away and yelled a derogatory statement.

After a lengthy shouting match, I insisted on talking to the person responsible for stopping a U.S. Diplomat. The oldest looking man in the group walked casually to the driver's side window. I asked the man to identify himself. He claimed to be a Comandante.

He asked, "Who are you?"

I responded, "I am a diplomat. Who are you?"

"I am asking the questions! What are you and your friends from the restaurant doing in Morelia?"

I guessed either a customer or employee at the restaurant was a snitch for this group of local enforcers.

I flashed my diplomatic credentials but did not give the Comandante enough time to see that it was a DEA badge. I said, "I am now dialing the U.S. Embassy so that they can contact your superiors. Your government would like to know that you are responsible for creating an international incident."

"You are in my city. Don't threaten me!"

I slowly raised my cell phone not wanting to startle the gun-toting men. I began dialing the number to the DEA office in Mexico City.

Without a word, the Comandante turned around and ordered his men to follow him. Just as quickly as they had moved in on me, they dispersed. Their vehicle lights were turned off so I could not read the license plate numbers.

I sat there in the dark for a few minutes to regain my composure. I thought, "Shit, I can't believe this happened to me again! I don't know how I come away unscathed from these encounters." In this case, I would never be found if these men decided to kidnap me.

I called my fellow agents to warn them. Our presence was revealed, the operation was compromised, and our logistics needed to be changed. I picked up my belongings and moved to a different hotel.

The next morning, the Assistant Country Attache (ACA) for the DEA office in Mexico City called me. The ACA asked, "Are you okay?"

"I'm good."

"We are concerned with your emotional and psychological reaction to such a traumatic event. If you feel like you need some type of counseling, we can provide it."

"That's not necessary, sir. I've been through this several times. Each time, I've walked away unharmed. I'm not meant to die yet because only the good die young."

The ACA continued, "Can you tell us who the men were that

surrounded you?"

"They never identified themselves. They appeared to be local cops likely tipped off by someone at the restaurant."

"Regarding your safety, do you wish to be evacuated from Mexico and returned to the United States?"

"No way. I'm staying in Mexico."

"Do you want to remain with the operation in Morelia or return to Monterrey?"

"I'll complete my tour." Intimidation would not prevent my determination to seek the killer of a fellow DEA agent.

I was ordered to take several days off from surveillance and remain inside my hotel room. The idea was for me to keep out of sight. I didn't have the patience to sit still and watch the unintelligent Mexican television programming. I was bored and felt confined.

A tattoo parlor across the street caught my attention and lured me to the quaint establishment. A young male tattoo artist greeted me in Spanish, "Good afternoon. Can I help you?"

I responded in Spanish, "I've always been intrigued on why someone would get a tattoo. Can I just look around at your work on the wall?" There were many photographs displaying the man's talent.

"Sure. What brings you to Morelia?"

I thought quickly, "I am visiting a friend attending the University. I had some 'down time' until this evening."

"Can I interest you in one of my works?"

"How difficult would it be to place Led Zep on my left arm?"

"That's it? I can draw a Hindenburg with Led Zeppelin written under it."

"I don't want to overdue it. Only rock and rollers will know what Led Zep means."

"Okay. It will only take about twenty minutes for two hundred pesos."

I said, "Life is short. Why not?" Most people have thought about getting a tatoo but few do it.

As the man was carving ink into my arm, he opened up about being an American hiding out in Mexico. He bragged about being a fugitive from justice in California and considered Morelia his new home. Unintentionally, I seemed to invite people to open up about themselves. They considered me a good listener. I limited his subtle inquiries about the crime until after the tattoo was complete.

A criminal history check revealed the fugitive owed thousands of dollars for child support. I regretted allowing the Deadbeat Dad to engrave the name of my favorite rock band on my bicep.

After my temporary assignment to Morelia, I returned to the Monterrey DEA Office. I was instructed to fly into Cincinnati, Ohio, and drive back in a specially designed bulletproof Chevrolet Suburban. It would be my assigned OGV while in Mexico.

The Suburban didn't make me feel any safer while assigned to Monterrey. I doubted the durability of the armor would protect my flesh from the multiple rounds of an AK-47. My cynicism was justified. I was psychologically scarred from the several intimate showdowns I had with the barrel of the *cuerno de chivo* assault rifles.

I didn't like the feeling of vulnerability and helplessness. It was something I would have to get used to for the rest of my days with the DEA and for what was in store for me.

Chapter 22 – Mortal Sin

It was extremely difficult for any U.S. agent to establish an informant network in a foreign country. In my situation, few Mexicans were willing to talk to any law enforcement officer, especially a *gringo*. With few sources available, gathering relevant information on the drug cartels was futile.

The pace of work didn't compare to the excitement of my days in El Paso and Ciudad Juarez. The lack of actual police work and inactivity took a toll on me. On a personal level, I turned to self-medication by double-fisting Mexican beers and Glen Levit Scotch.

After a year, a long-time DEA informant, nicknamed *El Diablo* (The Devil), contacted the Monterrey office and wanted to talk with anyone who would listen to him. Veteran agents avoided working with *El Diablo* because of his unreliability.

In the words of a senior agent, "We nicknamed him *El Diablo* because he looks like that ugly bastard on the Mexican Bingo card game, called *La Loteria*. Also, he's a piece of shit who works both sides. He'll try to gather intelligence on our operations so he can benefit with his own criminal activities. He's been 'black-balled' by the DEA yet we still work with him on occasion because of his connections."

I asked, "How can a man in his position hurt our efforts? He is a Comandante for the State Police in Tamaulipas, Mexico? He has firsthand knowledge about the Gulf Cartel and the up-and-coming *Zetas* organization."

The agent responded, "He got his hands dirty by allegedly committing several murders. We wonder how he has not managed to be killed. Our DEA heads said we shouldn't work with men like him. However, we both know the best informants are the ones committing the crimes."

Desperate for a productive informant, I arranged a meeting with the fifty-year old Comandante at a restaurant near the oldest brewery in Mexico, the *Carta Blanca Cerveceria*. I went alone since my cohorts did not like talking to the 'double agent'. He would be the most conniving person I had ever met and I didn't even know it.

I entered the restaurant and found *El Diablo* standing by the hostess. We didn't shake hands.

We were led across the dining area to a table near a twenty feet by ten feet glass water tank. There were no decorations or aquatic life inside the huge tank.

Like all cops, the Comandante and I instinctively tried to sit with our backs to the wall facing the entrance of the restaurant. I beat him to the advantageous seat. *El Diablo* sat across me using the reflection from the glass of the water tank to watch his own back.

While ordering our Bohemia beers from the waitress, a splash of water interrupted the exchange. A teenage girl wearing a tiny bikini jumped into the water tank. She swam playfully and erotically to each patron's delight.

El Diablo said, "Not a bad form of entertainment. Don't you agree?"

After a few mesmerizing moments, I responded, "This could be a very enjoyable meeting. I'll never look at a fish tank the same."

The conversation began with *El Diablo* describing his professional background and potential as a DEA informant. He expressed frustration with other DEA agents, because he was misunderstood and the information he provided was never appreciated. As the Tamaulipas State Comandante, he had insight to the escalating border violence and other activities pertinent to active DEA investigations.

I asked, "My supervisors are concerned about your affiliation with some murders in your area of responsibility. What do you have to say about that?"

"Your bosses expect me to be a virtuous, respectable person in my position. They don't have any idea what I need to do just to keep my job as a Comandante. I use discipline to send a message to those who disrespect me."

I thought, "That was blunt. No sugarcoating or denials by this man." I liked that. After many years of pursuing the members of the Juarez and Sinaloa Cartels, I believed *El Diablo* would be a useful source of information for getting acquainted with the Gulf Cartel and an up-and-coming drug cartel named *Los Zetas* (The Z's).

I balanced my desire to get in-depth, vital intelligence against the rumors of deceptiveness by the Comandante. I was confident we could establish a productive working relationship. So, I took a chance on the man. *El Diablo* was a necessary evil in the drug war.

The meeting ended with both of us going our own way. *El Diablo* returned to his home in Laredo, Texas. He bragged about his kids attending American schools and living like the *gringos*. It was safer for his family to be residing on the other side of the Rio Grande River.

I made a few heat runs through the downtown streets of Monterrey to avoid being followed. Agents working abroad were encouraged to take different routes between the DEA office and their residence especially after meetings with informants or Mexican cops. We didn't want the bad guys knowing where they could find our families.

The following week, *El Diablo* provided graphic photographs taken at several drug-related crime scenes. The bullet-riddled bodies were casualties of the battle between the Gulf Cartel and *Los Zetas*. This was exactly the type of documentation I desired.

On one occasion, myself and another DEA agent were looking at a photo of a naked body lying in the desert. Wild dogs had ravaged the unrecognizable corpse. We made light of the horrible sight with tasteless jokes. It was a defense mechanism used by those who regularly saw death.

Our secretary walked into my office and asked, "What are you guys laughing at?"

I said, "Something pretty graphic. I don't think you should see this."

"I can handle it. Try me."

I handed her the photo.

Disgusted, she said, "Let me get this straight. You think this is funny? You are laughing at the sight of a mauled and dismembered human being?"

Defensively, I said, "This is the type of photos my informant has been given me. These are just drug traffickers who shouldn't have been involved in the drug business."

The woman returned the photo, "You guys need sensitivity training. It is not normal to find humor in situations like this." She shook her head and returned to her desk.

El Diablo kept producing the photographs and I forwarded them up the chain of command. For some sanguinary reason, DEA Intelligence Analysts in Washington also enjoyed looking at the photographic representation of the violence prevalent along the border.

Aside from the photographs, the informant furnished compact discs containing personal information of tens of thousands of Mexican citizens. Addresses, telephone numbers, and vehicle registrations would be available at the touch of a key. This personal data was obtained illegally, but that did not keep it from being the disseminated to U.S. law enforcement agencies.

El Diablo helped me look good through the DEA channels. Agents throughout the U.S. and Mexico called me to request confirmation on what was once uncertain in their investigations. I compensated my prized informant with five thousand dollars. There were other smaller payments made to the informant as authorized by my supervisor.

On a spring afternoon, the lives of many people changed. *El Diablo* was in my office providing drug trafficking information when we were interrupted by a telephone call. I picked up the telephone and kept the conversation short. It was a personal call from my younger sister.

The Comandante saw that I was visibly upset, "What's wrong?"

I responded, "It's a private matter."

"Please, let me help."

"I was just informed that the kid who killed my cousin was released from jail in El Paso and is being extradited to Juarez. It is the only carjacking in El Paso history that resulted in a death."

"Why did he kill your *primo* (cousin)?"

"Not sure if it was an orchestrated hit by the Juarez Cartel or a random carjacking. My cousin took two to the chest for a stupid truck that wasn't even his!"

I explained that it was four years earlier when Bruno Jordan was murdered in the parking lot of a K-Mart Shopping Store. Bruno was exiting a new pickup that belonged to friend when a fourteen year-old thug walked up to him. The young killer pumped two nine-millimeter rounds at close range and then drove off in the pickup.

I continued, "The punk never gave Bruno a chance to beg for his life."

Several shoppers witnessed the murder and provided an accurate description of the gunman. A short time later, police officers found the suspect walking on a nearby street. The truck and the pistol were never located, presumably because they were transferred to another person in the murder plot.

El Diablo responded, "The *gringos* brag that they have a full-proof legal system. It sounds like a clear-cut case. Was the kid sentenced to life in prison?"

"No. The Mexican consulate had been putting political pressure on the sentencing judge and U.S. authorities to release the assassin. An appeal was filed and the piece of shit was acquitted. A convicted, cold-blooded murderer was released on a bullshit legal technicality!"

I continued, "Now, the killer has returned to Juarez and is hailed as a hero for beating the U.S. judicial system. He is gloating to the local media about the easy time he had while in juvenile custody."

I reached into the bottom drawer of my filing cabinet and retrieved a folder that I hadn't looked at since my cousin's death. I kept the newspaper clippings and a videocassette tape of the El Paso television news footage because I couldn't think of a reason to throw them away. I saved them for sentimental reasons. *El Diablo* looked at them, too.

El Diablo, a stone-cold killer, processed the information and conceived a devious plan. He stood up and said, "There's a guy in Juarez who owes me a favor. I'll have him look into it."

I did not respond. Common sense told me not to ignore the subtle proposition and tell him it was not his business. My law enforcement instincts told me otherwise.

El Diablo left my office without another word.

Many El Pasoans were shocked with the inept American justice system. As for Bruno's immediate family, they were devastated and left without knowing the motive for the murder.

Bruno's older brother, Phil Jordan, was the head of the El Paso Intelligence Center. There was speculation that the Juarez Cartel wanted to send him a message for his outspoken views in the media.

After Bruno's murder, me and the BTF *federales*, lead by Comandante

Mendoza, escorted Phil Jordan to the home of the killer's mother in Ciudad Juarez. The meeting was arranged to persuade the mother to have her son talk with the American authorities. Phil needed to know who ordered the hit on his youngest brother.

The mother refused to cooperate after another son was found floating in the Rio Grande River. The elder brother was murdered as a warning to the mother and kid brother not to talk to the *gringos*.

I couldn't understand how my cousin, a coat salesman at the Men's Wearhouse clothing store, could be killed. Meanwhile, I flirted with death on many occasions and was still alive. It just didn't seem fair.

The priest at Bruno's funeral said, "The Lord forgives those who have sinned against us including the boy responsible for Bruno's death. Now, we (the congregation) need to forgive the young man."

Most of the mourners didn't agree with the holistic opinion. Several family members turned to me and confided, "Do something." Since I was a law enforcer, they believed I could make things better.

January 20th was a day of celebration for me - my father's birthday and my wedding anniversary. It was also the day that Bruno was gunned down. In fact, Lily and I were in bed watching the local news after a romantic anniversary dinner when it was announced that someone was carjacked and killed. I responded, "Poor guy. That never happens in El Paso." Thirty minutes later I received a call from my sister telling me that it was Bruno.

While I had not forgotten about Bruno's senseless death, it had become simply a thing of the past. Now, here it was, front and center again. Melancholy set in and *El Diablo* was there to see it. Without realizing it, I let my personal feelings enter an arena with no room for sympathy. This crucial mistake numbered my days.

I reached for my portable player and lost myself in the soulful sounds of Stevie Ray Vaughn. Someone so talented taken away in his prime. The tragic death of a loved one can affect so many people. Just like Bruno's.

Chapter 23 – Elements Of A Crime

In the following months, *El Diablo* became more personal with our relationship. He invited me to social events with his family in Laredo. Out-of-the blue he would visit the U.S. Consulate just to see how I was doing.

El Diablo surprised me with a personalized Tamaulipas State Police leather jacket with my name embroidered on it. He also gave me Mexican police caps, patches, and trinkets as tokens of friendship. I shared the items with the other DEA agents who appreciated the informant's generosity and change of personality.

I should have seen it coming. There was a surreptitious motive for the unplanned visits and personal attention.

The informant confided in me about his father's heart attack that kept him hospitalized for several weeks in a Monterrey hospital. *El Diablo* said there were expensive medical costs in the thousands of dollars that his family could not afford. The informant pleaded, "I will work extra hard for you so I can make the money my family needs."

I told him I would ask my supervisor if the DEA could help. The RAC said it was near the end of the fiscal year with a surplus of available funds in the informant budget. In fact, there was $10,000 of unused funds that needed to be disseminated by the Monterrey DEA Office.

I made the mistake of mentioning the available amount to *El Diablo*. Telling an informant they have money coming to them is like teasing a heroin junkie with another fix.

By mid-September, *El Diablo* nagged me about the $10,000 payment. The informant was adamant that I needed to pay him the money he was promised.

I explained that there was a budgeting error and funds were limited in the CI coffers as first thought. I didn't tell him the RAC used the money for other informants who were more productive gathering drug trafficking intelligence.

As time passed, *El Diablo* became less productive and changed his attitude. Conversations with me were brief and no longer personal. Sporadically, he would call with coded messages about his friend in Ciudad

Juarez who was actively pursuing the whereabouts of Bruno Jordan's murderer. I disregarded the insinuations and didn't take them serious.

The FBI believed they were serious. For months, they had assigned a team of agents to monitor my every move. They established wiretaps on my cell phone, office telephone, and home telephone.

One evening, after I went home, they searched my office in the U.S. Consulate and found the old newspaper articles and videocassette recording. They corroborated everything *El Diablo* told them. The FBI believed the motive for murder was there.

Meetings between *El Diablo* and I were prearranged, conversations were recorded, and overt acts were orchestrated. The FBI was convinced they were doing something good by investigating a corrupt DEA agent with a personal agenda.

In October, a 3-on-3 basketball tournament for a local charity was held in Laredo, Texas. Me, my supervisor, and two other DEA agents traveled across the border to attend the tournament. It was an opportunity for us to bond and enjoy a weekend on American soil.

During the first game, I severely strained my back. I knew my chronic back problems would hinder me until I got rid of my beer belly. I could only watch my teammates play from a hard, wooden bench.

Frustrated, I began drinking the ice cold beer meant for the post-game celebration. The alcohol would hopefully alleviate the excruciating back pain that only intensified. I joked by claiming that the hops and barley in the beer had some medicinal value.

Our Monterrey team was eliminated from the competition by the early afternoon. The chilled beers would ease our disappointing loss against the kids half our age. We drank the rest of the day by the hotel pool. It became more than just a 'day drunk' as the beerfest went into the evening.

We discussed going to dinner so we went our ways to freshen up. As I was walking to my hotel room, I collapsed on the hallway floor due to severe back spasms. Two housecleaning ladies lifted me up and helped me to my room. I was embarrased yet gracious.

By the time we met for dinner, I was feeling no pain. The half bottle of Glen Levit Scotch complemented the fifteen beers in my system. My fellow hoopsters saw I was in agony and kept the suds coming. After many years of drinking, I had developed a high tolerance for alcohol. It was never an issue until that night.

It was around 7 p.m., when I received a call from *El Diablo*. The informant said he was near the restaurant and wanted to meet with me. I agreed to talk to him outside. The other agents who despised him had no desire to join us.

El Diablo arrived in an older model minivan that did not fit his stature as a murderous enforcer. He remained in the vehicle while I stood outside the driver's side window.

"*Que pasa, Comandante*? What brings you out at this hour?"

"Do you still want me to kill the kid who killed your cousin?"

I was used to my informant getting to the point. I responded, "I don't give a damn what you do! You keep talking about killing the punk but haven't done shit. Complete the contract with your connection and get it over with!"

Everyone has had a thought or wished that someone was dead. This wasn't the first time I thought about wanting someone dead. I had been thinking that way since working for the DEA. I didn't care if a piece of shit was killed - he deserved it!

I spoke *El Diablo* with our customary crude, vulgar language that we were used to exchanging. In my business, it was necessary to lower myself by talking to others using their type of language.

El Diablo said, "I can prove it to you this time. Do you want me to bring you his head?"

"Hell no! Are you crazy?"

"Does your cousin Phil Jordan know about this?"

"Why are asking about Phil? I hardly ever see the man."

The man asked many blunt questions and I foolishly responded. I was out of character and my careless words would make me pay the ultimate price. The drunken stupor was no excuse for the incriminating statements I broadcast.

The FBI audio microphones and video cameras recorded the damaging testimony. The evidence would be presented to the U.S. Attorney's Office and the acting-Administrator of the DEA.

In December, a rare high-level meeting was arranged between the DEA and the FBI. The gathering was necessary after a DEA agent and a FBI agent assigned to the Monterrey consulate were ambushed and nearly killed by Osiel Cardenas, a violent drug cartel leader in Matamoros, Mexico. A swift response by U.S. law enforcement was necessary to show the drug trafficker that his actions would not be tolerated.

There was no love lost between the DEA and the FBI. Differences had to be put aside. Two brethren of law enforcement were threatened. A unified effort by the elite agencies would establish a joint operation to apprehend the aggressor.

This would begin with an icebreaker at the Vermillion Bar and Restaurant in Brownsville, Texas. Ironically, that was the Monterrey DEA agent's favorite watering hole when we travelled to that city. Four DEA and five FBI agents sat at a large table sharing pitchers of draft beer and nachos. Everybody was cordial and determined to pursue the brazen drug trafficker.

Out of nowhere, *El Diablo* walked up to me at the table. I was shocked to see him there. I assumed the informant was contacted by my supervisor and instructed to help the U.S. authorities with the international operation. He had helped before with other joint investigations.

"Hey, what brings you here?"

El Diablo pulled out a Polaroid photograph from his coat pocket and handed it to me, "Here, this is for you."

The informant had given me many photographs of crime scenes. I looked at this photograph of a young man lying on the floor with blood oozing out of his head. I didn't know what this was about and didn't recognize the victim. The murder scene looked fake as if it was a staged production.

I asked, "Who is this?"

"It's the guy you wanted dead." He said it loud enough for the FBI agents to corroborate the topic of conversation between us.

Shocked, I stood up and I calmly said, "Follow me outside."

We walked out to the parking lot. I asked, "Where did you get this? This doesn't look like the punk who killed my cousin. This photo doesn't look real!"

"I did what you told me. You need to give me the money you promised me so I can pay my contact in Juarez. He killed the guy for you."

"That's crazy! I'm not going to talk about this now! I'll see you back in Monterrey in a few days. Here, I don't want this photo!" I tried giving it back but he wouldn't take it.

El Diablo pulled his hands away and said, "You keep it."

Foolishly, I placed it in my coat pocket. More evidence for the feebs.

El Diablo walked around the building and disappeared into the darkness.

I returned to the gathering of federal agents. After an hour of niceties, it was determined another meeting would be held at the U.S. Federal Courthouse in Brownsville, Texas.

The next morning, a FBI supervisor began by welcoming the agents from both agencies who came from surrounding areas, especially those from the Monterrey, Mexico office. He explained that coordinated efforts required specific duties from each person in the room. He asked for volunteers to lead special operations in Mexico. Without hesitation, I raised my hand.

The supervisor directed me to walk with him to an adjoining room. Sensitive information and Top Secret documents would be provided. I entered the room and was met by two FBI agents.

An agent said, "Sal, you are under arrest for Murder-for-Hire." Then he read me my Miranda Rights. When these rights are read to you, your life has just changed for the worse.

It took a few seconds to gather my senses from the punch in the stomach. I thought to myself, "*El Diablo*! That low-life, piece of shit! The FBI believed my informant and created a criminal case against the controlling agent. Cold motherfuckers! How long had the informant and the FBI been working on this?"

The other agent said, "The orders came from high above including the U.S. Attorney General. We have incriminating evidence. Would you like to see the evidence that we have against you?"

I responded, "It's not necessary. I know exactly what you have." The pieces came together. The FBI had instructed *El Diablo* to meet me when I was drunk in Laredo and set me up at my favorite watering hole in Brownsville. They knew I would be vulnerable there. I foolishly fell into a trap and I was mad at myself. I realized that *El Diablo* and the FBI had been setting me up for the last nine months.

I believed the credibility of the informant was tarnished and that his nefarious past would be exposed. *El Diablo* was a documented liar and considered black-balled, the worst title for an informant in the DEA. I said I could explain our relationship and my actions.

The FBI agents didn't want to hear it. They wanted me to confess and solidify their case. More importantly, they wanted me to flip on someone else. It would be my only way out.

"Tell us what part your cousin, Phil Jordan, played in this contract killing."

Again, Phil's name came up. I did not respond.

Phil called me occasionally to talk about family matters and his unrelenting efforts to find those responsible for killing his little brother. The conversations were recorded by the FBI. They wanted me to confess the true intentions of our cryptic conversations.

The last time I had seen Phil was one month prior in Dallas, Texas. Lily and I had traveled to see the Miami Dolphins play the Dallas Cowboys on Thanksgiving Day. It was an opportunity to watch two of the greatest quarterbacks in NFL history. Phil bought two tickets for us.

The FBI considered the trip from Monterrey to Dallas as part of the conspiracy to further the contract killing. Teams of FBI agents were vigilant and documented every move we made.

Phil was once the Special Agent in Charge of the DEA Dallas Division before making a lateral transfer to EPIC. On his way up through the ranks, Phil pissed off the Department of Justice and DEA managers when he spearheaded an Hispanic class-action lawsuit. The White leaders did not like the minority causing problems.

Another point of contention was Phil constantly talking to the media about international drug trafficking investigations when he wasn't supposed to. The FBI and DEA heads wanted to shut him up.

The FBI interrogators said they would help me if I would tell them about Phil's role in the murder-for-hire scheme.

I thought, "Fuck that!"

Being arrested is one of the most traumatic events in anyone's life. I tried to control my emotions and gather my senses. The shock would not subside. I thought of Lily and my family. I put my head down and sobbed.

My DEA supervisor came into the room and gave me a big hug. He was sobbing as well.

He said, "We didn't know this was going to happen. The FBI arranged this fake meeting to have you arrested. We were all set up!"

The federal statute for the alleged crime was Title 18 U.S.C. § 1958, Traveling and Causing Another to Travel in Foreign Commerce with the Intent That a Murder Be Committed. The elements of this violation include traveling between state or international borders and a promise to pay something of pecuniary value.

The FBI made numerous attempts to have me provide *El Diablo* with anything of pecuniary value, such as money, a personal weapon, or something to fulfill a crucial element of the crime. I never gave him any unauthorized payments or anything of value.

The FBI claimed that the supervisory approved payments made to my informant were in furtherance of the murder plot. More importantly to their case was the promise made to *El Diablo* of the $10,000 payment discussed between me and my supervisor.

As for traveling across state or international lines, the FBI orchestrated meetings by having *El Diablo* seek me out. The encounters helped the FBI agents capture their incriminating evidence because it was on U.S. soil.

Several efforts by the FBI to implicate Phil Jordan included a scheme whereby *El Diablo* called me while I was at my residence in Monterrey. The informant claimed he was at a payphone in Dallas, supposedly en route to Ciudad Juarez, Mexico, in furtherance of the contract killing. He needed $200 cash immediately to continue with the mission.

"You need $200? Are you kidding?" I denied the ridiculous request and hung up the cell phone on the very irate man on the other line.

El Diablo called again and insisted Phil Jordan meet with him anywhere in the Dallas area to provide the necessary financial assistance. The FBI coached the informant believing they had conceived a clever plan to get Phil involved with the conspiracy.

"You want to meet Phil? *Estas pendejo* (Are you stupid)?" Again, I hung up on *El Diablo* and the FBI wiretap. The informant tried calling several more times but I did not answer.

I knew exactly what the FBI had and how they would portray me. The prosecution would paint an ugly picture of me and present it to a judge, a jury, and the media.

The FBI would pick and choose only the incriminating evidence. They would never disclose the majority of the telephone conversations where I refused their failed entrapment attempts. They would use all their unlimited resources and personnel to present a compelling criminal case based on biased testimony and fabricated circumstantial evidence.

Perception is everything because reality is based on perception. In this case, I knew judgmental and prejudicial views would condemn me.

Police officers are held to a higher standard. They pledge an oath of integrity and dedication to fight the good fight. I needed to be made an example of a good cop going bad. I crossed the line, and to the judicial system, the thought was just as bad as the deed. Justice would be served, and I would get what I deserved.

After the FBI agents read my Miranda rights three times, I finally asked for an attorney. The interview was over and they were upset I didn't give up Phil. Once I felt the cold metal tightness of the handcuffs on my wrists, there was no way out after that.

I didn't want my wife, parents, and family to be embarrassed. I asked the FBI agents that the arrest not be publicized but I was in no position to ask for anything.

The overnight stay in the Hidalgo County jail was the longest night of my life. The constant noise of inmates talking, metal doors slamming, and the disbelief of being arrested made it impossible to sleep. The morning could not come soon enough. I just wanted to talk to my wife and tell her everything would be okay.

The next day, my mug shot was plastered on the front pages of local, regional, and international newspapers. The FBI claimed they arrested a rogue DEA agent who had a personal agenda and conceived a devious plan to kill someone. Everybody from the Cable News Network (CNN) to the El Paso television news programs broadcast the arrest. El Paso television stations and newspapers kept the story going as the FBI fueled their egos.

My parents were devastated and embarrassed. They received many telephone calls at their home, not of condolences but of inquiries. They refused to believe the rumors of their honorable son being capable of such an evil deed.

Lily was at the Monterrey government-leased home when she was told of her husband's arrest. The DEA agents wanted her to vacate Monterrey immediately. Her composure outweighed the shock. She refused to leave.

Lily realized she would not be coming back and wanted to gather everything of sentimental value. She piled anything that fit into her Chevrolet Trailblazer. The next day, Lily drove to the U.S. border to be with her husband.

Meanwhile, the FBI wanted to interrogate her. She had to know something about her husband's desire to assassinate someone. They believed she would add more to their case or possibly say something to insinuate her part in the murder-for-hire scheme. If that happened, they would use her arrest as leverage to get me to talk. Lily refused to talk to anyone.

The FBI wanted to execute a search warrant of our government-leased home. They wanted to find additional physical evidence in our homestead or in Lily's personal computer.

A U.S. judge denied the request for a search warrant. The judge felt the FBI didn't have enough probable cause for the overreach. It would be the only ounce of sympathy from the judicial system. The worst was yet to come.

The U.S. Magistrating Judge initially set a surety bond of $200,000 against me. Most defendants are issued a surety bond whereby a ten percent fee is paid by the defendant's family to a bail bond company. A self-employed friend of mine paid the $20,000 fee for my release from jail.

The judge ordered me to reside within the Southern District of Texas under the supervision of a U.S. Probation Officer. I was prohibited from traveling and needed to report my every move to a baby sitter.

I was ambushed by television and newspaper reporters upon my release from the Hidalgo County jail. Having made every effort to remain under the radar as a narc, I was now in the limelight.

I had plenty to say to the media in my defense but knew it wouldn't help my cause. However, I wanted just one thing to be published, especially in the Mexican media - *El Diablo* was a rat for the FBI! I hoped those in the underworld would read the newspaper.

Without a home, Lily and I humbly asked her parents to live with them in their modest home in Floresville, Texas. They were very accommodating. Lily and I went from a two-story mansion with all utilities and rent paid by the U.S. governement to Lily's childhood bedroom. All our furniture and personal belongings would be transported from Monterrey to my parents garage in El Paso. We didn't know where we would live in the near future.

As we arrived at the countryside residence, Lily noticed a telephone company linesman on a nearby utility pole. There was a white unmarked utility van parked next to the pole. She asked, "Isn't it a little unusual for them to be working on a Sunday?"

I knew it was the FBI setting up the equipment to wiretap my in-laws' home telephone line. They were going to make every effort to record any additional incriminating conversations made by me. I answered, "Yes. Please don't tell your parents. It will only upset them."

The FBI wasn't done. One week later, they pursued a malicious tactic and requested a court hearing for a bond increase. They wanted to keep me behind bars hoping I would break. They claimed I had lots of money since I paid for my initial bond fee. They argued that I must be considered a flight risk because of my contacts with the *federales* in Mexico.

The judge agreed with the FBI and exhibited his disgust with the high-profile criminal by setting an exorbitant $100,000 'cash bond'. The FBI and the U.S. Attorney's Office believed they had me by the throat again because there would be no way I could come up with that kind of cash.

Miraculously, a generous childhood friend withdrew all his personal savings to keep me out of jail. My friend knew he would get his money back from the court system after my case was closed. For me, this was merely a small victory in a winless battle.

The judge wasn't done. He ordered me be leashed like a dog. The tightness around my ankle from the Home Confinement Monitoring bracelet was secondary to the disdain I had for the federal judge. I was confined to my in-law's home. I couldn't go out into the public.

I believed if you screw up, 'Man Up', take the heat, and get on with your life. But the bastards kept kicking me while I was down.

DEA employees were ordered not to communicate with me or they would be disciplined. I was a pariah. The people that I had helped personally and professionally were nowhere to be found when I needed them most.

I was considered 'The Fixer' for many employees in the El Paso DEA office. I helped an agent from getting disciplined for wrecking his OGV while under the influence of alcohol. I had the vehicle towed and repaired before anyone noticed it missing. I helped another agent with his marital problems by talking to his wife and explaining his job description. She didn't believe he was working the non-banker hours. Another employee needed financial assistance so I helped her pay the bills. These were only a few minor examples.

Abandonment and betrayal are most painful when afflicted by those closest to you. There is a saying, "You find out who your friends are when you go to the hospital or when you go to jail." Now, I could count my true friends on one hand.

Vince Sellers ignored the order and called to console me. I warned him that the FBI tapped the phones. Vince responded, "Fuck those glory-seekers! As for the DEA, I'm not here to make any friends. I have all the friends I need to stab me in the back!"

Vince continued, "Aside from the misinformation from the FBI, there is a lot of gossip in our agency about you, and it's not good. Our own agents are claiming to have inside information that you plotted and paid for the hit. It's entertaining for these assholes to gossip and kick someone when they are on the ground. Don't count on any help from our people."

I asked, "What about Paul, Yvette, or Calderon?"

The FBI has been given permission by our administration to interrogate every DEA agent you associated with in the last year. They are trying to find out if you told anyone about your intentions. Remember that DEA stands for 'Don't Expect Anything'. Your so-called friends were never your friends!"

A quote came to mind by a William Shakespeare character, Leonato, "Done to death by slanderous tongues."

Vince added, "When they interviewed me, I told them I hadn't spoke to you since you left the El Paso office. Regarding the allegation, I told them you may have said something out of character but that you weren't that stupid. I was blunt about one thing. I told them if you really wanted to kill the punk, you would have done it yourself. You know exactly where he lives because we've been to his house in Juarez."

Vince continued, "This whole thing could have been handled administratively. Instead, our spineless acting-Administrator gave you up to the FBI."

"Why didn't he defend me?"

"He doesn't care about you! He is looking out for his own interests. He allowed one of his best agents to get fucked by the FBI so he can be endorsed by the FBI Director and get confirmed by Congress."

I was disgusted with the 'sellout' that eventually got rewarded with the title of DEA Administrator.

Vince asked, "Why don't you fight this shit in court?"

I responded, "I intend to. I can explain my actions and reveal the entrapment methods used by the FBI including the bullshit promised payment of $10,000. It just wasn't one incriminating act. It was a series of events that accumulated into circumstantial evidence. I said some stupid shit and the feebs ate it up!"

Vince said, "The propaganda machine of the feebs has spread the word that your actions created an open and shut case. They claim to have you by the balls!"

I realized, "I'm screwed. You know, if the government wants you, it will get you. We did it all the time."

"In your case, nobody was going to get killed. It was all talk initiated by the feebs. Actually, the FBI and your informant committed more of the alleged crime than you did!"

I wished others, especially an eventual judge or jury, would realize what Vince was saying.

Vince concluded, "As for giving the FBI what they want, it's your ass on the line. It's obvious they want your cousin, Phil." Vince would never encourage me to rat on someone else. He was only concerned that I would do what was best.

The option of blaming someone else was always on the table for me. Even as I was signing my termination papers from the DEA, a supervisor told me, "Damn, tell them Phil did it, and you can walk away from this! Nobody will blame you!"

It is human nature to defend yourself when accused of doing something you know you didn't do. I was confident I could explain the circumstantial evidence and vindicate myself. I recollected the times I met with *El Diablo* and could provide written documentation to show the payments were legit. Everything I did was authorized by my supervisor and witnessed by fellow DEA agents.

However, without the DEA on my side, I would be up the proverbial creek without a paddle. The evidence would be molded to conform to the answers they already had. There is a belief in the legal field whereby if your client is left explaining his actions while backpedaling, then you don't have a chance of winning. I would have a lot of explaining to do.

Retaining a good criminal defense attorney is like choosing a trustworthy used car salesman. You don't know who is going to rip you off.

My personal bank account of $7,000 was just a drop in the bucket needed for legal fees. The highly recommended attorney required a $20,000 retainer fee along with his meals and travel expenses paid. The $350 hourly fee included his time spent on reading reports, attending meetings, and all telephone conversations.

When I received the bi-weekly billing statements, I realized it was hopeless. Within months, my 401k Retirement pension was depleted. It would take years for Lily to pay off the debt. I couldn't afford to pay for the advocate that was supposed to be on my side.

Legal defense options were discussed. Entrapment seemed like the most obvious defense strategy, however, it was an extremely difficult defense to produce. Political reasons and the racial undertones were also considered, but I did not want to play the racial card.

Americans believe they are living under the fairest judicial system in the world. Those who have been subjected to the prosecutorial process know otherwise. The scales of Lady Justice are imbalanced by the heavy-handed prosecutor against the few rights available to the accused.

There is a selective form of law enforcement and prosecution instituted in the U.S. It begins with the power of discretion from the arresting officer. Then, the defendant is taken before a judge who may adhere to a formatted schedule to set a bond amount for release from incarceration.

Most defendants cannot afford to hire an attorney. They are represented by a court-appointed attorney who might work as hard as a paid attorney to defend them. Privileged defendants, those with money or political connections, are less likely to be prosecuted or receive the same punishment as those with no connections. These are just some variables that make the judicial system unfair and unbalanced.

The U.S. Attorney's Office threatened to file additional charges unless I pled guilty immediately. I knew the tactic well. Stack the charges and pressure the defendant to plead guilty, obviating trial preparation and a time-consuming trial. Expedition of punishment took precedence over the presentation of factual innocence.

There are no absolutes in life. For instance, "Innocent men do not plead guilty." A moral wrong had become a criminal act. I knew I was not totally innocent, but I was not totally guilty of committing the elements of the crime.

Many people told me, "I would have done the same thing. If someone killed any of my family members, I would kill the asshole myself!" Rationalizing my personal actions by wanting a murderer punished was considered honorable by most people however it was illegal in this case.

Reading my name versus the United States of America on court documents made me sick to my stomach. The country I nearly died for was now my adversary. The same federal prosecutors I had worked and socialized with were now going after me.

Throughout my DEA career, I had done things nobody wanted to do, and it had taken its toll. A product of my environment, I saw the world through cynical eyes. What was I to think when my livelihood was predicated in the foundations of deception and in a world where killing was customary? This didn't matter to the righteous enforcers at the FBI and the judicious prosecutors at the U.S. Attorney's Office.

The investigative tactics used by the FBI would never be scrutinized. Law enforcement officers and government prosecutors have immunity from criminal prosecution even when they falsely accuse, arrest or indict an innocent person. No apologies or compensation for the loss of employment for the victims of overzealous enforcers.

The U.S. Attorney's Office gave me a deadline. Take the plea immediately or the seven-year offer would be withdrawn. Additional charges would be created and a twenty-year prison sentence would be vigorously pursued.

Throughout my law enforcement career, I considered myself successful. I was a winner! Nobody likes to lose but I just got my ass kicked. I felt defeated. I was out of energy, out of legal options, and out of money.

Taking the high road was my only choice. An option that I would forever regret. I pled guilty to the murder for hire charge and accepted the eighty-seven months of incarceration in the Federal Bureau of Prisons. I would never be permitted to explain my side of the story to the judge or anyone else.

At the sentencing hearing, I was instructed by my attorney not to cause any doubt in the judge's mind or the case would go to trial. He said I couldn't afford it. My only words in the courtroom came from an edited apologetic statement to the court and the press.

The federal judge sensed my unwillingness to accept the plea agreement. Unless I said something about innocence or entrapment, he would abide by the recommended prison sentence. In fact, he considered giving me a higher prison sentence for the mafia-style plot described by the FBI in the criminal complaint.

Many letters were written to the judge for consideration during my sentencing. People who worked with me from the INS, U.S. State Department and other agencies wanted the judge to show leniency for someone who was kind, caring and professional. There were no letters submitted by any DEA personnel.

The judge said, "I'm reading all these letters from people saying how great of a person you are and asking me to show leniency. However, according to the criminal complaint by the FBI, I should give you a higher prison sentence for your mafia-style plot to kill someone."

The judge ignored my fifteen years in law enforcement and abided by the plea agreement designated by the Federal Sentencing Guidelines. He claimed his hands were tied and prohibited from applying a lower prison sentence because of repercussions from the U.S. Department of Justice.

After many years of walking into a federal courtroom as a witness for the U.S. government, I sat alone at the other table. I looked at the bailiff, court reporter, attorneys, and FBI agents shaking hands and joking around with each other. On that day, I was their enemy. I felt like an outcast.

The U.S. Attorney's Office notched a victory in the interest of justice with the punishment of a high-profile criminal. The arrest and prosecution of a corrupt cop was a success.

El Diablo was rewarded tens of thousands of dollars of U.S. taxpayer dollars for his righteous efforts. It was a hefty payday for him going to the FBI and presenting a DEA agent's head on a silver platter.

For the FBI agents who set me up, it was mental masturbation.

It hit me like a two-ton heavy thing. I was going to prison for a long time. My career was over in law enforcement and I was now a convict. I realized criminal justice, a sadistic oxymoron, was administered based on expediency rather than with facts or compassion.

I was permitted three months of freedom before self-surrendering to a federal prison in Kentucky. This would give me time to get things in order before the lengthy separation. My mindset was securing Lily's wellbeing while licking my wounds from the devastating financial setback. In my heart and mind, I was already incarcerated.

With ninety days and counting, I needed to devote the precious time with my parents. I wanted to comfort them as much as I needed their nurturing. I just prayed their debilitating health issues would not take them away before I got out of prison.

In my younger days, the drive from San Antonio to El Paso was enjoyable and relaxing. The transition from the fertile hill country to the vast desert landscape used to illicit invigorating and calming thoughts. The nine-hour journey was complemented with a twelve-pack of Bud Light beer and a pound of beef jerky from Wiatrek's Meat Market in Poth, Texas. The return trip included two bags of Martinez Brand pork rinds and a twelve-pack of Tecate beer.

On this trip, three cups of coffee and an energy drink were required. The panoramic view was obscured with despair and there was nothing to see. Only faint memories of the past and the many questions about the future occupied my mind during the long, tedious drive.

I kept my composure trying not to let my family feel the pain. Regardless of what I did with loved ones, the constant pain in my chest would not subside as I dreaded the inevitable. Words could not describe my overwhelming grief.

In my parent's garage, I packed away my business suits. The same suits I wore as the key witness in many federal court trials. I squeezed all my casual wear in a few cardboard boxes wondering if they would fit me in seven years.

I reached for the Creed compact disc and played "My Own Prison". The lyrics of the song described the stages of persecution and the sorrows of a man defeated by the unrelenting powers that be.

As I was sifting through my DEA memorabilia, I came upon two Exceptional Achievement certificates I had received. In a fit of anger, I ripped up the awards thinking, "It didn't matter how hard I tried. In the end, none of this mattered." I gave everything I had to an entity that had no feelings. I lost everything because of one man and the FBI!

I needed inspirational words to give me strength and overcome my fear of what lie ahead. Something wise and powerful enough to stay with me for the next seven years.

I turned to my father. It is difficult for a father to tell his son the right words about overcoming adversity. Especially when they are going to prison for a long time. I asked, "Dad, how am I supposed to get through this?"

A man of few words gave me the most relevant advice. He said, "Play it cool." Those three simple words put things into perspective and have guided me to this day.

With only a few days left, I needed to return to Floresville and be with Lily. As I was driving away, I looked back to see my parents crying and hugging each other on the driveway. It would be an image that would haunt me forever.

Lily and I spent our last night together unable to sleep. We lay side by side staring into the ceiling in disbelief.

She asked, "How can they lock you up for seven years? People who have committed worse crimes are sentenced to less time. It doesn't make sense. It was all talk. Nobody was going to get hurt!"

I clasped her hand. I came up with pragmatic answers and tried to assure her everything would be okay.

Then I said, "I am so sorry I let you down. You have been so loyal, never questioning my actions. You have your life to live and as much as it hurts to say this, you don't have to wait for me."

"Don't ever say that again! I will be here waiting for you. We will pick up the pieces." She cried the entire night.

Lily drove me to the San Antonio Airport. Against her wishes, she dropped me off in the departure lane. I did not want this to be a long, painful farewell.

I leaned over the center console. I caressed her lips and wiped away the tears trickling down her cheeks. I took off my wedding band because I didn't want to wear anything of value in prison. "Hold onto to this so you can put it back on my finger. I need you to be stronger than ever. We can do this together and not let those bastards get the better of us."

I kissed her on the lips, "Let's not say goodbye. Instead, let's just say, I'll see you soon."

I stepped out of the vehicle with my tote bag. She didn't want to leave me standing alone on the curb. I insisted she drive away. I could see her eyes filling with tears. Through the immense grief, she forced a fake smile and drove away sobbing. It would be one very long depressing year before we saw each other again.

I walked up to the airline ticket counter and asked for my boarding pass. The bubbly ticket agent asked, "No luggage to check in?"

"No ma'am."

"May I help you select a flight for your return."

I responded, "I'm not coming back for a long time."

Chapter 24 – The Sound Of The Keys

The U.S. Federal Bureau of Prisons (BOP) assigned most inmates to a prison facility within 500 miles of their hometown so they could be close to family members. This accommodated loved ones to visit inmates regularly during incarceration.

My family and I were not afforded that privilege. I was ordered to report to a low-security prison in Ashland, Kentucky - 1,200 miles away from El Paso and Floresville, Texas.

The BOP believed this distant facility would keep me far away from the Southwest border and would reduce the chances I might encounter someone I had arrested. If the prison officials were really concerned about my safety, they would have placed me in the safest facility known as a minimum-security camp, or Club Fed. Instead, I would be imprisoned behind high cinderblock walls and razor-wire fences.

According to the prison guidelines, I had pled guilty to a 'crime of violence'. Thus, I was considered a threat to society and would be placed in a facility with similar offenders. Also, my crime made me ineligible for any rehabilitative programs that could have reduced the prison term.

Prison officials did not consider providing me with an alias identity or fictitious name. I was just another criminal to them. I was left to fend for myself with my true identity.

I cut my hair short, shaved off all facial hair, and wore plastic frame glasses with thick lenses because soft lens contacts were prohibited in prison. I looked nerdy, nothing like my undercover days, and felt safer that way.

I had to reprogram myself and act like I truly felt - angry. I would use street lingo, prison jargon, and not let any law enforcement terms slip out of my mouth. I needed to stop acting like a cop and act like a con.

When I arrived at the prison, I stood at front entrance and was overwhelmed with the sight. The high razor wire fences that surrounded the facility terrified me. I froze for a few minutes wondering how I was going to survive in there for the next seven years. I couldn't turn back now.

I realized that crying would not help me and praying wouldn't do me no good. I took one more very deep breath of freedom and walked in.

The prison guard asked me, "You actually came from Texas to self-surrender?" He turned to another guard and said, "Hey, can you believe this guy came alone from down south. I don't remember anyone having the balls to do that."

The other guard approached me and asked, "You actually came up here on your own dime? Most convicts would have let the U.S. Marshal's Service pick them up and have the taxpayers foot the bill."

They returned to the issue at hand and ordered me to strip down, bend over and cough. This would be the first of many degrading events to come. Khaki clothing, a blanket, a towel, and a small bar of soap were provided.

My personal clothes, wallet, and watch were placed in a cardboard box and mailed to Lily by prison officials. She cried for hours after receiving the container back in Floresville.

I was escorted to a large two-story building lined with metal bars and inquisitive on-lookers. The heavy metal door that slammed behind me confirmed there was no turning back. I walked through the maze of countless bunk beds until I found mine. I climbed up the metal frame and jumped onto the upper bunk.

A Correctional Officer (CO) yelled, "Lights out!" The lights were turned off in the large bay area that had been in operation since the 1930's. With no modern conveniences, it looked and smelled like when it was first constructed during the Prohibition Era.

The darkness concealed the anguish on my face and the tears that trickled down my cheeks. As I lay my head down, thoughts raced uncontrollably, "This must be a nightmare! Someone please wake me up! There was some kind of mistake. The FBI, the DEA, or some politician needs to make an eleventh hour reprieve for me. I don't belong here!"

Hope is defined as believing in something. In prison hope is a worthless concept. Reality hit me, "I'm not going anywhere. This is my new home." I tried to soften the hard pillow. I turned it over to feel the cool side, but there wasn't a cooler side. I wouldn't find any comfort for a very long time. I lost all hope.

Few people sleep in prison. Throughout the night, there was constant movement, inmates talking, and unmannered sounds. The most distinctive sound was the clanking of the oversized metal keys that hung on the prison guard's belt. The keys used for the large metal doors. The sound let the inmates know the location of the hack, crude slang for a prison guard.

In my second week of incarceration, I was introduced to three staff members, called a Unit Team, who would monitor my progress. The Unit Team lectured me on what was expected of me for the next several years.

The female counselor said, "You need to participate in rehabilitative programs, get a job in the kitchen, and don't cause any problems." The standardized introductory was insulting and illustrated the ignorance of the Bureau of Prisons classification process. I kept my cool as the woman continued to lecture me. After fifteen minutes, she asked, "Do you have any questions?"

"Yes. Why am I being housed in a facility that houses drug traffickers and violent offenders? Can you please consider a transfer to a safer location?"

The response was, "You wanted someone dead! You are not going to get any special treatment from us!"

As much as I despised the fat GS-5 talking down to me, she was right. I would get no sympathy. I had to get used to the condescending attitudes and derogatory statements from the BOP staff and guards.

It didn't take long for inquisitive inmates to ask about my placement in the northern region of the United States. One inmate asked "If you're from Texas, why are you up north?" Like most inmates, he knew it was one of two reasons. I was either a snitch or a cop.

I deflected the insinuation by claiming the prison decision-makers had placed me in this distant location due to racial integration. "They need to send Mexicans up here to keep you White boys in check. I've already filed discrimination charges against these motherfuckers!" I hoped the fabrication would prevent any further personal questions from any of the two thousand inmates I was living with.

The inmate pursued his inquiry, "What are you in for?"

I needed to create a federal crime that would be believable. It couldn't be anything related to drug trafficking because I didn't want to be asked about the drug type and organization I was affiliated with. It would only lead to further questions. I kept it vague, "Money laundering."

"Why would they (the BOP) send you way up here for that?"

I responded, "No disrespect man, but you past your limit of one question per year." I smirked as if joking but it was no joke. I needed to develop tactful responses to prevent insulting any inquisitive inmates.

There were many aspects of prison life that I needed to learn quickly. First-time offenders were not provided with a "How To Act In Prison" handbook. I never had affiliated with anyone who had gone to prison. I was a cop who only associated with law-abiding citizens.

Prison nicknames were usually given based on the inmate's hometown or a physical characteristic. There was 'ATL' from Atlanta, 'Chi-Town' from Chicago and 'Taliban' for the inmate from the Middle East. Then there was 'Casper' who had pale skin and 'Pork Chop' who was overweight.

Some nicknames were considered forms of camaraderie or friendship. Others were derogatory such as, the 'Psycho', who had obvious mental issues, the 'Weenie Washer', a convicted pedophile, and 'Shakira', a Latin transvestite. These men had very lengthy and afflictive prison sentences.

I was given the nickname of 'Tex' because I was the only one from Texas in the facility. I never felt like a 'Tex', but it was safer than being called by my true name.

My first year of incarceration was wasted on retrospection. Dwelling on my past life of regrets and mistakes took up all my mental and emotional energy. Even cherished memories of family and friends wore me down and made me miss the outside world even more.

For months, I had a recurring dream that I was back in the El Paso DEA office. My former co-workers welcomed me back when they realized everything was a misunderstanding. The euphoria only caused heartache after I awoke. I'd wake up everytime thinking, "Shit, I'm in fucking prison! I'm in a living nightmare."

Prison is not a place to be soft. It is not a place to reveal your emotions or intimate thoughts to anyone. An inmate who exhibits any feebleness or complains about aspects of their incarceration is considered weak. Resiliency is necessary to overcome the administrative frustrations and individual challenges.

One must eliminate cravings of favorite foods and personal desires.

Amenities, pleasures, and favorite television programming will likely be unavailable while incarcerated. Then there is the recommended abstinence of vices like alcohol, drugs, and sex.

I promised myself two things while in prison. I would refrain from any sexual deviancy, and I would never shed a tear. To overcome any emotional or psychological lapses, I resorted to anger as my source of strength throughout my incarceration. I was mad at myself for falling into a trap, incensed with *El Diablo* and the FBI for setting me up, and disgusted with the people who turned their backs on me.

I was even mad at God wondering why he let this happen to me. He allowed pedophile priests to go unpunished and mass murderers to ruin countless lives! Yeah, I have the right to get mad at Him. He can take it!

I was given the name Salvador by my parents. In Spanish, it means 'savior'. Hell, I couldn't even save myself.

There are many unwritten rules that must be followed to survive in prison. Some include not staring at other inmates, don't talk too much, don't snitch, don't brag about yourself, and, most importantly, don't complain.

I listened to one inmate constantly complaining about his thirteen-month sentence. The 'soft joker' was determined to spend all his days in prison fighting for his freedom. The man said, "I was unjustly punished by a judge, a jury, and neglected by my attorney."

I turned to him and said, "You need to shut the fuck up! There are men doing twenty to thirty-year prison sentences. Nobody wants to hear any crying ass, bitching from you! Take a nap and your nightmare will be over." The advice was based on the philosophy that the more you sleep in prison, the less prison time you actually experience.

Another inmate used humor to scold the short-timer, "Stop complaining! You're not at Yale, you're in jail!"

Prison was like attending an all-male college with a mandatory course in human behavior. Everyone was living in a fish bowl, and people were looking at everything you did and said. You were forced to see the same individuals throughout every waking moment often for months, and sometimes for years. You saw their flaws, and often they would get under your skin. One needed to adapt to the uncongenial living conditions while ignoring the repulsive.

Many inmates were not housebroken. They didn't bathe regularly, use proper hygiene, or keep their bunk area clean. They didn't wipe the sink after washing their face, shaving, or brushing their teeth. They don't wash their hands after taking a shit.

They would sit on the toilet and admire their work of art instead of administering a 'courtesy flush' to prevent the foul odor from filling the air. Some would ignore the catchphrase of consideration, "Drop a load, flush the commode!" Come to think of it, this occurs in the free world, too. Any who has been in a public restroom has experienced the same disgusting behavior.

Prison was a melting pot of men with mental health issues and emotional problems. The angry men, serving prolonged sentences, were the ones society should worry about. The limited medical and educational programs can't heal the deep-rooted disorders.

Prisoners were warehoused in facilities made to accommodate half of the population. Prison administrators and the judicial system have ignored overcrowding. Depending on the age of the facility, inmates slept in two-man cells or open dorms housing around a hundred men. In these large bays, nicknamed sardine cans, bunk beds were aligned an arm's reach from each other.

Stories of rape, drug usage, and extortion were exaggerated. Sometimes rape was used as a punitive measure, but sex in prison was usually consensual. An inmate jokingly told me, "Don't ever sleep face down."

I responded, "You got that right! I have a one-way valve. There will be no in through the out door."

There was some violence, but most inmates tried not to lose their Good Time, that is, the incentive to reduce their prison sentence without any administrative infractions. Ideal inmates would receive one month off their sentence, after each year was completed.

The most common types of dispute between inmates occurred over television programming, telephone usage, and the microwave.

I noticed at times that all the televisions in each bay were tuned to music video channels. The Black inmates made a power move, slang for take control, by changing the channels to their liking and filling the airwaves with rap music. The White and Hispanic inmates avoided confrontation and found other ways to occupy their time.

On one occasion, I wanted to use the microwave oven for two minutes to heat up a bag of popcorn. With only one appliance made available to a hundred inmates, it was a prized amenity that required cooperation and sharing. An inmate had been using it for over an hour. Other inmates were denied access and walked away with their cold food in hand.

I wasn't going to be intimidated. At stake was a physical beating and I was sure to get the worst of it. Did I really feel that strongly about eating a bag of popcorn? I decided to make a power move on the man and check him, slang for confront him. I asked, "Mind if I use the microwave for a minute?"

The Black inmate making food for his crew did not turn to acknowledge me but said, "You need to wait."

I said, "I've been waiting an hour."

The inmate played with his corn rows on his head then turned towards me, "I'm still using it. You need to wait about another hour before I'm done, *amigo*."

With plenty of built up anger, I got in the face of the larger Black man saying, "First of all, I'm not your *amigo*. Second, take a break or I'll break the microwave over your fucking head!"

"You flexing on me?" Flex is slang for challenging someone.

Another Black inmate stepped between us and said, "C'mon, don't do this! Let the man get his popcorn on!"

The man removed the Tupperware container filled with rice and chicken. He placed it on top of the other six plastic bowls.

I placed the bag of popcorn inside the microwave oven. I pressed a button and stared at the fuming man standing in my intimate space. It was a very long two minutes.

I enjoyed eating a bag of popcorn in the television room. It was one of the few pleasures available to me. I wasn't going to let anyone jack my rec, slang for interrupt my recreation.

Most inmates tried to keep whatever dignity they had left during the lowest point of their lives. They kept busy with their job assignment or whatever hobby was available. Some leaned on another for emotional and psychological support. Sharing a hardship with another seemed harmless but could be very dangerous.

Much like the American populace, prison guards considered inmates as third-class citizens. Guards and staff were indifferent to inmate requests because prisoners had lost all their rights. Phrases used ad nauseam by guards when addressing a disgruntled prisoner were "You got what you deserved", "You should've thought about that before you committed the crime", and "Don't do the crime if you can't do the time."

Inmates rarely experienced any form of humor. It was not accepted or normal to be laughing during the worst time of your life. Oddly, I found a few accounts of humor while incarcerated.

An young Indian inmate with a last name of Patel told me, "Apparently Jesus must be spending his precious time in American prisons."

I responded, "Why would you say that?"

"Because alot of inmates say they found Jesus in prison."

I smiled. He was making a point. The most hypocritical people in the world are those 'fakers' that claim they are walking with the Lord but don't practice what they preach. In fact, they act reborn when it is convenient for them. They are the most perverse of sinners.

Another incident occurred when four inmates became gravely ill. Medical staff could not figure out the source of their unique ailments, especially the high levels of mercury in their blood stream.

After days of interrogation, one of the men admitted they had been trapping pigeons on the rec yard and cooking the substitute for 'yard bird' as fine prison cuisine. The poison that nearly killed the inmates came from the toxic pigeons that drank industrial wastewater from a reservoir at a nearby paper factory.

Another sick nugget of humor occurred when an inmate assigned to trash can duty found a used tampon in the Unit Manager's office. For days, the inmate marketed his prized product by offering a whiff of the bloody item for a price of three postage stamps. Postage stamps were a primary source of currency in prison. The man made a killing!

The jokester later admitted to me, "I actually smothered the tampon with a packet of ketchup. These fools thought they were getting a whiff of Ms. Kelly's monthly visitor!"

I couldn't help but laugh.

The orderly continued, "I know what she really smells like."

"What do you mean?"

"After she leaves from work, I get to smell her office chair. I can tell when she isn't wearing any panties."

"You are one perverted dude."

Chapter 25
Don't Expect Anything And You Won't Be Disappointed

Two men in business suits, who identified themselves as OPR investigators, visited me in prison.

They wanted to know if I was willing to give up other DEA employees for some questionable activities. The names of supervisors and agents were provided to me along with their alleged violations.

"You want me to tell you what my former co-workers did so you could build a criminal case against them?"

One man said, "There would be benefits for your cooperation. Just like it was offered to you regarding your cousin Phil."

They thought since I was abandoned by the DEA, I desired revenge by disclosing the illegal activities conducted by other agents.

I deduced by their conversation and mannerisms that they were actually FBI Special Agents. They wanted to arrest other DEA personnel while making me a final offer to implicate Phil Jordan in my case.

I kept the meeting brief and said, "Get the fuck out of here. I have nothing to say."

The men rose from the plastic chairs, turned off the mini-recorder, and departed with their tails between their legs.

I thought to myself, "The only opportunity I had to reduce my prison sentence just walked out the door."

A significant event occurred after that encounter. It was a Saturday morning in the rec yard when my life took another unexpected turn. A prison softball league had been formed by the inmates. I was selected as the head coach by the Hispanics which included Cubans, Dominicans, and Mexicans.

During the game, I noticed many of my teammates eyeballing me. I wondered why many of them were acting different and not saying a word to me throughout the game.

After the game, my full name was announced over the public address system telling me to report to the Lieutenant's office. I knew it was never a good thing for an inmate to hear their name announced to the entire compound.

I walked into the office and was handed a Gentlemen's Quarterly Magazine (GQ) with an eight-page story about myself. The article displayed photographs of me. The article described an upcoming book titled, "Down by the River", by author Charles Bowden.

After my arrest, Mr. Bowden wanted to interview me. At that time, I did not trust anyone with my personal or business affairs. I had just been burned by *El Diablo*, the FBI, and the DEA.

Concerned with legal implications, I provided the author with vague and non-legal aspects of my arrest. The interviews were published nationally for everyone to read, including federal prisoners.

Inmates were permitted to receive magazine subscriptions and books from the outside. The information found in them usually spread quickly in the compound. As I flipped through the pages, I realized many inmates were made aware of my background and wanted to wring my neck. Cons despised cops, especially ex-cops living in their midst.

In the past year, several inmates had confided in me about their criminal cases. I must have given the impression that I was a caring person and wouldn't repeat their confessions. I was told many things I didn't want to hear. Those same inmates would be the first in line to shut me up.

The Lieutenant asked, "Looks like you are famous!"

I responded, "I'm going to get my ass kicked."

"Do you think you can fade the heat?"

"Hell no!"

"We can put you in solitary confinement until things cool down."

"That will take months. I can't go back with these guys."

"You leave me no choice. If you feel your life is in danger then I have to do something about it. I'll have an orderly gather all the belongings from your locker."

For my safety, I was taken out of the general population and placed in solitary confinement. Prison officials use politically correct terms, such as

Special Housing Unit (SHU) or segregation, in an attempt to humanize the isolation. Inmates refer to it as 'the hole'.

One must imagine being enclosed in a small restroom without a shower stall. A metal-frame twin cot, toilet, metal and tiny metal sink are the provided essentials. Then, fathom living in this enclosure for months or years.

Detachment from other humans can cause the mind to wander. With no visual or intellectual stimulation, the imagination may extend beyond the limits of normality. There was no way to ignore the paralyzing state in these conditions. Few brief events distracted me from the neurosis and preoccupation with my anger and depression.

Physical exercise was limited to push-ups on the floor, stomach crunches on the cot, and pull-ups by wrapping a bath towel on the highest part of the sliding metal door. Thoughts crossed my mind of ending the nightmare by wrapping the towel around my neck. I calmed myself as I paced for hours back and forth in the 6' by 10' cell.

I detracted from the overwhelming boredom by reading outdated, overused paperback books distributed by an orderly. Some books had missing pages, graffiti, or boogers stuck to the pages.

During solitary confinement, interaction with another human came only when a meal tray was slipped between the steel bars. I refused to initiate conversation with the CO's because I despised them. They continually denied my requests to use the telephone so I could update my wife of my circumstances.

Handcuffs and shackles were customary for the walk from the prison cell to the shower stall. The showers were offered whenever the CO's felt like it, usually every three to four days.

Deprivation from necessities and hygiene required adaptation. For instance, clean underwear was distributed just twice per week. I had to turn the boxer shorts inside out then reversed to provide me with a sense of cleanliness.

Two cells away from me, there was an inmate with mental problems who constantly complained to the CO's. He knocked on the metal gates for hours taking breaks while he napped. He talked out loud as if he were conversing with family members. The CO's didn't care to keep him quiet because they were in another room behind a heavy metal door.

For weeks, the inmate sang out loud the same song over and over. I came to dislike the catchy pop song, "Sweet Dreams" by the Eurythmics.

My only connection to the free world was my Sony Walkman. The invisible airwaves provided moments of restrained joy. I found a distant radio station that played blues artists like John Lee Hooker, Albert King, and Sonny Boy Williamson. These underappreciated pioneers of blues music were the roots for many classic rock groups and artists.

I heard a groovy tune by Muddy Waters called "The Blues Had a Baby and They Called It Rock and Roll." The 'wah-wah' of the bluesy harmonica took me to a place outside the metal cage and provided solace during another low point in my life.

With no television viewing available, I listened to sports announcer, Brent Musberger, eloquently describe my beloved Los Angeles Lakers winning the NBA Championship. I held back my joy because there was nobody to high-five.

On rare occasions, I was taken to the rec area for a change of scenery. I would have an hour to walk around in a larger cage. With nothing more than a discarded, deflated basketball available, I would toss it against the chain-link enclosure. I would reminisce back to the days of playing with my childhood buddies at Ramona Elementary in El Paso. I would transcend beyond the prison, the inmates, and the CO staring at me.

The greatest elation came from the fifteen-minute telephone conversations with my wife. The telephone calls were permitted, usually once or twice per week, depending on the mood of the prison guards.

I was never advised of the anticipated length of confinement in 'the hole'. I had prior experience regarding the submission of administrative forms within a governmental entity. However, not knowing my immediate future was absolutely frustrating.

I would lie to Lily saying I was comfortable and optimistic about the pending move to another facility. Now that my true identity was broadcast to inmates throughout the country, I hoped the prison officials would come to their senses and realize that I needed to be transferred to a safer level facility.

As for people on the outside, they were busy with their own lives. Correspondences from my few friends and relatives began to thin out as time went by. For most, it was a chore to sit down and write a letter.

Today, I had been anxiously awaiting on one specific envelope. Sent by someone with an alias name and fake address, it finally arrived. "Bad things happen to bad people" was scribbled on the envelope.

Inside was the front page of a borderland Mexican newspaper. The headline in bold letters claimed a Mexican State Police Comandante and his bodyguard had been assassinated near the police headquarters in Matamoros, Mexico.

Details in the article said unknown assailants sprayed the bodies with bullets as the men sat in their sedan. There were no witness accounts and no arrests had been made. The article had praises from the FBI claiming the Comandante of the State of Tamaulipas was an honorable cop who assisted with joint U.S. law enforcement efforts. His noble service included arresting a corrupt DEA Special Agent in a Murder-for-Hire plot.

The article mentioned a briefcase containing $20,000 in cash that was found next to *El Diablo*'s limp body. The FBI did not comment on that. They knew there was no credible explanation for any police officer to be in possession of $20,000 in cash.

I liked to believe it was the dirty money the FBI rewarded *El Diablo* for setting me up. The double-crosser died before enjoying all of his ill-gotten gains. Avarice, or greed, is considered a deadly sin. *El Diablo* paid the penance for eternity.

Poetic justice can be very gratifying. I was elated and very content.

I put the newspaper down. I wondered who was responsible for killing the corrupt cop. Maybe it was 'him'? I had helped him as a DEA Agent and he considered me a friend. Before I reported to prison, we both knew it would be our last encounter. 'He' asked me for a few personal details regarding *El Diablo*. I told him what I knew. It was likely a favor that could never be repaid.

On the other hand, *El Diablo*'s identity as a snitch was plastered in the Mexican media after my arrest. I had made it clear to the newspaper and television reporters that the Comandante set me up. Anybody who wanted to know the whereabouts of the lowlife didn't have to look very hard.

Through a narrow window across the hallway, I could see a U.S. flag hoisted high on a metal pole at the front entrance of the Ashland, Kentucky prison. I saw fireworks in the distance beyond the flag. It was Independence Day.

For most, it would have been an awe-inspiring sight and uplifting event. For me, there was no feeling of patriotism. There was only the dreadful thought that I would never again feel pride for my country.

I thought to myself, "I proudly saluted the symbolism of the flag and defended the U.S. domestic and foreign policies. America was considered the world's police and I was part of that elite force."

One must not confuse patriotism with faith in God. Patriotism means loyalty and allegiance to the actions of a government and its leaders. It is naive to believe that a government is always right. Patriotism includes the right to question, dissent, and protest, whereby faith in God is based on His love and forgiveness. Everything I had believed in faded.

My disdain for politicians was based on their blatant lies. The two Hispanic U.S. Congressmen I had met before reporting to prison, promised to help me, but they lied. They sat in front of me and pretended to care about reducing my lengthy prison sentence. They said they would contact prison officials after I served part of my prison sentence and request leniency.

Friends and family members called and wrote letters to the politicians but to no avail. Staff members claimed the Congressman would look into my situation. Like most politicians, they did not want to associate themselves with a criminal. There was no financial gain for them and it would only tarnish their wholesome reputations.

The Prison Warden made a rare appearance in the SHU. I had only seen the Hispanic warden from a distance. I wondered, "Why would he leave the comfortable confines of his office and visit us rejects in the hole?"

I thought, "There aren't many Hispanics in this part of the country especially one with political pull. I was certain the Warden would empathize with me and help one of his peeps get a transfer to a facility closer to *la familia!*"

I stood up from my bunk to shake the man's hand through the metal bars, but the Warden did not reach out.

He looked at me and said, "I had to come and meet you. You're a celebrity."

I responded, "I don't feel like one." I continued, "Warden, knowing my background, don't you think the Bureau of Prisons would consider it safer for me to be placed in a minimum-security camp?"

"I don't think so."

"Sir, I'm not asking for special treatment. I'm not a flight risk, and I shouldn't be considered a threat to society. The prison population now knows about my past. At least, can you transfer me closer to my family in Texas?"

The warden laughed out loud, "Hell no! We're going to send you farther away. You are classified a violent offender and we need to keep you safe."

The warden walked away before I could reach through the bars and choke some sense into the bureaucratic asshole.

I had enough of the ignorance. I yelled, "Don't walk away, you fucking coconut!" I then muttered, "Brown on the outside but White on the inside."

It was nearly two months in 'the hole' before the Bureau of Prisons found another place to keep me incarcerated. Just as the Warden stated, the decision makers would send me farther away from my home.

Along with thirty other inmates, I was placed on a modified transport commercial bus. The conveyance was used to transfer inmates between prison facilities. On occasion, the Bureau of Prisons punished disruptive inmates by constantly moving them between facilities, referred to by inmates as Diesel Therapy.

I found it difficult to eat the bologna sandwich and drink the carton of juice with my wrists shackled to my waist. The inconvenience did not take away the joy of seeing the free world without the obstruction of razor wire. Looking through the metal bars on the windows, I saw passing cars with regular people enjoying their freedom. I felt the excitement of a child on an amusement park ride!

Before reaching our final destination, we needed to make a stopover.

As the bus slowed down to enter a tunnel into the Atlanta Federal Penitentiary, I was overwhelmed with the ominous sight. The external view of this facility illustrated why prisons were coined, The Big House.

The towering cinderblock walls blocked the rays of sunlight, and suddenly it was dark. Waiting at the entrance were several large Black prison guards carrying various weapons. They yelled out orders and led inmates like cattle into their stalls.

I was placed in solitary confinement until another transport bus was available to take me to my new residence. Not knowing how many days I would be in 'the hole' only tested my worn-out patience and limited sanity. No phone calls were permitted, and human contact was non-existent.

I became familiar with a 'penitentiary shower'. It took one minute to walk in shackles from the prison cell to the shower. Three minutes to lather and rinse with the cold water, then one minute to return to the cell. Sometimes a tiny bar of soap was provided. The experience was enhanced with a vociferous prison guard insulting and shoving each inmate during the five-minute excursion.

Not knowing what lay ahead in my prison sentence, I had to come to terms with myself. I knew the second year of incarceration would be devoted to introspection. Recognizing the past and accepting the current circumstances would provide enlightenment. This could only be achieved by not suffering with regret anymore.

I committed my share of sins and needed to ask God for forgiveness. It took days to conjure up a seemingly endless list of sins. It was difficult to admit the evil deeds yet necessary for me to move on. I confessed to Him every bad thing I could remember. I pleaded for absolution and strength to make it out from this temporary purgatory.

The animosity and ignorance of the Bureau of Prisons led me to another dangerous facility. After ten days in the penitentiary, I was transferred to another low-security prison in Petersburg, Virginia. Now I was 1,500 miles away from my family. Also, with nearly eighty percent of the inmate population being Black, I stood out.

The handcuffs came off followed by the waist chain that was connected to the ankle irons. I rubbed my wrists. I walked into my 8' x 10' cell where my cellmate was lying on the bottom bunk reading an Essence magazine. The muscular Black man looked over his magazine and nodded. There were no formal introductions or handshakes in prison.

I could hear the music blaring from the ear buds of my new 'cellie', slang for cellmate. The song was titled, "Who We Be" by rap artist DMX. The rhythmic sound and harsh lyrics of an angry Black man described the systemic cruelty of the American judicial system.

I stepped on a plastic chair to step up to the top bunk. I lay there for a moment to absorb my new surroundings. Oddly, I thought of a joke I once heard. A small White man was placed in a prison cell already occupied by a large Black man. After the guard locked the cell door and departed, the Black man asked his new cellie, "Are you going to be the husband or the wife in this cell?"

The White man replied meekly, "I'd like to be the husband."

"Alright. Now come over here and suck your wife's dick!"

My new cellie was named Pork Chop. We learned to get along for about a year because we kept to ourselves and didn't talk very much.

As for my new surroundings, I kept to myself for days. My primary concern was "Down By The River" written by Charles Bowden that was about to be published and marketed throughout the U.S. My true identity and past occupation would be revealed.

Federal inmates would have access to the publication. I needed an ally to protect me from the other inmates.

I befriended a large, muscular orderly nicknamed Animal. With a name like that, I knew I would have a fighting chance of protection from any aggressors.

I bought his friendship with a pack of cigarettes and a pint of ice cream from the commissary. We shared Ramen Noodle meals on occasion. We spiced up the packages of noodles with canned mackerel or canned chicken. This was considered fine cuisine in the joint, slang for prison.

Animal did me a favor and hustled a pair of steel-toed boots. While most inmates walked around in sneakers or soft shoes, I wanted to be prepared for a fight. I wore the boots for the rest of my incarceration. Some inmates wondered why I wore the uncomfortable footwear. I responded, "I can't afford the high-priced tennis shoes sold at the commissary."

I had been there several weeks before my true identity was exposed. Since inmates received magazine subscriptions, someone recognized the displaced newcomer nicknamed Tex from a recently published GQ Magazine article.

Two very large Black men approached me in my cell. One of them said, "Let me holla at you. You need to come see Slick."

I recognized the name. Everyone in the compound knew the Black gang leader, or shot caller. I wasn't given an option. I had to talk to the man or get my ass kicked.

I needed an advocate so I asked Animal to accompany me to the meeting. I quickly explained my past and he didn't say anything. The fellow felon agreed to walk with me.

I had seen inmates disciplined by other inmates. They were taken to a secluded area and punched repeatedly in the torso. This way the bruises were covered by a shirt and not visible to prison guards who would initiate an investigation. On other occasions, I had seen inmates beaten to a pulp.

Animal and I walked to a cell surrounded by several large Black men. I feared being raped and was determined to fight to the death before that happened. I thought of scenarios where I could defend myself. I looked around for anything in arm's reach that could be used as a weapon.

I saw a Huggy Bear-looking man lying on his lower bunk. A scrawny, frail body was not what I expected for the most powerful man in the compound. It looked as if the inmate had his share of heron, slang for heroin. No salutations were exchanged.

After a lengthy stare down, Slick asked, "What are you in for?"

I responded, "I was punished for being a dirty cop." That's how I was viewed in the free world. I wasn't about to lie to the shot caller.

"Why did 'The Man' send you here?"

"I arrested a lot of Mexicans. They are doing time throughout Texas. They would like nothing better than to get payback on the man who sent them to the joint."

"You ever arrest any East Coast players or D.C. (Washington D.C. area) gangstas?"

"I was assigned to the Southwest border and arrested mostly Mexican drug smugglers. I never arrested any of your people."

The shot caller listened and contemplated the fate of the narc in front of him. He said, "Snitches get stitches while cops get killed. How should we handle this?"

"I am now a convict just like you. I just wanna do my time without any problems. I understand you gotta do what you gotta do."

Animal broke the tension by saying, "Listen to me, Slick. I stand here vouching for Tex. We broke bread together, and he is going to help our people with his library skills."

Earlier that week, I had formatted and typed a letter for Animal. I then prepared the envelope and mailed it to his attorney. Aside from sharing a meal, I was confident that the small favor would go a long way. These acts of kindness would eventually save my life.

Slick asked, "Do you know how wiretaps work?"

I responded, "Yes."

"I want you to explain it to me."

I provided a cliff notes version of the probable cause necessary to obtain legal authorization and a general description of the required electronics. He probably could have gotten a better explanation from any one of his homies if he just asked them.

My vague description must have been enough for the shot caller. He said, "I'll get back to you if I have any more questions. If anybody fucks with you, let Animal know about it."

Animal and I nodded. We slowly exited the prison cell keeping our eyes on the unmovable bodyguards lining the walls.

I am forever indebted to Animal. I never knew his real name. He is still serving a thirty-year sentence regarding a murder.

To show the Black community that I was one of them, I signed up for the flag football league. Flag football and basketball were the only physical contact sports permitted by prison officials. I would be the only non-Black in the league.

Disregarding my medium physique, the team captain directed me to play the center position. It was a decision made to show all inmates that he wasn't going to be soft with me. He did this because the largest of the opposing team members would line up against me in the nose guard position.

For weeks, I was punished by the likes of 'Big Al', a 300-pound Black man with anger issues. I held my own until my right knee gave out in the playoffs. I was carried off the field on the shoulders of teammates as everyone chanted, "Tex, Tex, Tex." Very similar to a closing scene from a popular sports movie.

After showing my bravery, I had few problems with Black inmates. The respect rippled through the compound.

The Arian Brotherhood inmates thought of me as one of the smartest Mesicans they ever met.

The Italian-American inmates, some tied to the Gambino family, appreciated my attendance in their Sunday Catholic mass. In fact, since I worked in the Chapel, I was instructed to conduct the masses after the Catholic priest assigned to the prison was arrested for child molestation. Prison officials and the Catholic Church had been hiding the priest in the facility since the molestation occurred twenty years prior.

As I walked in the rec yard, the mobsters would greet me with their deep, New York accents, "Yo, Sally!" On occasion, they invited me to partake in their extravagant Italian-style meals made with sausage and fresh vegetables smuggled out from the kitchen. They had connections who worked in the kitchen, the commissary, laundry, etc.

However, there were inmates who tried to express their displeasure with a narc living amongst them. They would bump into me or spit on the ground as I walked passed them. Many flexed on me but didn't take any action. Others just wanted to annoy me.

An inmate convicted for online solicitation of a child tried getting close to me. He thought since both of us had few friends, we could run together, slang for fraternize. The difference between us was that he wanted a friend and I didn't.

The pedophile tried breaking the ice with crude humor. He crossed the line when he commented on a female guard walking away from us in the rec yard, "She's got an ass of a ten-year old boy."

After listening to his perverted humor, I responded, "Let's get something straight. Smart I like. Smartass I don't. Take your jokes somewhere else." After that, the inmate kept his distance and that was fine with me.

In another incident, a young D.C. thug entered the television viewing room and changed the channel to a rap music station. The punk ignored several inmates who were watching the news program, "60 Minutes". Nobody said a word since inmates wanted to avoid confrontation or any administrative infractions.

Negotiating with a punk like him would be ineffective and likely dangerous. The safest option for everyone was to ignore the power move by the disrespectful intruder. A decision had to be made whether to allow the punk to flex on everyone in the room or check him.

I got up and turned the television knob to the previous program. I remained standing by the television waiting for the next move.

The punk said, "Hey, whatcha doin'?" He stood up and reached to change the channel back to the music video station.

I did not move my hand and calmly said, "We were watching our program. If you touch me, you and I are going to 'the hole'!"

The punk put his right hand in his pant pocket as if reaching for a shank, slang for a sharp weapon.

I responded, "You pull anything out of your pocket and I'm going shove it up your ass! Now, get the fuck out of my face before I bitch-slap you!"

An older Black inmate sitting in the back of the room announced, "Youngster, don't mess with 'Tex'. Word is he is a stone-cold killer." Prison rumors weren't very accurate.

The punk took a few steps back and rambled on for several minutes, stomping his feet and making false threats. "I heard about you! Don't get it twisted that me and my homies ain't gonna mess with you!"

I said, "Bring it on."

The confrontation was interrupted by a guard yelling, "Chow time!" It was the standard announcement to the inmates that breakfast, lunch, or dinner was served. All the inmates, except for me, scampered out of the television viewing room and walked briskly to the chow hall. I wanted to make a point by holding my ground and waited for the news program to finish before heading to the cafeteria.

I always walked alone, and ate alone. I despised small talk, and did not want to make friends with anyone. It was nothing personal, just a precautionary measure.

I stared at the poor imitation of Mexican food splayed before me on the tray. I tried to remember how my mother's red chile enchiladas smelled and tasted. I thought, "How long has it been since I've had authentic Mexican food? Hell, how long has it been since I've had any decent food?"

The cafeteria was at capacity because the dinner was the best meal served in weeks. Fried chicken was the finest cuisine ever served in the joint. It was almost impossible for the cooks to mess up the grub.

A biker-looking inmate sat across from me at the long, metal table. We acknowledged each other's presence with a simple nod.

He initiated a conversation, "If you had to choose between a bottle of your favorite liquor, making love to a woman, or eating a steak, which would it be?"

There was no doubt it would be making love to Lily, but I'd play along. Looking the tablemate in the eye, I said, "I'd love a ribeye steak cooked medium rare and charred."

"I knew it! You're the third guy today who said steak!" The biker added, "I never come to the chow hall except for days like today. I make my meals in the microwave. I've eaten so much damn rice in the last four years of incarceration that I could feed all of China."

I appreciated the witty survey but didn't want to extend the encounter. I rose from my seat and knocked twice on the table. This gesture was customary and showed respect to fellow diners, rather than saying aloud, "Excuse me." I bussed the plastic utensils and tray and took them to the dishwashing window.

Exiting the cafeteria, I was patted down by a hack searching for food being smuggled out of the chow hall. I hated being frisked. I limited my conversations with staff members and guards. They looked and talked down to me since I was just another convict to them. I disliked them as much as they disliked me.

On the slow walk to the prison library, I passed a sixty-something year old inmate who had nineteen years remaining of a thirty-year sentence for selling two pounds of crack cocaine. In my eyes, the man was fading by the day as the Grim Reaper had a better hold of him than life did. I wondered how anyone could endure such a lengthy prison sentence.

I felt sorry for the man. I had to find a way to stop and just say something nice to ease the man's misery.

The old man beat me to the punch, "Look at all those cars in a line with their headlights on. Must be a funeral."

I looked through the razor-wire fence to a country road outside the prison. I realized the man had been locked up for so long that he wasn't aware most automobiles were manufactured with day-running lights. I didn't want to insult the man's lack of intelligence by explaining the modern technology. So I just nodded.

I said, "I've seen you at the library. If there is ever something I can do for you like typing or legal research, please let me know."

"Son, I ain't got nobody on the outside. I got no skills or jobs waiting for me. Prison is my life and my death." The old man walked away leaving me standing alone.

I remained looking outside the prison through the razor-wire fence. I placed myself inside the passing vehicles to feel the sensation of coming home from a day at work. I desired to stretch my imagination looking for any connection to the outside world.

I relished the distant roar of a blaring horn from a train on the unseen railroad tracks as I rode the conveyance while on vacation. I found myself on business trips with the sight of a commercial airliner flying high above the rec yard. The fantasies were therapeutic yet painful.

Staring into the distance, I noticed a maroon GMC pickup. It was similar to my OGV while assigned to the El Paso DEA office. Reverie set in.

Richard McGee called me on my cell phone, "Hey buddy, I have a huge favor to ask. You don't have to do this, so don't feel obligated."

"What is it?"

"We just intercepted a conversation on the wiretap. One of the main targets is going to meet with others at the Electric Q discotheque in Juarez. This could be a great opportunity to identify members of this organization. My surveillance units are busy tailing other targets throughout El Paso, and I don't have anybody available."

Actually, there were no agents in the El Paso office that would be willing to go solo across the Rio Grande River. Knowing where McGee was going with this, I asked, "Are you saying this could be dangerous?"

"Of course. Everything over there is unsafe."

"Well, danger is my middle name."

"You are the best! The meeting is taking place shortly. Be careful!"

Without hesitation, I drove across the International Bridge of the Americas into Ciudad Juarez. I arrived at the discotheque and saw five men standing near the front entrance.

It was still early for the partygoers. There were only a few vehicles in the parking lot. It was difficult to find an advantageous location to park and not be seen by the targets.

I found a spot between two parked vehicles and was able to take several photos using a 35mm SLR camera and the zoom lens. The setting sun provided sufficient lighting for the unobstructed photographs.

After a few photos, I repositioned myself on the southern side of the building to call McGee for further instructions. Before I finished dialing, a black Chevrolet Suburban pulled up behind me. The vehicle was positioned to block my pickup against the wall of the discotheque.

A young Mexican man exited his vehicle, raised his arms, and shrugged his shoulders, as if to ask, "What are you doing on my turf?" He must have seen me taking photos of his crew.

I recognized the man from a previous surveillance operation. The man recognized me, too!

Appearing around the corner of the building were four men walking briskly towards me. One of them was a Mexican police officer dressed like the Frito Bandito character with large caliber bullets reflecting in the sunlight. The other men were carrying automatic rifles.

"Shit," I thought, "I've been burned!" Now, I was trapped by the black Suburban and outnumbered. I had to think and act quickly.

My initial thought was to ram the Suburban and force an opening to escape. This would take less than fifteen seconds, which would unfortunately be enough time for the bad guys to spray me and my pickup full of bullets. I kept the engine running as this option appeared to be the only way out.

The alternative would be to talk to the drug traffickers and reason with them. Maybe they would understand that I was doing my job and following orders, just like them.

I knew better and thought, "That's not going to happen."

I stood on the step on the driver's side door and said more forcefully yet calmly in English, "Hey, you need to move."

I repeated, "Didn't you hear me? I'm in a hurry, so move!"

The man looked confused and angry. He returned to the open driver's side door likely to retrieve his weapon.

I got down from the step and nudged my Glock with my elbow for reassurance. I reached behind the seat to retrieve my Colt sub-machine gun. I chambered the first of thirty-two 9mm rounds. I placed another full clip on the front seat within arms reach.

I intended to shoot the Suburban driver first then use the bed of my pickup as cover to spray the others with bullets. They were now getting very close.

As I turned towards the Suburban, I was shocked to see it slowly rolling in reverse. The man struggled to gain control of his vehicle. There was a small opening!

Without hesitation, I jumped into my pickup. I backed out, punched the accelerator, and sped away. Still in disbelief, I focused on driving as fast as possible without getting into an accident.

Looking back through the rearview mirror, I saw the Suburban gaining ground. I set my sights on the Bridge of the Americas. It was rush hour, and the traffic lanes would be extremely long.

McGee came over the DEA radio, asking for my location.

I answered, "I don't have time to talk! I just got burned, and I'm hauling ass for the free bridge!"

McGee hollered, "We picked up talk on the wire. Get out of Juarez now! The bad guys are looking for your truck. The Mexican police are going to plant coke in your truck and have you arrested!" If that happened, I would never come out alive from a Mexican jail.

I approached the Mexican border checkpoint. I could see the uniformed officers scrambling and pointing my way. They must have been notified to stop and detain the man in the maroon GMC pickup.

I took another glance in the mirror. It revealed the facial expressions of the front seat occupants in the Suburban and their long-barrel weapons taking aim at me.

The northbound lanes entering the United States were backed up nearly a mile long. There was no way I was going to get jammed up and become a sitting duck. I veered my truck into the southbound lanes and took my chances with oncoming traffic.

The Mexican police officers froze. They were shocked to see the brazen driver speed by their inspection booth.

I kept my head low just in case a trigger-happy cop would take a shot at me. I focused on the apex of the bridge. The imaginary international line meant the Mexican police couldn't pursue me passed that point.

After several evasive maneuvers, I made it to the American side of the bridge. I forced myself between two vehicles in the outermost line of traffic.

Two angry U.S. Customs Inspectors saw the aggressive driver and ran towards him. They had their right hand on their pistols ready to draw and fire, if the inconsiderate man tried another dangerous maneuver.

I displayed my DEA badge through the front windshield. It was clearly seen by the inspectors. I identified myself and explained the dilemma.

The inspectors believed the incredible story and escorted me through the U.S. checkpoint.

As I awoke from my remembrance, I still wondered how I survived the predicament. How and why did the bad guy move the Chevrolet Suburban? Did he accidentally nudge the gearshift while reaching for his AK-47? Was this a case of divine intervention?

I thought, "I wasn't meant to die that day. Someone upstairs must have something planned for me. Shit, if I knew going to prison was part of His plan, I would have rather died that day!"

Back to reality. I needed to quell my desire to be outside the fence because it only caused emotional instability. I slowly walked to my prison cell thinking of how much I hated reflecting on the past. It only made me miss the wildest days of my life. A life that I loved.

I climbed up onto my upper bunk. I tried to finish a two-page letter to Lily. It was difficult to write upbeat letters with something positive when overwhelmed with depression. I laid the pen down on the mattress and reclined on my bunk.

I put on my headphones and turned the radio dial to a local classic rock station. Being aired was Led Zeppelin's, "Nobody's Fault But Mine". The irony of the title and lyrics were relevant to the reasons for me being incarcerated.

The dim rays of the setting sun broke through the metal-barred window. The same window I looked out at night to find the moon. I wondered if Lily was staring at the moon at the same time.

The prison was located around the sacred land where Robert E. Lee gave the Confederacy's last stand against Ulysses Grant. Any American citizen would have considered standing on this area as holy ground. I couldn't appreciate the historical relevance. This was the site of my incarceration.

I unfairly despised everything about the East Coast. The tall, dense trees limited my view and made me feel more enclosed. The humidity, the adverse weather, and gray clouds mirrored my gloom.

I knew it would be a long time before I saw the beauty of a desert sunset. I desired to feel the cooling sensation of a passing storm in the middle of a dry summer. I even missed the unwelcome springtime dust storms that swallowed the entire city of El Paso.

I thought, "Don't get emotional. Take it one day at a time. Another day in prison is over. Only a couple thousand more to go."

I never wore a wristwatch while incarcerated. Seconds, minutes, and hours were paltry in an eighty-seven month prison sentence. I ignored looking at calendars because I did not want to compute my bit (slang for prison sentence) in days, weeks, or months. I preferred to measure time in seasons.

Prison is about routine. My routine included a daily visit to the prison library. It was the quietest place in the compound. I saw the regulars working on legal remedies for themselves and for other inmates.

There was money to be made as a jailhouse lawyer. Many inmates wanted someone to research their case and pursue any remedy available. It would take weeks or months of research. I helped inmates with their judicial appeals by formatting and typing their motions. That was as far as I went. I didn't want to pretend to be someone I wasn't like a swindling wanna-be attorney.

I made time to lose my beer gut especially since I was on the wagon. I hit the weight pile (free weights) three times a week. I worked out alone never relying on a spotter. Other inmates saw me going solo and asked if they could join me. I respectfully denied their requests.

On one occasion, there was a blizzard that dumped several inches of snow on the East Coast. None of the inmates left the comfortable confines of their living quarters except for me. I had the entire rec yard to myself. I hit the weight pile for two hours and jogged throughout the afternoon.

The prison guards in the watchtower must have wondered who the crazy inmate was alone in the frigid weather.

I cherished the solitude and felt a sense of achievement by overcoming the adverse weather conditions. I found tranquility in the midst of a storm.

Prisoners believe they relinquished their right to compassion when sent to the joint. Feeling the extremes of elation and devastation had to be repressed. Joy is inappropriate during the worst time of your life.

While incarcerated, inmates miss many special occasions with loved ones. Personally, I was most disappointed that I was unable to attend my little sister's wedding and my wife receiving her Master's Degree. Photographs provided some solace for my absence.

Tragedies were difficult to handle. My heart was broken when I learned that my beloved aunt had passed away. Around the same time, my father suffered a stroke soon after visiting me in prison.

I was frustrated that I could not be with my parents to console and comfort them. I encouraged them to remain healthy so we could reunite and mend the wounds together.

Then there was the ordeal of rejection. I saw many inmates receive a "Dear John letter", that is, an inmate's spouse or significant other expressed their desire to move on with their life in a correspondence. The inmate is left to maintain his sanity and subdue his emotions.

One Christmas Eve, an Italian Mafia member named Frankie and I were watching the Catholic Midnight Mass from the Vatican. Nobody in the compound was stirring, except for an inmate from New York who walked by the television room. Something told me to go after him and insist he join us to watch the somber programming.

No words were spoken throughout the annual religious ceremony. Tears filled the eyes of the three of us as we sat missing loved ones on that holy night.

Two weeks later, the New Yorker approached me. He said, "I want to thank you."

I responde "For what?"

"When you invited me to watch television on Christmas Eve, I was walking throughout the building looking for the highest rafter. I wanted to hang myself that night. You saved my life."

I just listened.

"I received legal documents that day. My wife filed for divorce. She said she couldn't hold on anymore and wants to divorce me."

I said, "You don't have to explain anything to me."

"I want to. I have nobody else to talk to. The last time I saw her was when we were coming home from a romantic dinner. As I pulled into our driveway, we were ambushed by the FBI. They slammed both of us onto the hood of my car and handcuffed us with our hands in the back. I stared across the hood into her frightened, tear-filled eyes. That was the last time I saw her."

I could have extended the conversation and asked personal questions to console the man but preferred not to say anything. While in prison, I changed. I was not the same compassionate person who took the time to listen to others problems.

The inmate ended the conversation, "I just wanted to thank you."

I was one of the fortunate ones. My wife sent me encouraging letters and family photos on a weekly basis. We talked on the telephone twice a week, but she cried at the end of every conversation. My heart broke a little bit more with her every whimper.

It had been a year without seeing her. Lily traveled alone cross-country to visit me. She had nobody to guide her through the prison visitation process.

Visitors needed to arrive before dawn and line up outside the prison walls. Women and children waited several hours while prison officials slowly scrutinized each visitor. The hours of visitation were limited to only a few hours on the weekends. Sometimes, families were turned away because of overcrowding or delayed with only minutes to spend with loved ones.

Most prison guards treated family members as second-class citizens. Visitors were degraded with stern instructions and humiliated by the invasive body searches.

Lily saw an elderly woman visitor set off a metal detector and denied entry. The woman lost her place in line when she went to a nearby Walmart to purchase a new bra.

Upon her return, the prison official said loudly that the newly-purchased bra would not be permitted unless she removed a thin support wire built into it. After a trip to the women's restroom where the wire was torn out, the embarrassed woman was finally allowed to enter the visitation area and see her son. Many mothers, daughters, and wives were forced to go braless. This was an embarrassing and self-conscious dilemma for women.

For inmates, the emotions ran high during visitation. Prison etiquette was not to stare or talk to another inmate's family members. Some fist fights ensued in general population because an inmate felt another inmate disrespected him by looking at his girlfriend or wife.

Even so, one couldn't ignore the tremendous joy of seeing a child hugging his father. On the other hand it was sad knowing the father was not there to teach his child to ride a bike or throw a baseball. A father could only regret not being there to nurture and guide the child through their wonder years.

Lily tried to make the best of the situation with an upbeat attitude. She scanned the items in the vending machine for something I would like. She selected pork rinds and Reese's Peanut Butter cups.

She asked if we could take a picture together. Since cell phones and cameras weren't permitted in the visitation area, an inmate trustee was delegated as a photographer. I refused because I didn't want any mementos of my incarceration.

Lily said she ran into people back home who said, "Tell Sal, hello."

Instead of making me feel better, it only made me angry. I responded, "Fuck the 'hello'! Why don't they write and tell me themselves? I helped out a lot of people when they needed assistance. Where are they now? If they really cared, they could help by giving you some money for this trip or send me something."

Lily said, "Don't get upset. They are just trying to be nice."

"Salutations don't mean shit! It's what a person does that is important. People who step up and take initiative by helping us out are the ones I respect. The ten cents an hour that I make doesn't pay for the phone calls." The prison hourly wage was a far cry from the $70,000 per year salary I was making with the DEA.

Lily calmed me and said some have asked if she needed anything to let them know. However, she was too embarrassed to ask for money.

The most difficult aspect of the two-hour visitation was at the end. It was hard to see her leave. The scent of perfume and touch of her soft skin could barely make up for the many years without lovemaking. A prison guard interrupted our lengthy hug and passionate kiss.

We didn't say goodbye, instead, "I'll see you soon." She vowed to wait for me. We discussed vague plans for the future and assured each other everything would be fine. Not knowing what lied ahead of us was almost as agonizing as our separation.

I painfully watched Lily walk through the sliding steel gates of the visitation room without me. The gates slammed shut, she glanced back and threw me a kiss. It would be another six months before we saw each other again.

Chapter 26 – Short-Timer

After four years of incarceration, the Bureau of Prisons decision-makers had forgotten about my past. I was sent closer to home. Although it was a lateral transfer to another low-security prison in Big Spring, Texas, I would be only four hours away from my wife and family.

I was handcuffed, shackled, and taken to an airport runway by the U.S. Marshals Service. Surrounded by the heavily armed guards, I was escorted up the rolling stairwell leading into a commercial airliner known as Con Air. About fifty inmates were flown from the East Coast to the Oklahoma City federal prison transfer facility.

As the jet airliner accelerated and rose from the runway, I was overjoyed. I couldn't believe I was leaving the East Coast. I was going home! The sack lunch consisting of a plain bologna sandwich, bag of chips, and an orange, was the finest airline cuisine I ever tasted.

The bus ride from Oklahoma City to FCI-Big Spring was just as exhilarating as the flight on Con Air. The open highway and splattering of mesquite trees provided the scenery I longed for. I saw people in cars engaged in conversation and could hear their Texas twang. There was nothing that could have dulled my excitement! I spoke too soon.

Our Friday afternoon arrival was untimely as we were told we could not enter the general population until the following Monday. The welcoming committee, or Receiving and Distribution staff, responsible for processing incoming prisoners had already gone home and did not work on weekends.

I was placed with six other men in a prison cell designed for two men. We spent the entire weekend without any reading materials, rec time, or opportunity to shower. We made small talk, slept on the cement floor, and watched each other take shits.

I was sent to a facility that housed men I had arrested as a DEA agent in El Paso. I recognized several inmates, including one I sent to 'the joint' for two decades. I avoided talking to all of them. Every preventive measure was implemented to keep me from being identified as the narc who set them up.

I would not tell prison officials of the dilemma. I had been warned from the very beginning of my bit, "If you believe your safety is an issue then prepare to remain in solitary confinement for a lengthy time." I would rather take my chances of not being recognized than being sent to 'the hole' and getting transferred to another facility far away.

There were many inmates from the El Paso area. To disassociate myself from *El Chuco*, I claimed to be from San Antonio. To prevent any recognition of my real name, I introduced myself as Zep, because of the tattoo on my left bicep.

However, there were several close calls regarding my past occupation. My first week in general population, an inmate from my hometown approached me and said, "You look familiar. You from El Paso?"

I responded, "Only visited once or twice."

"Really? I'm sure we've met."

I tried to deflect the stare of the inmate with humor, "You know us Mexicans. We all look the same."

The inmate reacted agitated, "I'm not joking around."

I had to turn the conversation and take another approach, "I know prison is not a place to joke around. I definitely don't play like that. You got me confused with someone else. Now, excuse me." I turned and walked away.

I recognized the inmate. While stationed in El Paso, I had conducted surveillance and testified against the drug trafficker during a DEA investigation. As for the issue at hand, the inmate had a daily subscription for the El Paso Times. I prayed the man wouldn't remember seeing my face plastered on the front page of the publication several years ago.

This inmate was a shot caller for the Texas Mafia. I knew I would be killed by midnight if the man recognized the former narc that put him in prison ten years prior.

Then, there was a Black inmate who was transferred from FCI-Petersburg to FCI-Big Spring. The inmate recognized me, "Tex! I see you made it closer to home."

I said, "Yeah. I'm only a few months away from ending this nightmare. Why did you get punished and sent out here?"

"You know, segregation."

I knew that wasn't the truth. The inmate must have snitched on someone in the Petersburg joint and was sent far away for his safety. However, I was in no position to contradict the man.

He added, "Right after you left the compound, a helicopter landed outside the joint. Guys started a rumor that it was there to pick you up. They believed you were still working undercover."

"Damn prison rumors." I begged him not to disclose my true identity to the inmates in Big Spring, "Bro, please don't tell any of these Mexicans about my past. I'm too short to be put in the hole."

"Don't sweat it. I got my own battles to deal with. Just keep these 'eses' (slang for Mexicans) off my back if the racial shit gets heavy."

The man and I gave each other a bro hug. We rarely spoke to each other after that day.

Another incident that nearly exposed my identity occurred about a year into my stay in this facility. The majority of Mexicans in this prison were pressured to show their loyalty to one of several regional gangs.

A Mexican Mafia gang banger asked, "*Ese*, who do you run with?"

I responded, "I run alone."

"You said you are from 'San Anto' (slang for San Antonio) yet your homies wonder why you don't hang out with them."

"I'm a short-timer, *carnal*. I don't need to get caught up in any shit right now."

"Well, they want to know if you are going to help them jump the White boys today."

I asked, "*Que rollo* (What happened)?"

"Yesterday, an old Mexican man using crutches put his food tray on a table next to the chow line. There were some White boys eating at that table. While the old man reached over to get something to drink from the soda fountain, a White boy put the old man's tray on the floor!"

I responded, "Holy shit!"

The gangster continued, "The old man didn't say anything. He reached down to pick up the tray but his *camaradas* (buddies) told him to leave the tray on the floor because he wasn't a dog. The Mexican shot callers told the White leader to have the punks apologize to the old man. The punks don't want to."

"Are the *gringos* going to punish the punks?"

"The problem is the White leader doesn't want to discipline the youngsters for disrespecting the old man so we need to discipline the White boys."

Reluctantly, I asked, "What can I do?"

"We are going to jump all the White boys tonight. It will be after sundown so the prison cameras don't identify us. We need to know if you are going to help us."

I knew I had to commit or suffer repercussions. "*Orale* (Okay)."

The Mexican gang banger walked away.

It went down sooner than later. It was like the reenactment of the Battle of the Alamo. The Mexicans swarmed in waves. The White men were surrounded, outnumbered, and brutally beaten. For every Caucasian, there were four or five Mexican men kicking or punching them.

The onslaught was over by the time the prison's Emergency Response Team established their attack position. When the dust settled, hundreds of bodies were strewn throughout the rec yard. Most were inmates who listened to the guard's orders of, "Faces on the ground!" The other bodies were the pulverized victims. All this happened because of one person's act of racism and stupidity.

The facility was in lockdown for weeks. Prison lockdowns are similar to solitary confinement. Inmates are unable to leave their bunk area, forced to spend their time playing cards, reading paperbacks, or engaging in lengthy, shallow conversations with their cellie.

All two thousand inmates were punished until those responsible for causing the chaos were identified. Many men were sent to the hole until it reached full capacity. Many inmates licked their wounds in private while others suffered permanent physical injuries.

The racial animosity lasted for months.

An inmate summarized the psyche of the prison compound, "Animals are adaptive. We are animals. We need to get along, or we kill each other. To the outside world, we are rejects and the unforgiven. Nobody can understand what we've endured until they have been through this shit themselves."

Paralleling my psyche was the music coming from a local radio station. High school students were allowed to play any kind of music they wanted on Saturday nights. I was acclimated to new rock groups like Disturbed, Godsmack, and Breaking Benjamin. The heavy metal sounds and passionate lyrics inspired me during my transition to a remorseless life.

The last year of incarceration was dedicated to preparing for an unknown occupation. I read as many books as possible regarding job opportunities. It felt like a hopeless quest. There were few occupations in the outside world that would hire a convicted felon. My only passion of law enforcement was unattainable and I had no idea what I would do for employment.

Charles Bowden visited me during this time. He was a man who showed little emotion but was very caring inside. As our visitation was ending, he asked, "What can I do for you?"

I was caught off-guard. Nobody had asked me that for many years. It took me a minute and I responded, "I don't know what I am going to do for a living." Without a word, Charles turned and walked towards the exit.

A few months later, I was visited by two highly-respected attorneys, Samuel Bayless and Rick Russell. I had never met these men but they were Charles' friends. They came to offer me a job and eventually helped me with my road to redemption. I am forever indebted to these men.

As my prison sentence was coming to an end, I needed to calm my anxiety and frustrations with uncertainty. I relied on weightlifting, softball, and handball. Like most everything in prison, the activities were made available only to pass the time away.

There was one inmate that liked competing against me in handball. For months, we met on the weekends and became fierce competitors. Conversations were limited to our playing strategies. We never discussed personal matters.

One day, another inmate asked me, "Do you know that guy you've been playing handball with?"

"I know his name is *Chuy* (nickname for Jesus). He's from somewhere south of Matamoros, Mexico. That's about it. Why?"

"It is rumored he was a *sicario* for the Gulf Cartel. He is credited with nineteen kills for the cartel."

I responded, "No shit! I guess the feds didn't do their homework. The *vato* is a short-timer."

The inmate continued, "If they found out about the hits (murders) this guy did he would be doing life in a pen (penitentiary). You know he's going back to what he did best."

"You're telling me my handball partner is a stone-cold killer. Call me a skeptic but it's hard for me to believe any prison rumor."

"Well, inmates talk about each other all the time. What else do we have to do?"

Inquisitively, I asked, "What's the rumor about me?"

"Nobody is talking about you. Should we?"

"Only if you want to talk about someone with a boring life as a teacher who got caught up with money laundering. Now, I ain't got no job or no money. That's all anybody needs to know about me."

The elusive response was enough to end our conversation. My words and actions in the joint were improvised throughout the years to keep me alive. It would be a long time before I could actually be myself.

Chapter 27 - Road To Redemption

After six years living behind the razor wire, I was reassigned from FCI-Big Spring to a Halfway House in San Antonio. Since I was considered a model prisoner and didn't receive any infractions, I could spend the last six months of my prison sentence outside the fence.

I was permitted six hours of freedom. Lily would pick me up in Big Spring and drive me to San Antonio.

Prison officials provided me with a few departing gifts – no name clothing and generic dress shoes. I left everything else behind because I did not want any mementos of my incarceration. I walked out of the joint with the wrinkled clothes and was met with the biggest hug and kiss I had ever received. Lily and I held each other for a few minutes although it felt like an eternity.

The warmth of the sun on my body felt better than ever before. Everything felt better outside of the fence. Our priority was to find the nearest motel.

Someone told me not to look back at the prison when driving away. Doing so would jinx me by coming back to the joint. There were no sentiments with anyone or personal attachments to anything back there. I was moving forward and never looking back.

In order to get acclimated to the real world, I needed to be gainfully employed. I was ordered to work at a nearby car wash that hired the majority of the inmates for minimum wage. I advised the staff that an attorney, named Samuel Bayless, would hire me as a paralegal at his law office in downtown San Antonio. Also, Mr. Bayless needed my assistance due to his failing health.

The Halfway House administrators refused to allow me to be unleashed in the public without a controlled environment. They believed it was easier for them to keep an eye on me in the confined area of the car wash. It was another regimented aspect of the BOP that lacked common sense and was unwilling to loosen its grip on me.

One counselor, who was also a Black Baptist preacher, recognized the irrationality. He supported me and took responsibility of monitoring the atypical inmate. He was not like his bone-headed associates and I was grateful.

After being released from the halfway house, I was punished with an additional three years of federal parole called supervised release. I may have been out of the prison system but felt like I was still incarcerated.

I was required to report monthly to a pencil-dick Federal Probation Officer who treated me like just another convict on his list. The meetings consisted of explaining my efforts to better myself by balancing a checkbook, maintaining a steady job, and avoiding contact with any other felons. His demeaning lectures as to how I should adapt to society and change my evil ways added to my disdain of the criminal justice system.

I learned that one mistake can have permanent punitive consequences. Although having first-hand experience at both ends of the criminal justice system, I am prohibited from serving on a jury. I was an experienced marksman, yet forbidden from owning a weapon to protect my family or anyone else. As for job opportunities, most companies will not hire a felon, even one who sacrificed so much for this country.

I am usually judged immediately when someone hears of my arrest and conviction. The stigma of being branded a convicted felon affects how people view me. Judgments are easily made through ignorance. Knowing the truth requires time and effort. I'm not going to waste my time to educate anyone simply for their acceptance.

Today, there is the recurring nightmare that haunts me. I am overwhelmed with joy by being reunited with my family after serving my prison sentence. The happiness turns to fear when prison officials order me to return to prison. They tell me there was a miscalculation in my original eighty-seven month conviction and I need to complete the rest of my prison sentence.

I return to prison only to realize nobody tells me how many days I am going to spend incarcerated. I feel helpless and confused by the ineptness of the prison officials. They are not trying to give me a release date! It is a sickening nightmare that still wakes me drenched in sweat and a fear of being victimized.

The emotional and psychological scars will never heal. I have become desensitized by the cruelty experienced as a narc in the drug war and solidified by being a convict.

I had met an inmate with prior military experience who was diagnosed with Post Traumatic Stress Disorder (PTSD). His fellow felons nicknamed him, *Loco*. Without any apprehension, he said, "I heard about you being a cop. You experienced some heavy shit like I did in combat. Just like me, I know you have psychological issues to deal with. If you didn't get PTSD after being a narc then you certainly will get it after being locked up in prison."

I agreed, "I'm pretty sure we all have PTSD."

There is no way to make up for lost time. I devote my time to only a handful of people. Especially important to me are those who helped Lily while I was in prison. The benefit is that life becomes less complicated when you can count your true friends in one hand.

Today, I am a successful bail bondsman. I can relate to my clients because I've been in their shoes. I provide insight to their legal options and guidance through the judicial process. For those who disrespect my kindness and fail to appear in court, I turn into a bounty hunter and implement my past investigative and surveillance experience to hunt them down. I notify local police officers to effect the arrest since I don't have that authority anymore. It gives me a false sense of being a cop again.

I know everyone must be held accountable for their mistakes. Many people believe I got the punishment I deserved. Some feel otherwise. Condemnation nor sympathy can change the fact that I lost my career in law enforcement, lost my freedom for seven years, and ruined my reputation.

The people who put me in prison will never be held accountable for their ill-advised persecution. I believe they will eventually meet their Maker who will enlighten them about their so-called noble efforts. Hell, they may even bump into *El Diablo* while in their eternal nether world!

I find closure believing, "I may forgive, but I won't forget." My mind goes back to a song by Linkin Park, "In The End." The lyrics describe a man who gave his all to what he believed in then lost everything except for the memories that haunt him.

I have had many titles – college grad, State Trooper, Special Agent, convict. The only label that means anything to me now is 'Daddy'. I have found that you don't know what true love is until you have a child. The love you feel for a child changes your perspectives. Everything else is secondary.

My only child was a premature son, born four months early, who weighed one pound, one ounce. With a ninety-nine percent mortality rate, he was a miracle kid who overcame the odds. The hospital staff instructed me to think about funeral arrangements. Me and Lily visited him everyday for the first four months of his existence. Upon his release, Vincent could not be placed in a day care because of a high risk for infections. Unable to find a job, I became a stay-at-home Dad for the first two years of my son's life.

I wonder when I will tell my son that I am a convicted felon. Vincent has only heard the stories of his father arresting bad guys. Will he be disappointed learning of my arrest and incarceration? Will he need to defend his father's honor from ridicule? Will he even believe this story?

REFLECTIONS

The U.S. Sentencing Commission was responsible for the Federal Sentencing Guidelines used by federal judges and juries for sentencing in federal cases. In the Commission's charter, a violation classified as a federal crime requires a more severe prison sentence than one who had been convicted of a similar crime under state law.

There are longer prison sentences for those found guilty of far lesser crimes under the federal statutes than those who commit violent crimes at the state level. People are punished under the guise of rehabilitation. Incarceration is all about retribution.

The guidelines need to be revisited, as the punishments do not fit the crimes. Lengthy prison sentences tear the fabric of a family causing irreparable damage. Unfortunately, there are no politicians willing to spearhead a reevaluation. If they appear 'soft on crime', it would be political suicide for their careers.

The defendant is forced to accept the applicable penalty from a formatted chart. Personal and professional backgrounds are irrelevant to the impersonal sentencing process. First-time offenders are categorized according to the regimented sentencing guidelines with little forgiveness. This is not to say that America needs to be lenient on repeat offenders or violent criminals. Fool me once, shame on you; fool me twice, shame on me.

Upon their release from confinement, ex-cons try to mend personal relationships and regenerate their livelihood. Those who did have a career lost it after their arrest. With limited opportunities for gainful employment, convicted felons will pursue any means available to make a living.

When you read or hear about someone being arrested, don't take it for face value. Just because someone is arrested doesn't mean they were guilty of something. Know that there is always more to the story. Consider the motives behind the alleged crime, whether there was a fulfillment of the elements that constituted the crime, and the investigative tactics used by the law enforcement agency.

As for me, I admitted my mistakes and explained my actions. I wasted seven years of my life in prison and continue to feel the unending punitive measures as a convicted felon. For those who believe I deserved to be punished, they should be pleased to know that I am serving a life sentence.

LEGEND OF ACRONYMS AND JARGON

BOP	Bureau of Prisons
BTF	Binational Task Force
Buy/Bust	Undercover purchase followed by arrest(s)
CI	Confidential Informant
CO	Correctional Officer
DEA	Drug Enforcement Administration
DPS	Department of Public Safety
EPIC	El Paso Intelligence Center
The Eye	Agent with direct visual observation of a target
El Chuco	Affectionate term for El Paso
Federales	Mexican federal agents
FCI	Federal Correctional Institution
Flash roll	Currency displayed during undercover operation
The hole	Solitary confinement
Madrina	Underlings for Mexican police
Mule	Drug courier
MFJP	Mexican Federal Judicial Police
OGV	Official Government Vehicle
PD	Police Department
Plaza Agents	Mexican police assigned to the local city
PGR	Procuraduria General de la Republica
SO	Sheriff's Office

Made in the USA
Las Vegas, NV
20 October 2021